Saint Sebastian

St. Sebastian

Roman martyr; little more than the fact of his martyrdom can be proved about St. Sebastian. In the "Depositio martyrum" of the chronologer of 354 it is mentioned that Sebastian was buried on the Via Appia. St. Ambrose ("In Psalmum CXVIII"; "Sermo", XX, no. sliv in PL, XV, 1497) states that Sebastian came from Milan and even in the time of St. Ambrose was venerated there. The Acts, probably written at the beginning of the fifth century and formerly ascribed erroneously to Ambrose, relate that he was an officer in the imperial bodyguard and had secretly done many acts of love and charity for his brethren in the Faith. When he was finally discovered to be a Christian, in 286, he was handed over to the Mauretanian archers, who pierced him with arrows; he was healed, however, by the widowed St. Irene. He was finally killed by the blows of a club. These stories are unhistorical and not worthy of belief. The earliest mosaic picture of St. Sebastian, which probably belongs to the year 682, shows a grown, bearded man in court dress but contains no trace of an arrow. It was the art of the Renaissance that first portrayed him as a youth pierced by arrows. In 367 a basilica which was one of the seven chief churches of Rome was built over his grave. The present church was completed in 1611 by Scipio Cardinal Borghese. His relics in part were taken in the year 826 to St. Medard at Soissons. Sebastian is considered a protector against the plague. Celebrated answers to prayer for his protection against the plague are related of Rome in 680, Milan in 1575, and Lisbon in 1599. His feast day is 20 January.

source: www.newadvent.org/cathen/13668a.htm

Saint Sebastian

A SPLENDID READINESS FOR DEATH

KUNSTHALLE wien
KERBER VERLAG

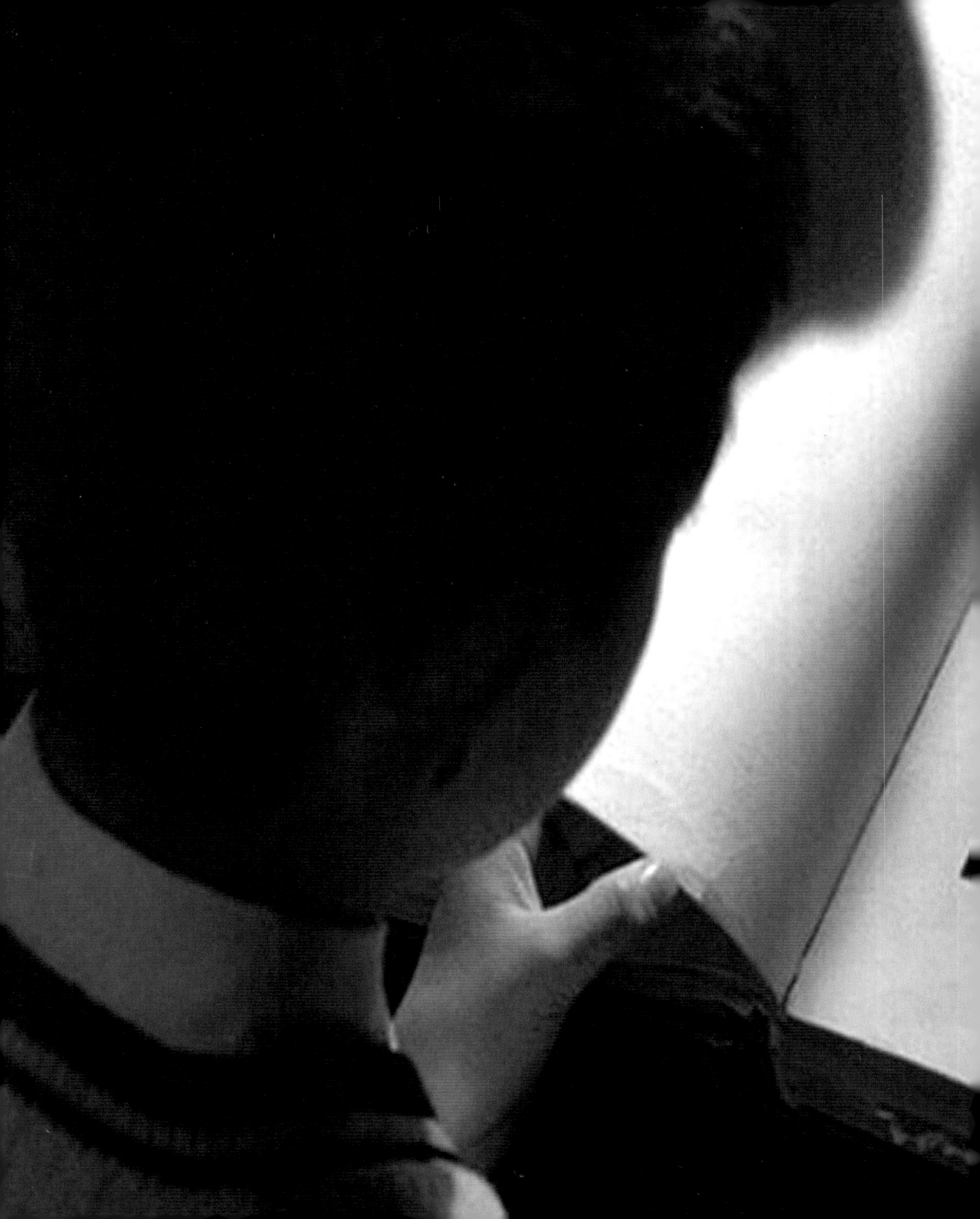

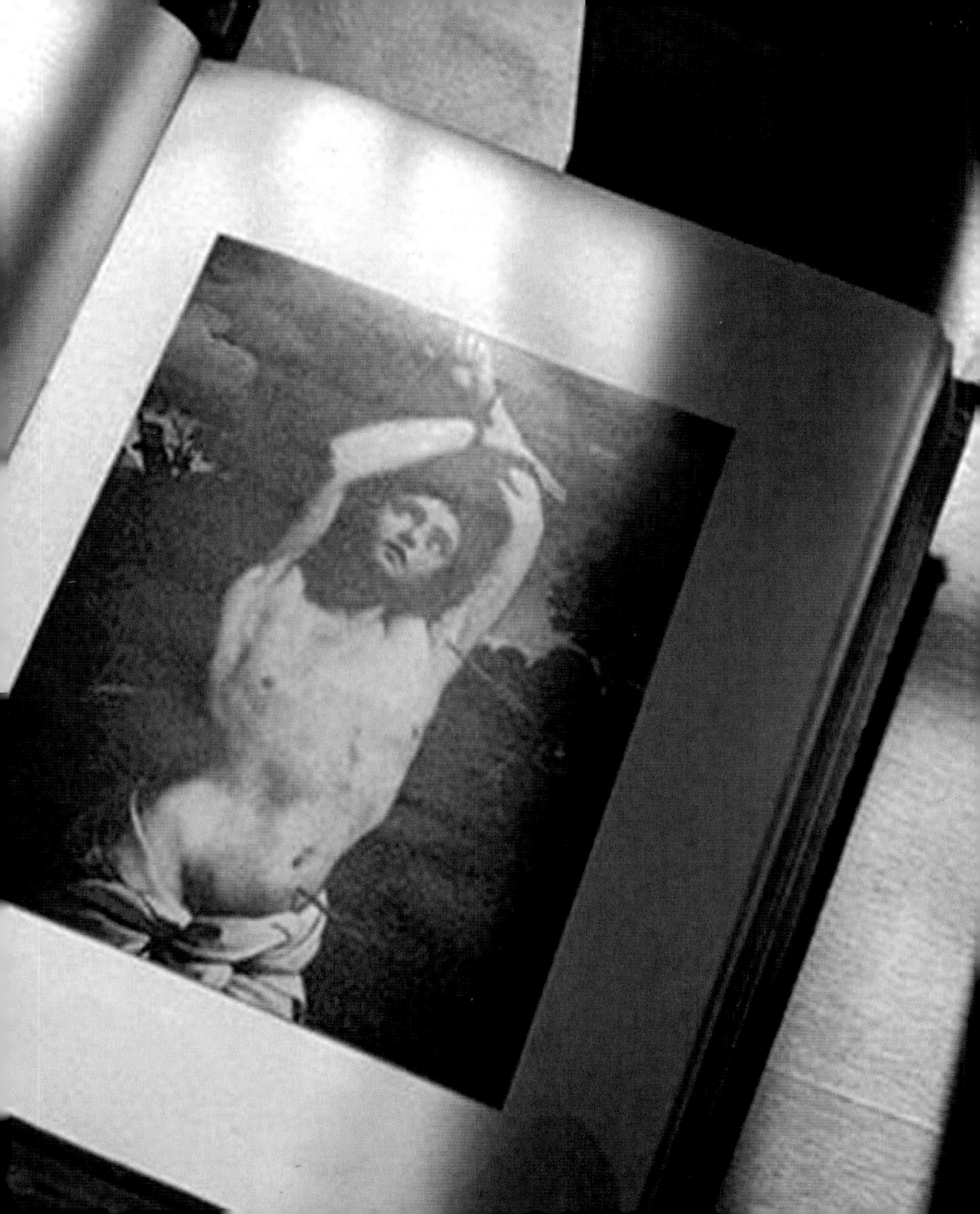

For Susanne

ACKNOWLEDGEMENTS

We gratefully acknowledge the generosity of all the artists and authors for making available their works and ideas. Further to this, we wish to thank all the individuals and institutions listed mentioned below for their support. They all, with their contributions, have made this project possible:

Sponsors:
British Council
Italian Cultural Institute, Vienna

Lenders:
Ron Athey, Los Angeles
Collection of Ghirlandi Lega Baldini, Faenza
Baudoin Lebon, Paris
Gerd Bergfleth, Matthes & Seitz Verlag, Munich
Laura Betti, Rome
Peter Blum Edition, New York
Louise Bourgeois, New York
Galerie Daniel Buchholz, Cologne
Chris Burden, Topanga
Cheim & Read, New York
Paula Cooper Gallery, New York
Kirby Dick, Los Angeles
Dvir Gallery, Tel Aviv
Marc Enguerand
Galerie Frank, Paris
Gagosian Gallery, New York
Sammlung Stephan Götz, Stuttgart
Howard Greenberg Gallery, New York
Galerie Karsten Greve, Cologne
In-motion Pictures, London
Jay Jopling / White Cube, London
Richard Kaye, New York
Laika Films, Brussels
Sigalit Landau, Tel Aviv
LETTER Stiftung, Cologne
Evan Lurie, New York
James Mackay, London
Mai 36 Galerie, Zurich
Sebastian von Mayreck, Havanna-Paris
The Museum of Modern Art, New York
Musiksammlung der Österreichischen Nationalbibliothek, Vienna
Makiko Nagaya
Luigi Ontani, Rome
Collection of John und Amy Phelan, New York
Pratt Contemporary Art, Kent
RW Work Ltd., New York
Salzgeber & Co. Medien GmbH, Berlin
Carlo Santoli, Avellino
Collection of Fabio Sargentini, Rome
Kishin Shinoyama
Sommer Contemporary Art, Tel Aviv
Teatro di San Carlo, Naples
Sammlung Walter Sudol und Steven Johnson
Warner Bros. Film GmbH, Hamburg
Collection of Wendy Williams, New York
The Estate of David Wojnarowicz und PPOW, New York

We also thank:
Konrad Bayer, Lord Byron, Gary Grant, Hedy Lamarr, Thomas Mann, August Graf von Platen, Walter Pater, Pittigrilli, Jane Russell, Walter Serner, Edith Sitwell, Evelyn Waugh, Oskar Wilde.

←《 Still from: PAUL SCHRADER, *Mishima*, 1985

Table of Contents

Forward

"If mediated lives, he figured, why not mediated deaths?"
THOMAS PYNCHON

Saint Sebastian: the patron saint of soldiers, of homosexuals, of plague- and AIDS-sufferers. Personified Sebastian: a sado-masochist icon, a death-loving, androgynous dandy, the very embodiment of the exemplary suffering of the artist. Scandalous Sebastian: his provocative and sensuous representation by Fra Bartolomeo was hung down by monks for fear that it might engender sinful thoughts in women. Equally, the première of the opera, *Le Martyre de Saint Sébastien* by Gabriele D'Annunzio and Claude Debussy in Paris in 1911 turned into a full-blown scandal when it was revealed that the role of the Christian Saint was being played by Ida Rubinstein, a woman, a Russian, and Jewish to boot. The arch bishop threatened to excommunicate theatregoers attending the five-part *ballet sacre*, which drew parallels between the Christian martyr and the demi-god Adonis, himself the issue of an incestuous relationship. The struggles involving power, rebellion, bans and beliefs, which lie at the heart of St. Sebastian myth, continue on to weave a web well into the 20th century, outlining a boundaries-transcending drama "between the secularisation of the sacred and the sacralisation of the profane" (Joachim Heusinger von Waldegg).

The myth of St. Sebastian is further illuminated in the exhibition from the perspective of contemporary artists. In so doing, however, the eye also catches glimpses of historical climaxes, such as the première of the aforementioned *Martyrdom of St. Sebastian* opera of 1911 or the painter of the Sebastian motif *par excellence*, Guido Reni. He it was who rendered his hero the most ambiguously: at first glance one caught sight of an anaemic youth lethargically surrendering to his suffering. Yet behind this facade one perceived the contours of an ecstatician in the flesh, fully submitting himself to his masochistic lust for life. The motif of a Sebastian glancing up to heaven with a "divine, passionate gaze" (Oscar Wilde), enjoying his pain and sorrow as if in a trance, "exhausted by the very nearly voluptuous helplessness of his agony", (Marguerite Yourcenar), is mirrored in the works of Luigi Ontani, Kishin Shinoyama, the film-maker Bavo Defurne and the photographer Eikoh Hosoe. Hosoe und Shinoyama set the stage in their respective series *BA RA KEI (Killed by Roses)* and Death of a Man for the Japanese writer and excentric aesthete Yukio Mishima to take the part of Sebastian, who was thus to become one of the central characters upon whom the cult of Sebastian would be projected in the second half of the 20th century. Thus it is that Paul Schrader (*Mishima*), David Wojnarowicz und Cerith Wyn Evans explicitly refer back to Mishima. According to his autobiographical novel, *Confession of a Mask*, Mishima experienced his own Coming Out while examining a reproduction of Reni's Sebastian. "The arrows [he wrote] have drilled themselves into the taut and breathing young flesh and consume the body from within with tortures of the utmost agony and ecstasy." After the failure of his assault on the headquarters of the Japanese armed forces and a solemn expression of loyalty to the emperor, Mishima committed suicide by way of seppuku, intent on following his idol to the last. The artist "suffering in exemplary fashion" (Susan Sontag) is also represented by Chris Burden, particularly in his performances, *Doorway to Heaven* und *Shoot*. In the latter, the artist is intentionally being shot at. The pleasure experienced in feeling pain and the pleasure of causing pain are shown in Kirby Dick's documentary film, *Sick: The Life and Death of Bob Flanagan, Supermasochist*, depicting the life of Bob Flanagan and his partner and tormentress, Sheree Rose. Sado-masochist traits with a direct reference to Sebastian are also evident in the works of Ron Athey and in Joel-Peter Witkin's *Queer Saint*. Witkin's Sebastian is a fragmented character, skeleton-like, robbed of his own in-the-flesh reality. He is horrific as a martyred monument, counteracting all those aesthetic representations of homo-erotic fantasies. The divergent ascriptions of gender in St. Sebastian, of the sort frequently discussed in Gender Studies, are another theme of the exhibition. Louise Bourgeois focuses on a female Sebastian character in her works on *Sainte Sebastiénne*, as well as in a sculpture from 2002, shown in this exhibition for the first time. The great variety of faces of Sebastian is one of the reasons for his many and diverse sub-cultural appropriations. Social groups such as the gay community and the AIDS-scene during the 1980s repeatedly identified with the saint who, through his association with the plague, would draw suffering upon himself, in order that others might be saved (David Wojnarowicz).

Sebastian, then, runs through the polarity of the world, existing between desire and abstention, between suffering and redemption, between the agony and the ecstasy, between life and death, between male and female identifications.

Our thanks are due to the team of the Kunsthalle Wien, in particular Angela Stief (curatorial assistant), Simone Sentall (production) and Maria Haigermoser. We also gratefully acknowledge all our sponsors and loaners, without whose willingness and cooperativeness this project would not have been possible.

Gerald Matt and Wolfgang Fetz

Richard A. Kaye

St. Sebastian: The Uses of Decadence

If ever there were a religious rubric that has acquired urgent resonance in the twenty-first century, it is surely "martyrdom," a term that recently has acquired charged, contradictory meanings. Once upon a time martyrdom signaled not only religious truth but a lived religious truth, one that might be emblazoned on the body. Lately, however, the concept of martyrdom increasingly has acquired almost wholly negative associations, evoking terrorists, reactionary fundamentalists, and all who frustrate liberal dreams of a well-ordered self, immune to absolutism, fanaticism, and extremity. Of course, psychoanalytic thought long ago determined that religious martyrs were unknowingly masochistic, a view first presented by the French physician Jean-Martin Charcot, who published a collection of medieval art works in 1881 illustrating the thesis that religious experiences were manifestations of hysteria. As the art historian Colin Eisler has explained, "A psychoanalytic age has reduced martyrdom to a complex."[1]

St. Sebastian, with his popular devotees among those with and without religious affiliations, is a striking counterpoint to such claims. Sebastian's classic Renaissance pose of youthful, beatific, pious surrender to a grisly, arrow-ridden fate, has proven to be of enduring fascination to writers and artists interested in non-normative forms of desire. For unlike other Christian martyrs, whose piety rendered them obsolete in an age of secularization, Sebastian suggested a different kind of martyr, one who had an inherent but ever-mutating perversity. "Little more than the fact of his martyrdom can be proved about St. Sebastian," noted Klemens Löffler in the *Catholic Encyclopedia* (1912), but his followers continue to embellish the saint's legend.[2] Unlike the medical models that defined homosexuality in the nineteenth century, the "cult" of St. Sebastian insisted on the unfathomable mystery, aesthetic beauty, and moral integrity of the martyr's "outsider" status, especially as suggested in the Renaissance iconography of Mantegna, Guido Reni, and Perugino, artists whose versions of St. Sebastian were admired by both nineteenth-century and modern artists. Meanwhile, for women artists such as Frida Kahlo, Louise Bourgeois, and Ana Maria Pacheco, all of whom were less beholden to Renaissance models than their male counterparts, Sebastian was an alluring symbol but one who must be radically reconfigured.

The history of St. Sebastian as a signifier of male victimhood, masculine beauty, homoerotic desire, and sado-masochistic display is long and intricate, having many of its sources in a highly coded nineteenth-century discourse of Aestheticism and Decadence in which Catholic symbols held a special symbolic power. In Oscar Wilde's *Picture of Dorian Gray* (1890), the decadent protagonist dons a cloak adorned with the symbols of St. Sebastian. The French Symbolist painters Gustave Moreau and Odilon Redon celebrated a Sebastian of androgynous, ethereal qualities. The martyr functions as a semi-covert acknowledgment of a repressed homosexual secret in Thomas Mann's

Death in Venice (1911), whose Aschenbach worships St. Sebastian as a "new kind of hero" for whom suffering was not "merely passive." In Stefan Zweig's novella, *Confusion*, a student visits his tormented bisexual professor and discovers two works in the older man's office, an "attractively scaled down bust of the Paris Ganymede" and besides it a "St. Sebastian by an old German master, tragic beauty set, probably not by chance, besides its equivalent enjoying life to the full."

Why has St. Sebastian come to stand for various forms of erotic mischief and homosexual consciousness? Zweig's juxtaposition of Ganymede and Sebastian is instructive, for St. Sebastian's varying legends and images are a more oblique, modern emblem of the emphatically homoerotic Ganymede, the comely youth abducted by Zeus to serve as cub-bearer to the gods. Whereas the details of Ganymede's story are inherently homoerotic, Sebastian in many ways had his homoerotic meaning foisted on him, symbolically, by those who saw his arrow-ridden state as evoking homoerotic fantasies. Additionally, those who wished to see the saint as a homosexual icon chose to see the arrows perforating his svelte, handsome body as an image of homoerotic penetration. Important, too, have been the many accounts of the saint's life in which he reveals his Christianity in a dramatic fashion. Sebastian's story thus becomes a kind of "coming out" narrative, a tale of confession that modern artists can adapt to represent the contemporary gay male, who discloses a homosexual "secret." Confession, as Michel Foucault has argued, is the means by which modern individuals conceive of their sexuality. Sebastian, a figure of oblique eroticism, given that he is a solitary subject in Medieval and Renaissance painting, is construed by many of his admirers as "homosexual" because his classic pose of blissful receptivity may imply homoerotic bliss. St. Sebastian successfully replaced earlier "myths of homosexuality" – Ganymede and Zeus, Hadrian and Antinous – because, whereas those mythic narratives are narratives of homoerotic love, Sebastian's myth and image revolved around questions of homosexual identity.[5]

In May 1911, St. Sebastian was the focus of his most notorious twentieth-century incarnation, the appearance of Ida Rubinstein as Sebastian at Paris's Chatelet Theater with music by Claude Debussy and a text by the Italian poet D'Annunzio. The carnage of World War I produced a spate of indelible images depicting soldier martyrs as St. Sebastian, most notably in Egon Schiele's 1915 self-portrait (fig. 1) of himself impaled with bayonet-like arrows. Numerous artists of homosexual affiliations have not only drawn on St. Sebastian's imagery to convey forms of homosexual traumatic experience and heroic suffering, they have done so in sharply personal and confessional ways. The Japanese novelist Yukio Mishima's *Confessions of a Mask* (1949) features an adolescent boy who is sexually aroused by a Guido Reni Sebastian, while his developing masochism, linked to his new-found homosexual awareness, becomes a metaphor for his enslavement to a Japan that in a post-war era is given over to Western-style capitalism. Here Sebastian emerges as a symbol of that part of the self (especially the sexual self) that cannot be assimilated into mainstream culture, but which paradoxically locates itself in cultural totems. Eikoe Hosoe's photographs of Mishima as Sebastian (➳ p. 44)

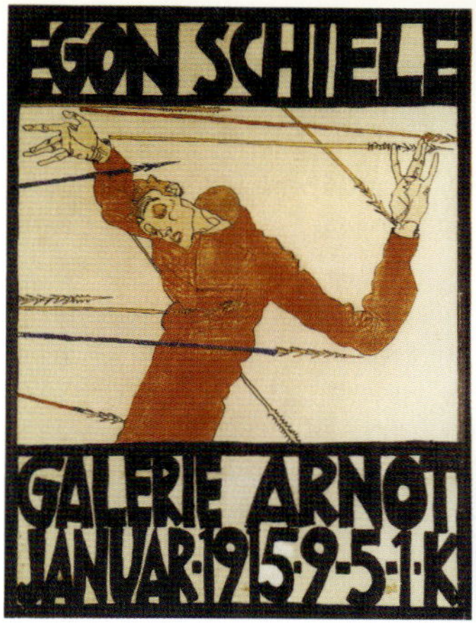

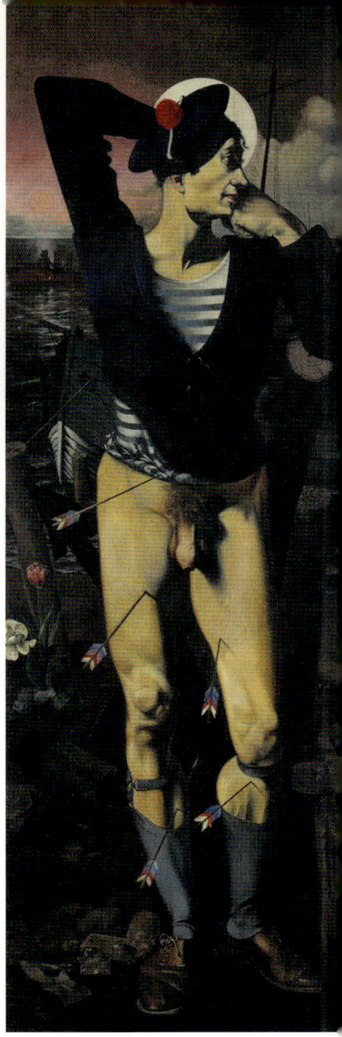

acquired grisly retrospective meaning in 1970 when Mishima committed seppuko, Japanese suicide, by driving a sword into his abdomen. Hosoe's photographs, some of which appeared in his series *Ordeal by Roses (BA RA KEI)*, have become archetypal twentieth-century images of exhibitionistic self-torment, notable for their adoption of Surrealist techniques to the imagery of St. Sebastian.

Two of the first pictorial representations of Sebastian that relied on an emphatically homoerotic visual vocabulary were the French painter Albert Courmes' *Saint Sebastian* (1934, fig. 2), in which the martyr is depicted as a preening sailor, naked from the waste down, and the American artist Marsden Hartley's *Sustained Comedy (Portrait of an Object)*, (1939, fig. 3), in which Sebastian is tattooed with images of sailors, muscle-builders, and butterflies. Modern gay accoutrements thus serve to interpret Sebastian's sexual ambiguity as homosexual. The "gay allure" of the *St. Sebastian* by the photographers Pierre and Gilles partly arises from the stylistic excess of their technicolor approach. (Similarly, Keith Haring and Gilbert and George fashioned St. Sebastians as camp icons.) Eschewing camp aesthetics, Derek Jarman's film *Sebastiane* (1975, ➻ p. 52) follows the exile of Sebastian, a Christian Adonis, who becomes the friend of fellow soldiers and then the semi-willing target of their arrows. The film exploits Sebastian's reputation as a saint who inspires, but does not necessarily reciprocate, homoerotic passion. Sebastian ultimately inspires the violent enmity of his homosexually tormented commanding officer Severus, who orders Sebastian's execution. Indebted to the nineteenth-century photographs of Baron Von Gloeden, Jarman's film is a medi-

fig. 1: EGON SCHIELE, *Selfportrait as St. Sebastian*, 1915

fig. 2: ALFRED COURMES, *Saint Sébastien*, 1934

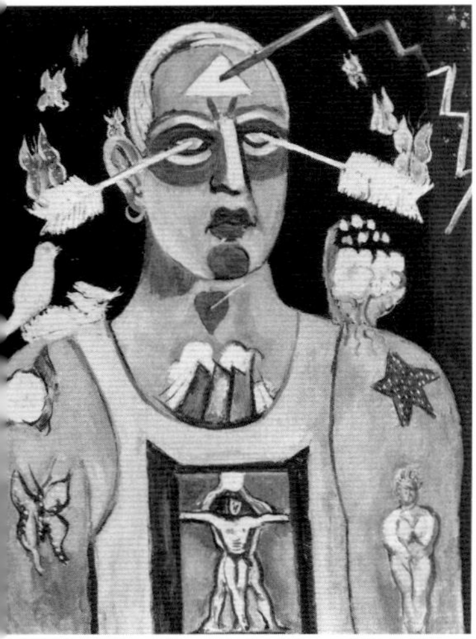

fig. 3: MARSDEN HARTLEY, *The Sustained Comedy (Portrait of an Object)*, 1939

tation on the sources for homophobia in the repression of same-sex desire. Peter Weigl's *The Martyrdom of St. Sebastian* (1984) is, contrastingly, a lushly colorful, intensely dramatic passion play. With a golden-haired martyr and a Debussy choral music establishing Sebastian's power to perform miracles, the film insists on the emotional links between religious belief and homoerotic desire. In a more politically charged identification, Ron Athey's self dramatizations as the martyr in the 1990s featured Athey's own body (➻ p. 18). Rejecting the well-oiled, wiry saint incarnated by Mishima, Athey impersonated a Sebastian of modest physical allurements, offering a Gay Everyman caught up – but rebelling against – the reactionary forces of contemporary history. More recently, Sebastian symbolizes those besieged by AIDS, either homosexual men or intravenous drug users, whose syringes are suggestively arrow-like. Drawing on the martyr's medieval role as a plague saint, David Wojnarowicz's *Bad Moon Rising* (1989, ➻ p. 92) depicts Sebastian as a limbless torso against a pattern of US dollars, an implicit critique of the money apparatus determining AIDS.

While Sebastian's appeal for many gay-identified artists has a long tradition, the martyr's value for women artists is one of the less noted but in some ways most mysterious aspects of Sebastian's saintly power. Several years before Mishima sought out Sebastian as an icon – but in a similar meditation on the tensions between civilization and the primitive – the Mexican artist Frida Kahlo drew on the imagery of St. Sebastian for several of her works completed in the 1930s and 40s. These include *Broken Column* (1943, fig. 4) and *Memory of the Heart* (1937, fig. 5), in which a clothed Kahlo is pierced by a single rod and stands next to two dresses suspended on strings, and *Wounded Stag or The Little Deer* (1946, fig. 6), in which Kahlo has inserted an image of her own face on the head of a arrow-riddled stag. As with Mishima, Kahlo's identification with St. Sebastian doubtless stemmed from her own experience as a "pierced" figure. As a young woman Kahlo was wounded in a 1925 streetcar accident in which a iron rod pierced her body, an incident that was to cause her lifelong physical and psychological distress. Kahlo's own body had been, in a sense, the arena for a grotesquely similar fate as that met by the Sebastian of legend. Unlike Mishima's Guido Reni-indebted devotion to Sebastian, Kahlo's Sebastian images radically depart from the traditional Renaissance iconography of the martyr. Her anthropomor-

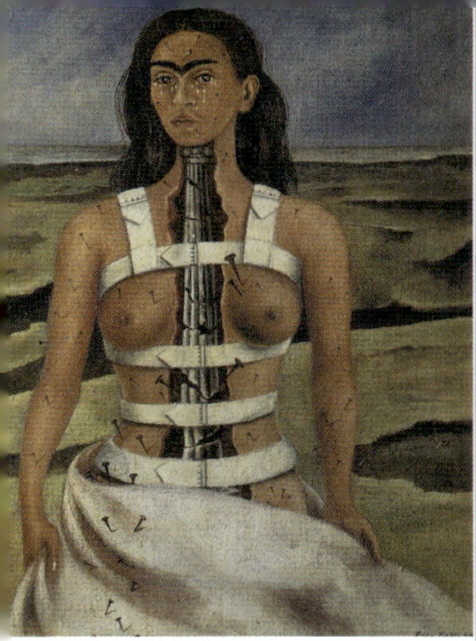
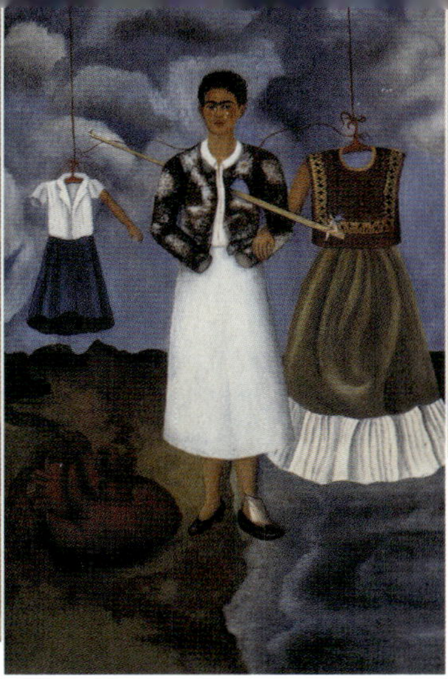
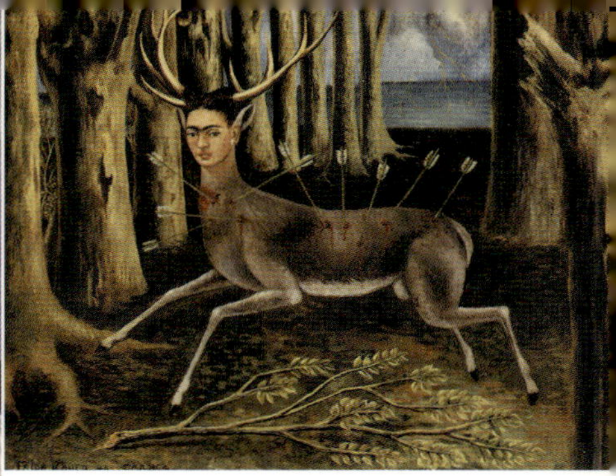

fig. 4: FRIDA KAHLO, *Broken Column*, 1944

fig. 5: FRIDA KAHLO, *Memory of the Heart*, 1937

fig. 6: FRIDA KAHLO, *Wounded Stag or The Little Deer*, 1946

phized stag, a totem of animal grace, harbors a playful primitivism of proto-feminist import that mocks the solemnity of martyrdom as depicted by Renaissance male masters as well as the heroics of masculine self-surrender embodied in Mishima's grisly photographic self-portrait. *Memory of the Heart* (fig. 5) offers us a Kahlo as latter-day Christian martyr but also, with the work's large, bleeding heart, an evocation of Kahlo's Aztec ancestry, whose rituals included sacrificing hearts torn out of living people. The "civilized" modern woman cannot quite repress the remnants of a barbaric epoch. Unlike Kahlo, Louise Bourgeois is a rigorous formalist known for favoring austere abstraction, evident in her *St. Sebastienne* (1947, ➻ p. 22), a semi-abstract figure in which a red heart is pierced by arrows. But Bourgeois's investment in Sebastian imagery encompassed a figurative representation of a female figure running away from arrows, an image that Bourgeois explained as a "self portrait of a person who is very happy and running and then suddenly realizes that she has antagonized certain people. She gets shot at. Then she is transformed from a nice sweet creature into a mean, feline person."[4] With a similar accent on the proto-feminist dimension in St. Sebastian imagery, Ana Maria Pacheco's sculptural works, drawings, and paintings devoted to St. Sebastian from the 1990s (some of which evoke Latin American contemporary political torture) insist on a female witness-protector's shock before the sado-masochistic rituals of male political power (➻ p. 68).

These images are powerful testaments to Sebastian's enduring and unruly power, a martyr beloved by gay male artists but continually adopted by all who require a potent symbol of sexual disorder, political or personal rebellion, or beatific self surrender.

1 Colin Eisler: *Painting in the Hermitage*, New York: Stewart, Tabori, and Chang 1990, pp. 300-1.

2 Klemens Löffler: *The Catholic Encyclopedia*, Vol. XIII, New York: Robert Appleton Company 1912.

3 For a more extensive discussion of these issues see Richard A. Kaye: "'Losing His Religion': St. Sebastian as Contemporary Gay Martyr," in: Reina Lewis and Peter Horne (eds.): *Outlooks. Gay and Lesbian Visual Cultures*, London: Routledge 1996; Essay: "'A Splendid Readiness for Death'. T. S. Eliot, the Homosexual Cult of St. Sebastian, and the First World War," in: *Modernism/Modernity*, May 1999.

4 Interview with Larry Rinder, in: *Louise Bourgeois: Drawings and Observations*, Berkeley: University Art Museum 1995, p. 147.

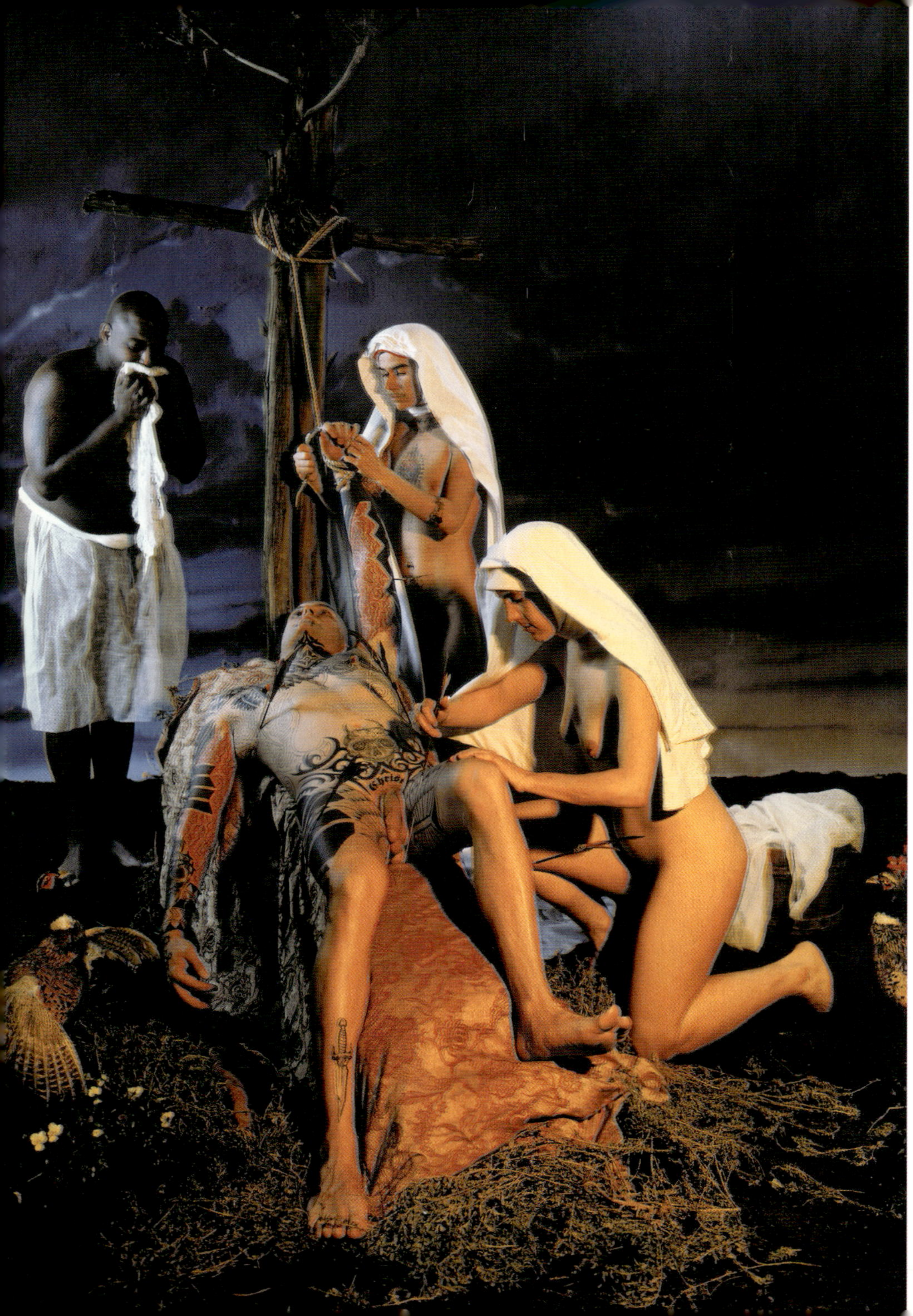

Ron Athey

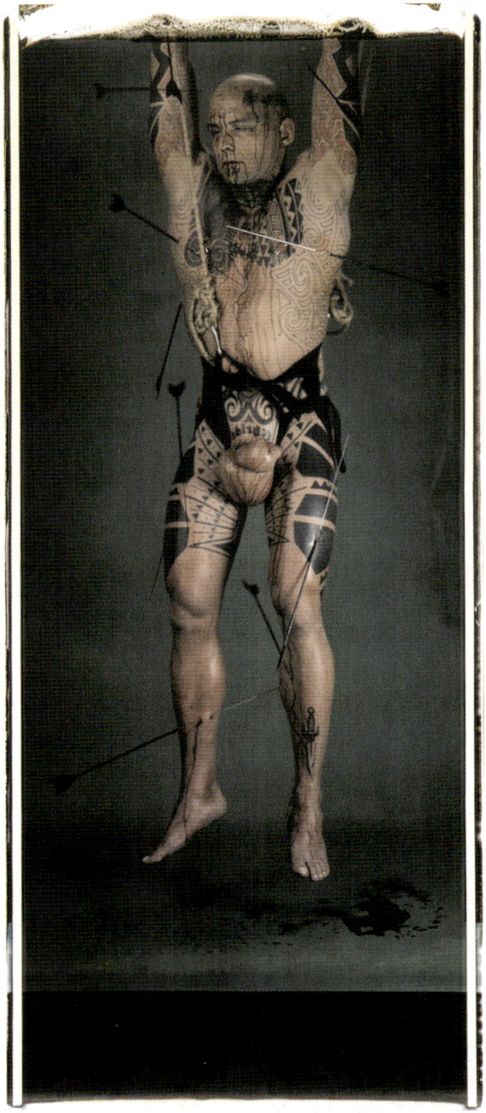

In 1981 I lived in a hotel in an industrial section of downtown Los Angeles. I had been injecting crystal meth-amphetamine for two years and was on a particularly long run, I hadn't slept in almost seven days. As was usually the case with hallucinations, I suddenly felt quite normal and rested, then looked around me and saw that St. Sebastian was martyred on every utility pole. Dozens, maybe hundreds, of tall, skinny St. Sebastians (they had the exaggerated appearance of someone who'd been stretched), were arrowed to the rough wood poles. Spectacularly, the hallucination did not evaporate upon closer examination.

I was in active addiction and having prophetic drug-induced visions in the year that was the start of the AIDS deaths. Within ten years I wouldn't be able to count how many funerals I had attended, and even though drug-free, the image kept returning in my mind: the Sebastian of ruined beauty. This image appeared in three of my performances over the next 12 years, in the final version, as in the giant Polaroid, with disfigured genitals (the temporary result from infusing one liter of medical saline solution). I only recently found out that he was the saint prayed to in time of plague.

Like the plague, the theater is the time of evil, the triumph of dark powers that are nourished by a power even more profound, until extinction. – The theater, like the plague, is in the images of this carnage and this essential separation. It releases conflicts, disengages powers, liberates possibilities, and if these possibilities and these powers are dark, it is the fault not of the plague nor of the theater, but of life.
(Antonin Artaud: *Theater and its Double*)

Ron Athey

RON ATHEY
Saint Sebastian, 1997
Sebastian Suspended, 1992

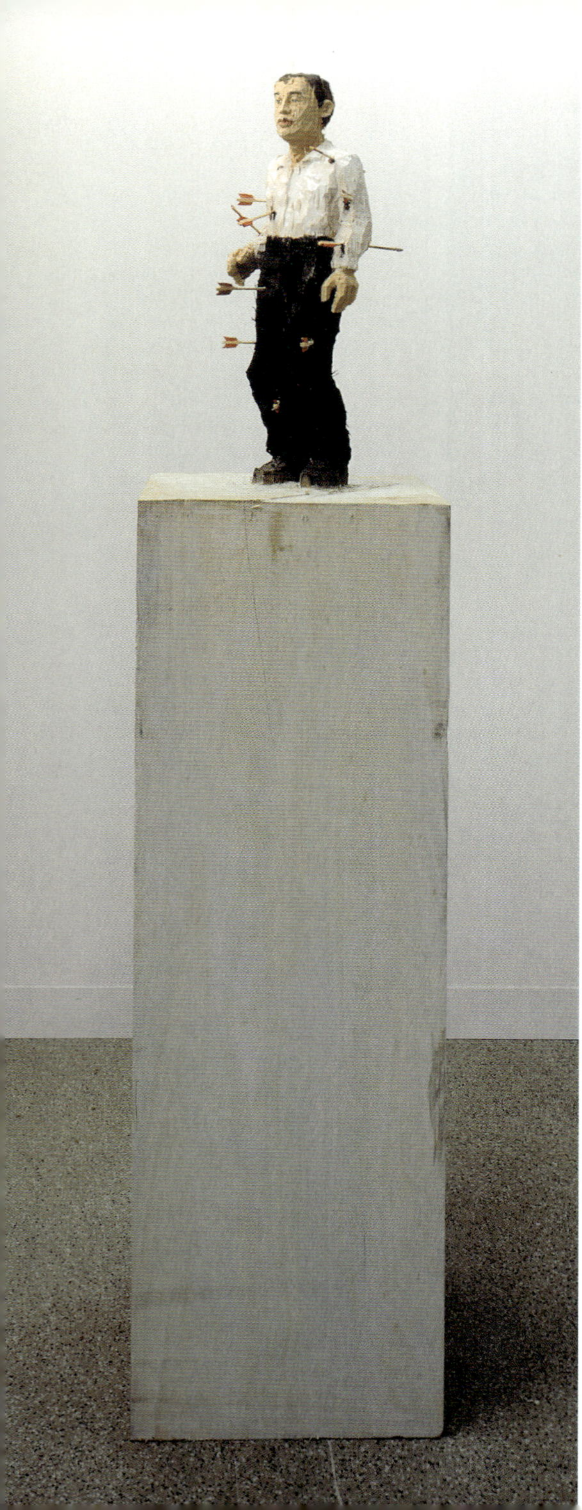

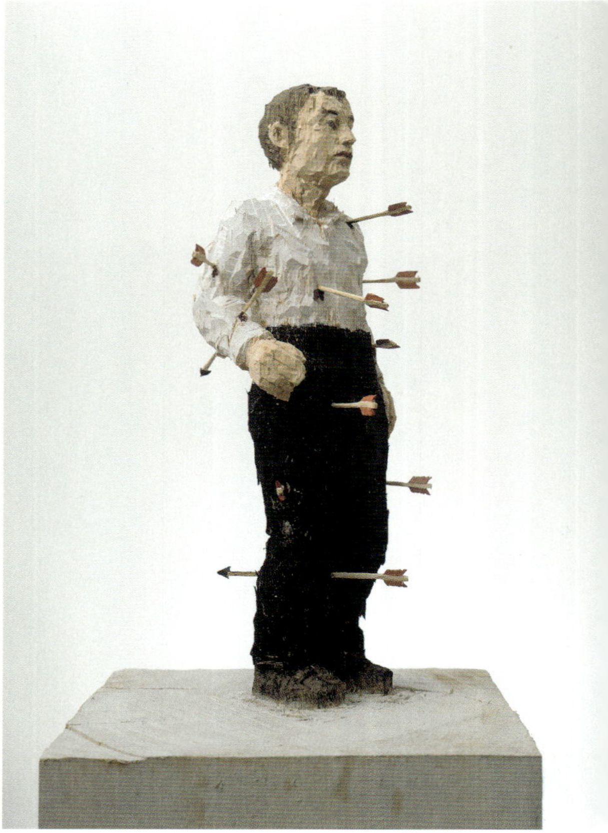

Stephan Balkenhol

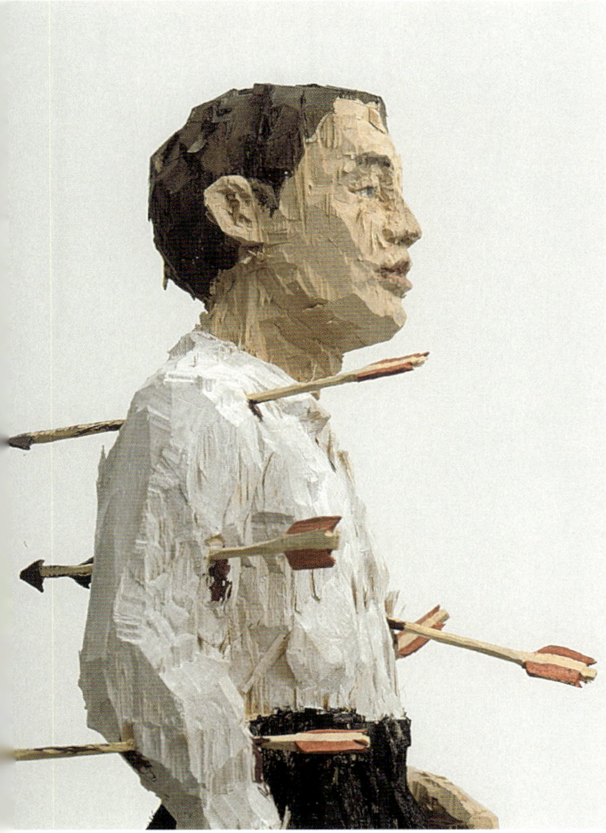

STEPHAN BALKENHOL
Märtyrer, 2003

My sculpture, "the man in the black trousers and the white shirt", is being martyred – I am a martyr and the viewer can become a bit of a martyr too.

The image of Saint Sebastian has aroused compassion in all times. And pleasure in sharing suffering. After all, suffering - especially imagined suffering - can also be very sweet. The artist as an exemplary actor can be either a conqueror or a martyr. He carries his body and soul to the marketplace, reveals his innermost parts and extends himself beyond the limits of his physical and mental possibilities. He carries his cross as a representative of humanity ... he is profoundly vulnerable.

To be exemplary in one's actions can also be a privilege: to become immortal and, perhaps, to be ennobled through martyrdom. The idea, or "message" lets him forget all dangers – a martyr values his idea more highly than physical comfort. Fulfilment through self-denial.

My sculpture, Saint Sebastian, is not really suffering. It shows us a man who could be Everyman, who is suddenly hit by arrows in the midst of his everyday life – for whatever reasons.

The possibility of such an attack – which could hit anyone – interests me.

In principle, everyone could become a martyr, by making himself open to attack, by taking risks for his convictions – setting his entire existence at risk.

But I am not at all interested in glorifying martyrdom. My position is more like that of Brassens: "...Mourir pour des idées d'accord, mais d'une mort lente..."

Under some conditions it can be harder to live for one's convictions than to die for them.

STEPHAN BALKENHOL

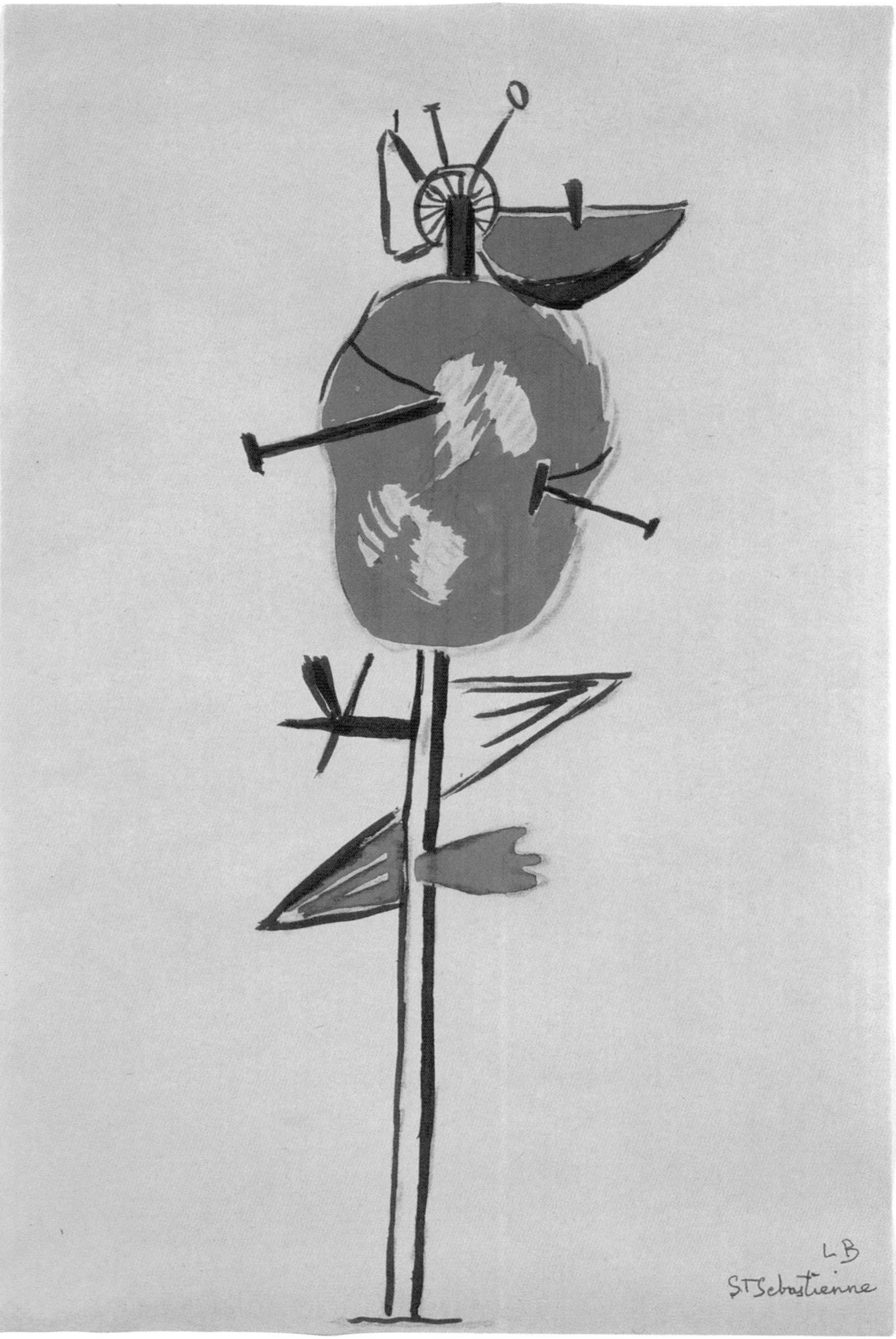
LB
ST Sebastienne

Louise Bourgeois

St. Sebastienne is a self portrait. It's a state of being under attack, of being anxious and afraid. What does a person do when they are under siege? You better understand why you are being attacked. Is it provoked? Is it revenge? Do you fight back, or do you run for cover and retreat into the protection of your own lair? That is the big question.

LOUISE BOURGEOIS

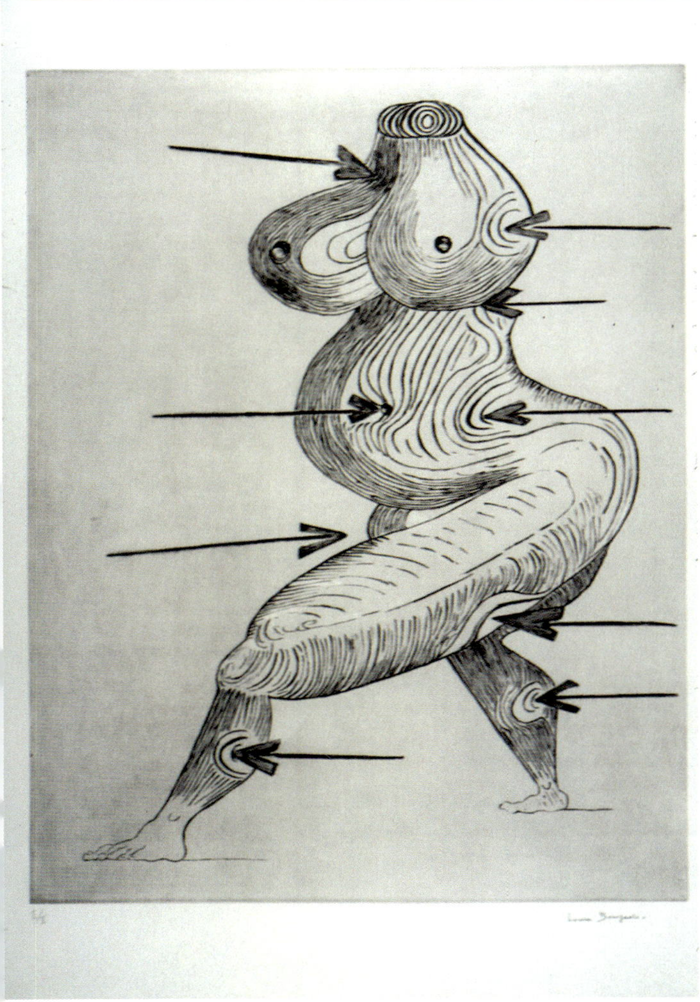

LOUISE BOURGEOIS
St. Sebastienne, 1947
Sainte Sebastienne, 1992

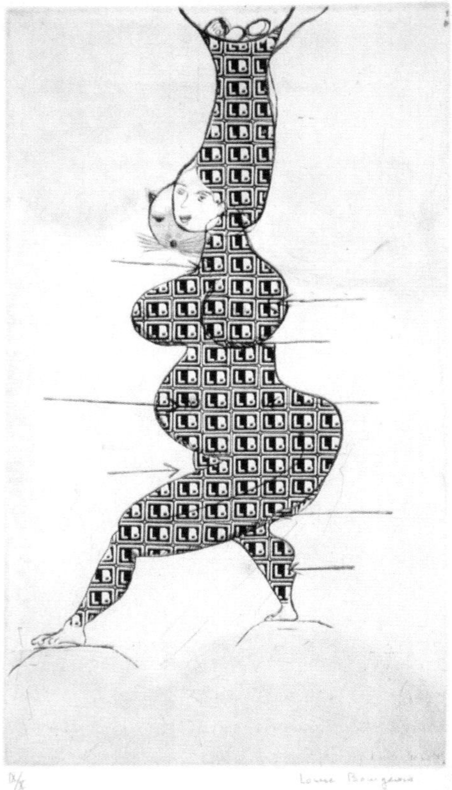

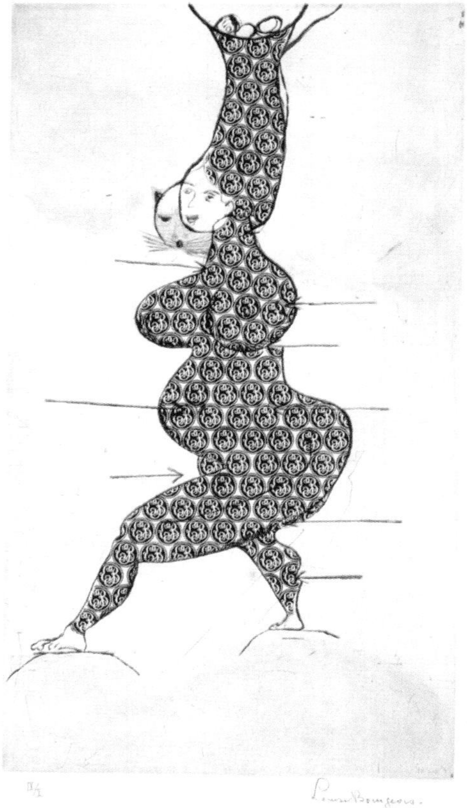

LOUISE BOURGEOIS

Stamp of Memories II, 1994

Stamp of Memories I, 1993

St. Sebastienne, 2002

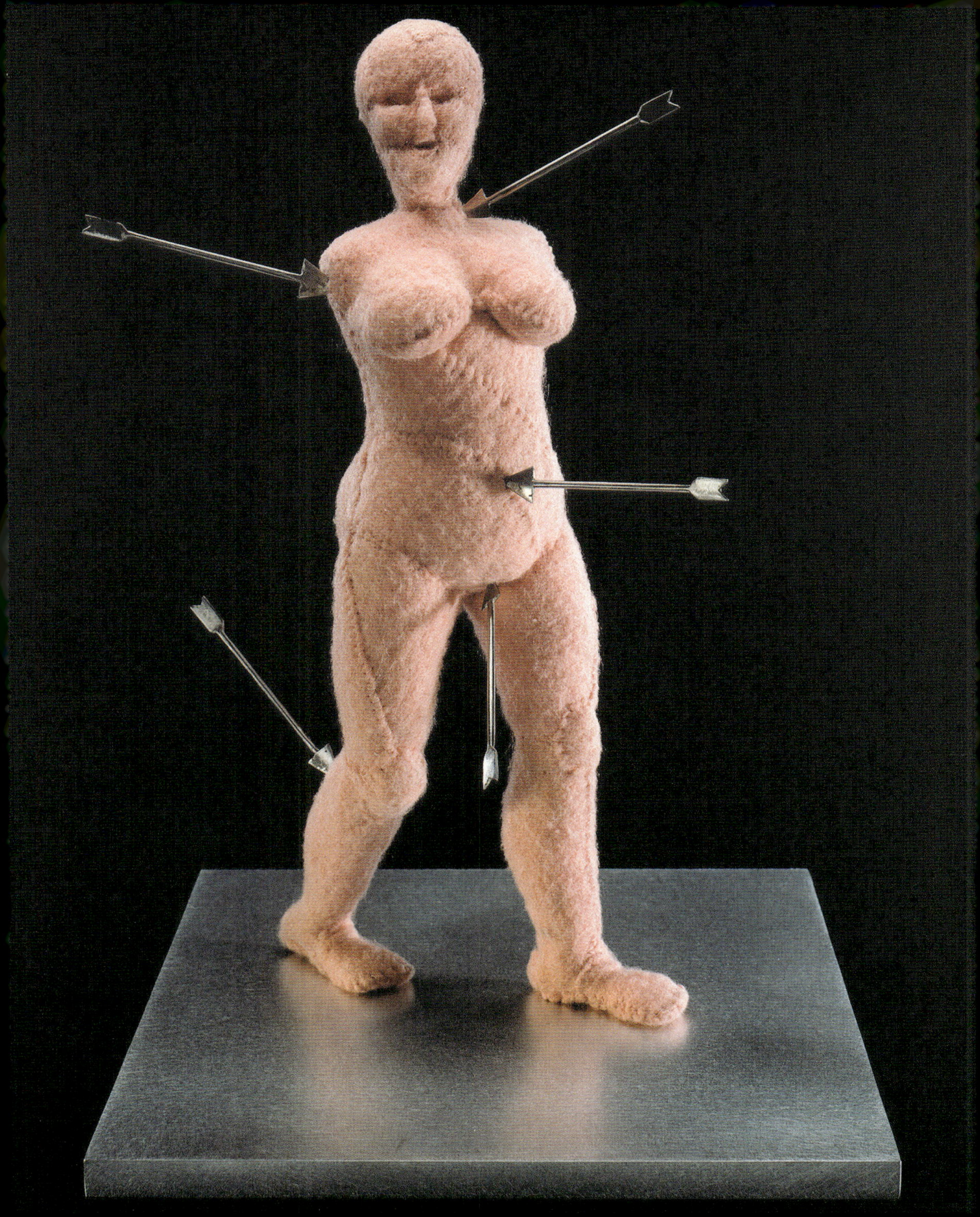

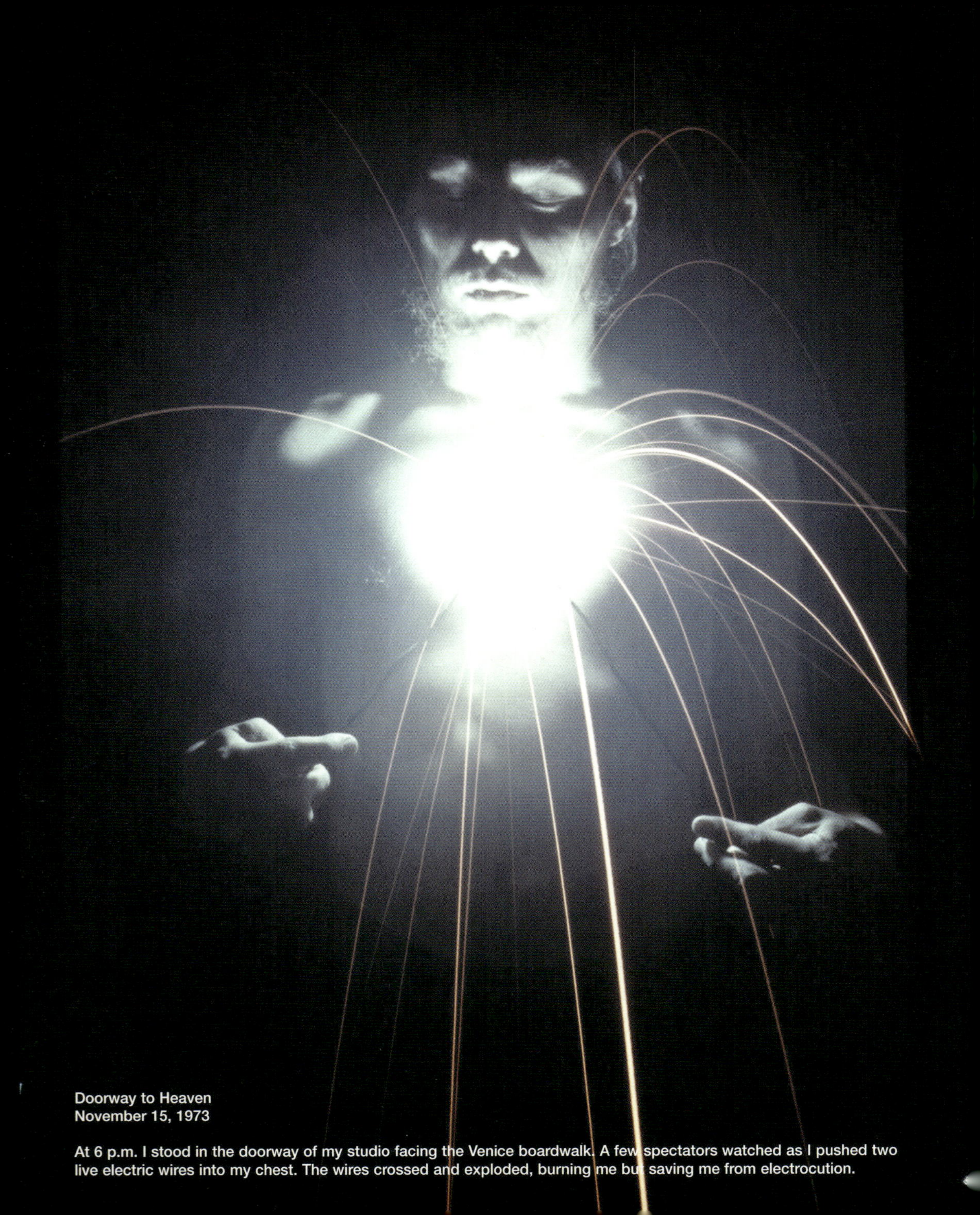

Doorway to Heaven
November 15, 1973

At 6 p.m. I stood in the doorway of my studio facing the Venice boardwalk. A few spectators watched as I pushed two live electric wires into my chest. The wires crossed and exploded, burning me but saving me from electrocution.

Chris Burden

In the photograph *Doorway to Heaven* (1973) there is a portrait of the artist transfigured in meditation. Fine beams of light emerge from his breast, lighting the darkness of the room and drenching the relaxed face of the artist from below in metaphysical light. Behind the radiant surface there is high tension, in the true meaning of the words. The photograph is part of the performance *Doorway to Heaven*, where Burden makes his body an instrument, as he does in many of his works. Here again he provokes a borderline experience. *Doorway to Heaven* is indeed not as spherical and contemplative as one might assume at first sight.

In the *Legenda Aurea* Sebastian is at the doorway to heaven and escapes certain death from the raining arrows only to die in the end anyway, driven by an insatiable yearning for death. Burden also risks life, and seems even to expect it and challenge it, looking towards both it and the coming pain with his eyes closed. The source of the light is not to be found in extraterrestrial fields but is the result of Burden's scientific experiment: the artist inserted two ends of electrical leads in his breast, which led to a short circuit. The photograph shows the moment before the nerves could carry the pain of the burns to his brain. The camera reacted more quickly than the systems of the body and also outwitted the perceptions of the people watching the performance, who could barely register this tiny moment of intact beauty with their naked eyes. In this case, the photograph has lived longer than the reality and demonstrates a situation that is almost fictitious, when pain and pleasure merge, as they do in the case of Sebastian.

Angela Stief

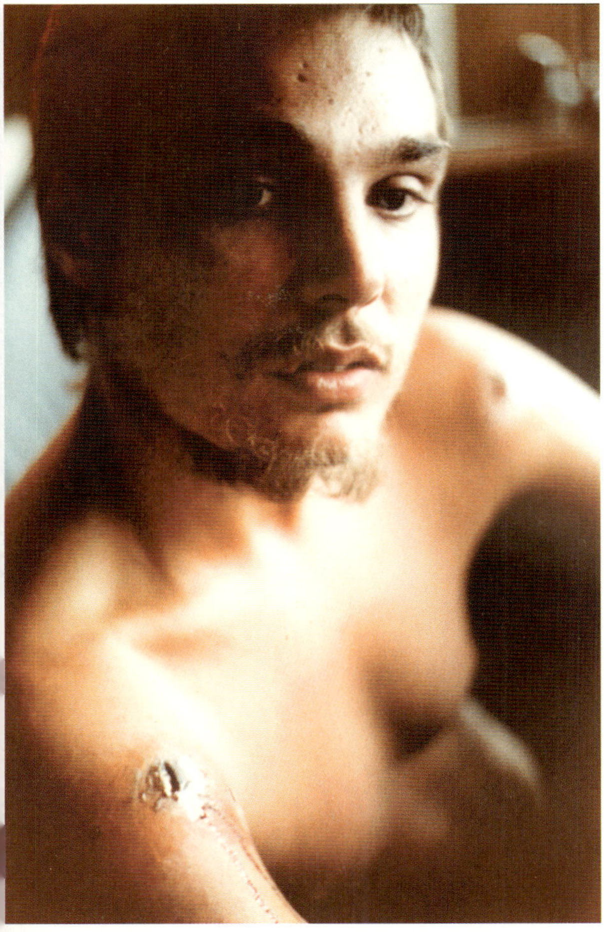

CHRIS BURDEN, 1973

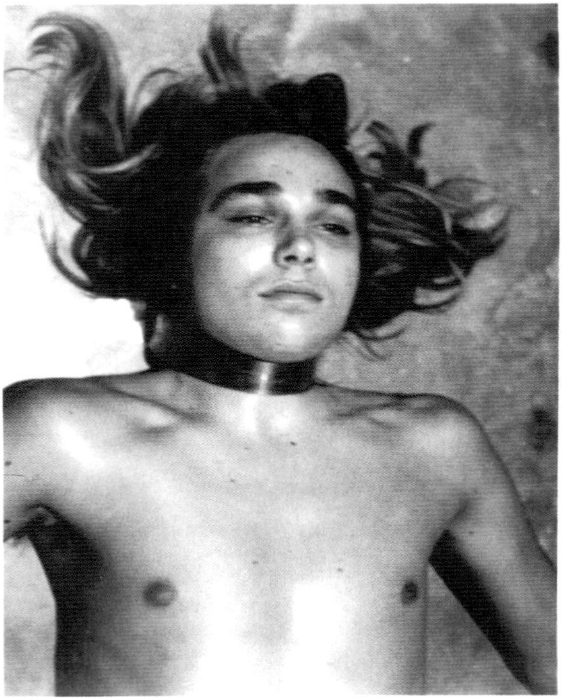

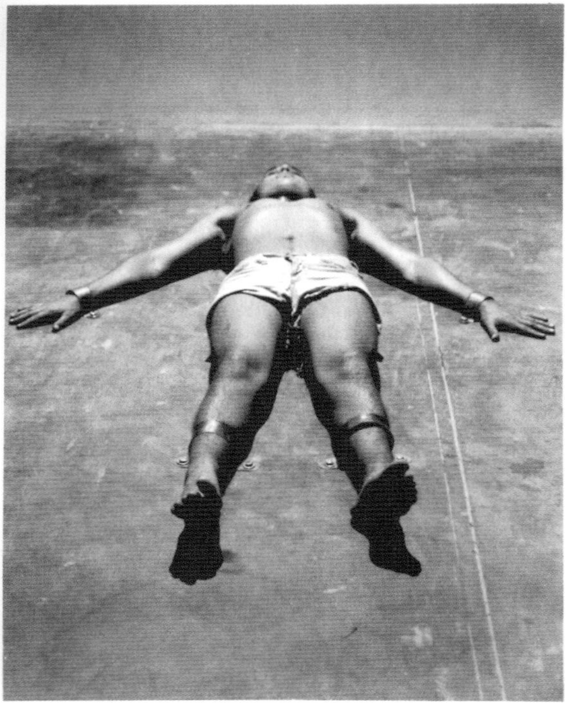

Prelude to 220, or 110
F Space: September 10-12, 1971

I was strapped to the floor with copper bands bolted into the concrete. Two buckets of water with live 110 lines submerged in them were placed near me. The piece was performed from 8-10 p.m. for three nights.

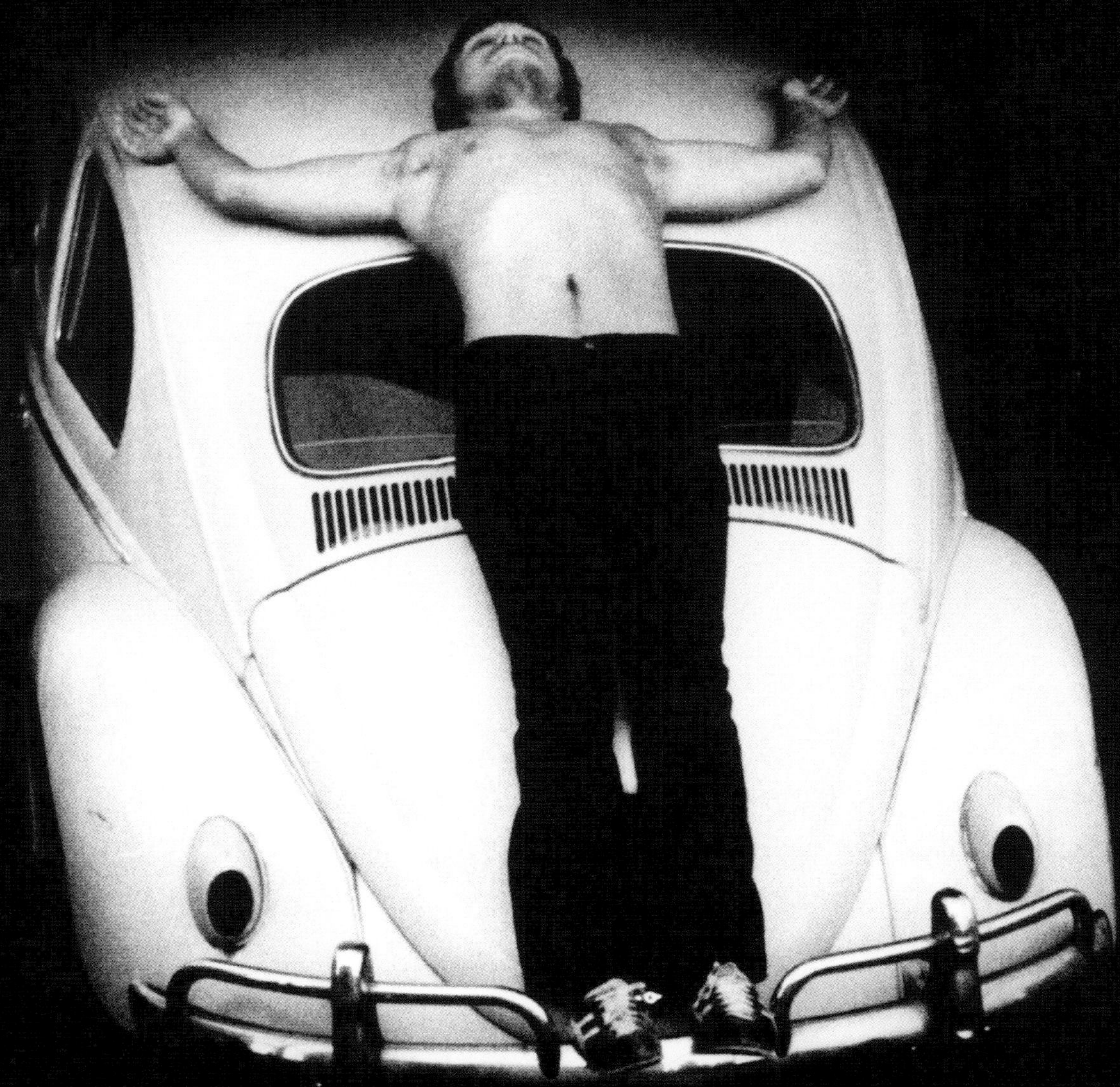

Trans-fixed
Venice, California: April 23, 1974

Inside a small garage on Speedway Avenue, I stood on the rear bumper of a Volkswagen. I lay on my back over the rear section of the car, stretching my arms onto the roof. Nails were driven through my palms into the roof of the car. The garage door was opened and the car was pushed half-way out into Speedway.
Screaming for me, the engine was run at full speed for two minutes. After two minutes, the engine was turned off and the car pushed back into the garage. The door was closed.

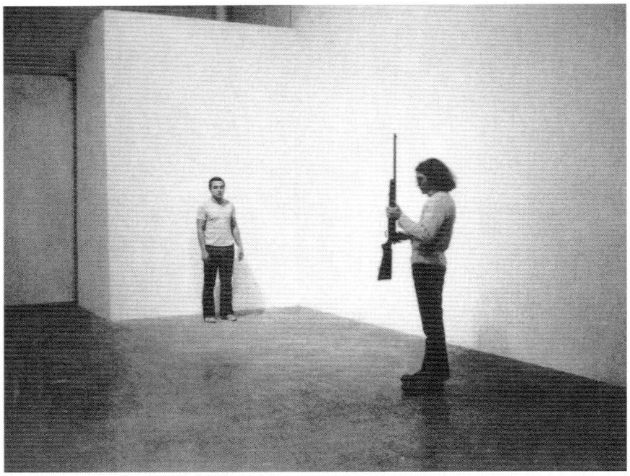

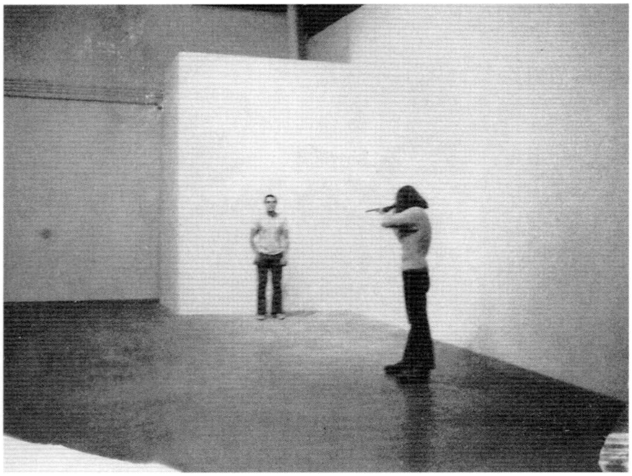

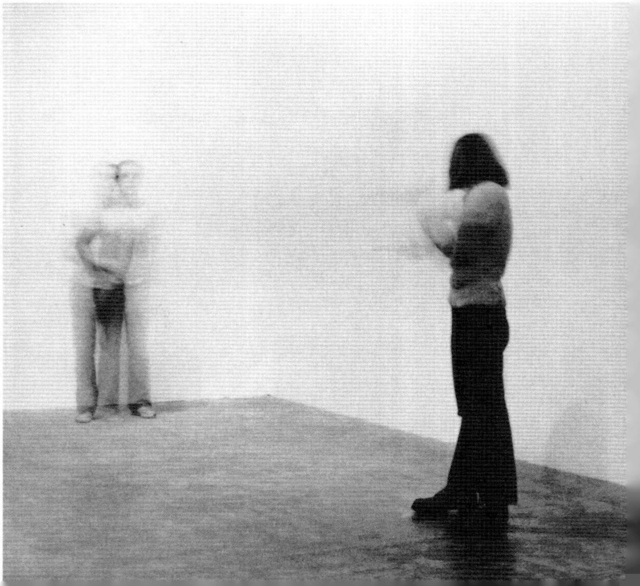

CHRIS BURDEN, *Shoot*, 1971

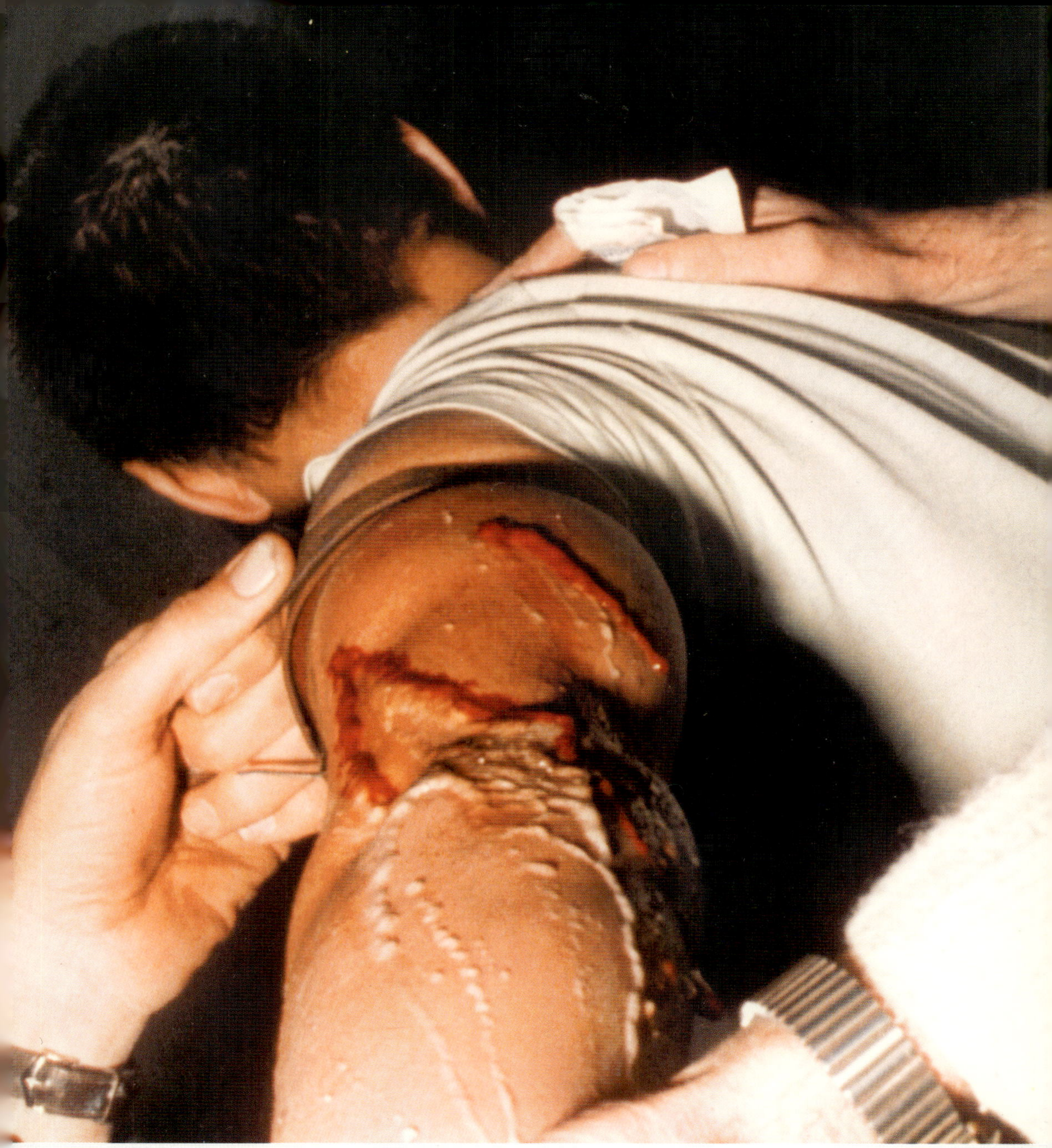

Shoot
F Space: November 19, 1971

At 7:45 p.m. I was shot in the left arm by a friend. The bullet was a copper jacket 22 long rifle. My friend was standing about fifteen feet from me.

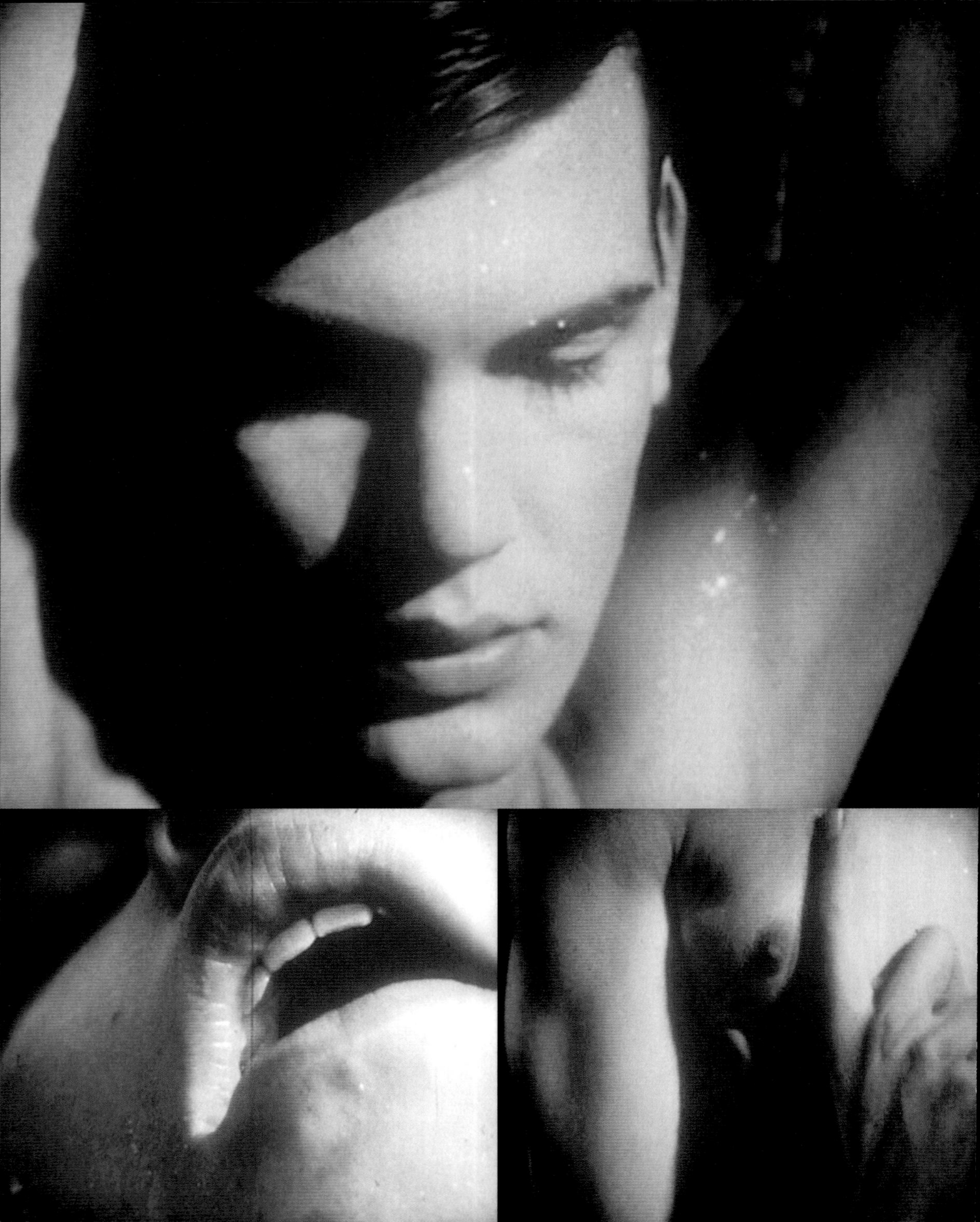

Bavo Defurne

Film is a medium very fit to express simple interpersonal relations and plot-driven adventures. Expressing abstract, universal and heavy emotion, intrapersonal struggle, general longing or "Weltschmerz" in film is a challenge. Even more, if the film is only about 10 minutes long. My personal strategy to go about this is to use archetypes. By archetypes, I mean characters so universal that we all know them and we as viewers are aware of the emotions they represent.

In my short film work, I use The Sailor, The Boy Scout, The Schoolboy and the Saint to represent various aspects of male desire, of absolute and universal longing. Those chameleon characters are used as templates. They have some invariable features, but other features are left blank for the artist to fill in his message. This way of working is for me a strategy that yields speed and clarity in artistic expression. Those advantages are especially good for short films. It gave the works the chance to succeed in making the cross-over from experimental film elite to wider audience.

I unregretfully enjoy using these templates. We share a big heritage and I feel it would be senseless and pretentious to throw all this away. It is a big waste to start from scratch, it doesn't get you far. A template could easily be called a cliché, and I don't think this is bad at all. The word cliché means "an original from which one prints". The specific artistic expression is situated in the act of printing, not in the original itself. The act of using clichés is essentially an act of confronting the heritage with the actual.

I feel that Saint Sebastian is a very exciting template to work with. He is the ultimate chameleon. He has been part of the artistic vocabulary of many many artists with as many messages. He is, after Jesus, the most popular male nude in Catholic iconography.

Historically, there is almost nothing sure about him. Sebastian was a Christian, a martyr, and possibly a Roman soldier. All the rest is legend. So the original cliché is almost empty.

The arrows that we now recognize as main ingredients were only added in the Middle Ages, centuries after the saint had made his first appearance in Christian iconography. Arrows stand for sudden death, arrows symbolized the plague, Sebastian was a popular Plague Saint. Early Sebastians were stiff and un-erotical. Artists showed no interest for the physical beauty of the saint. Lots of blood and a huge load of arrows showed the saint's pain. Renaissance and the knowledge of anatomy meant a big change for Sebastian. His

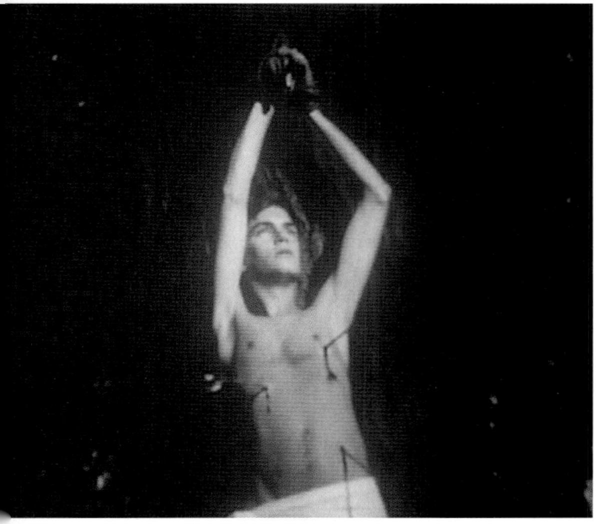

Stills from: BAVO DEFURNE, *Saint*, 1996

positions became more diverse and difficult to draw. His arms were often pointed upwards instead of bound behind the back. His body started to move and curve, his muscles developed. Romantic depictions introduced a yet more sensual, sensitive saint, with more attention to facial expression, and only very little blood and arrows.

Today as yesterday, Sebastian is an exciting template for stories of pleasure and pain. My film *Saint* starts off from the Catholic martyr legend. But I do not stick to it, I open the film to different readings. There is a rescue theme added: as soon as the saint is condemned, some boys try to rescue him by attempting to kill the Emperor. A lot remains unsaid, but the images are loaded with lust, romance, and pain. About what? This is open to the viewer's imagination and interpretation, altough the longing of the male body is surely one of the main themes, as are death and sacrifice.

I am personally interested in the link that Sebastian has to AIDS. He is a young, beautiful man struck by sudden death. He is a saint who protects against the plague, an epidemic more than once compared to AIDS. For more than the last century, Sebastian has been related to male homosexuality. And although the reality is that AIDS is now an issue of the whole world, gay male communities are far more aware of the threats. The fear of death due to AIDS, and the inevitability of death once a person was contaminated, were very important themes when I was developing this project, in the early nineties. I think these feelings have inspired me in the creation of the Saint Sebastian I brought to the screen.

This is only one of many readings of my film. I myself have many of them, and every audience again reacts differently. The last word will never be spoken. It excites me tremendously to see how this work without dialogue keeps on feeding many, many readings. This effect that the Chameleon Saint has both on artists and viewers, is a sign of the huge powers the saint has over us.

Saint was filmed on Super-8 and I hand-processed the negative myself. Like the people, plants and animals that appear in the film, the film stock itself felt as if it was organic, its very unpredictability enabling me to achieve richly contrasting tones. I loved the tactile – almost erotic – touch of the film material. Like Genet's *un chant d'amour* and, to a certain extent, German Expressionist cinema, *Saint* tries to create maximum impact with very simple, low-tech tools, leaving much to the viewers' imagination. The dark, furry images add mystery and body to the whole.

Bavo Defurne

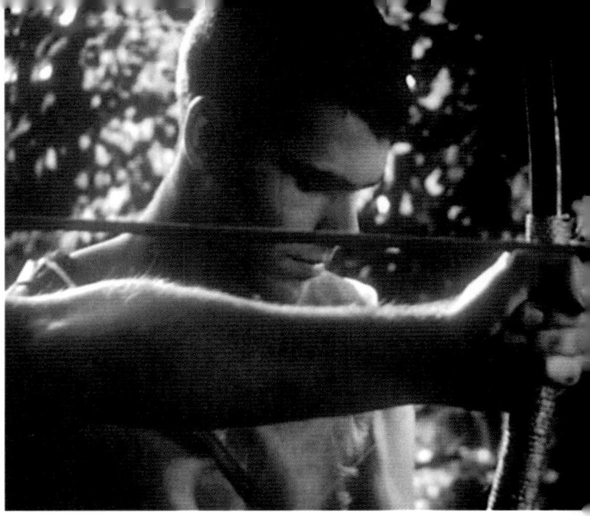

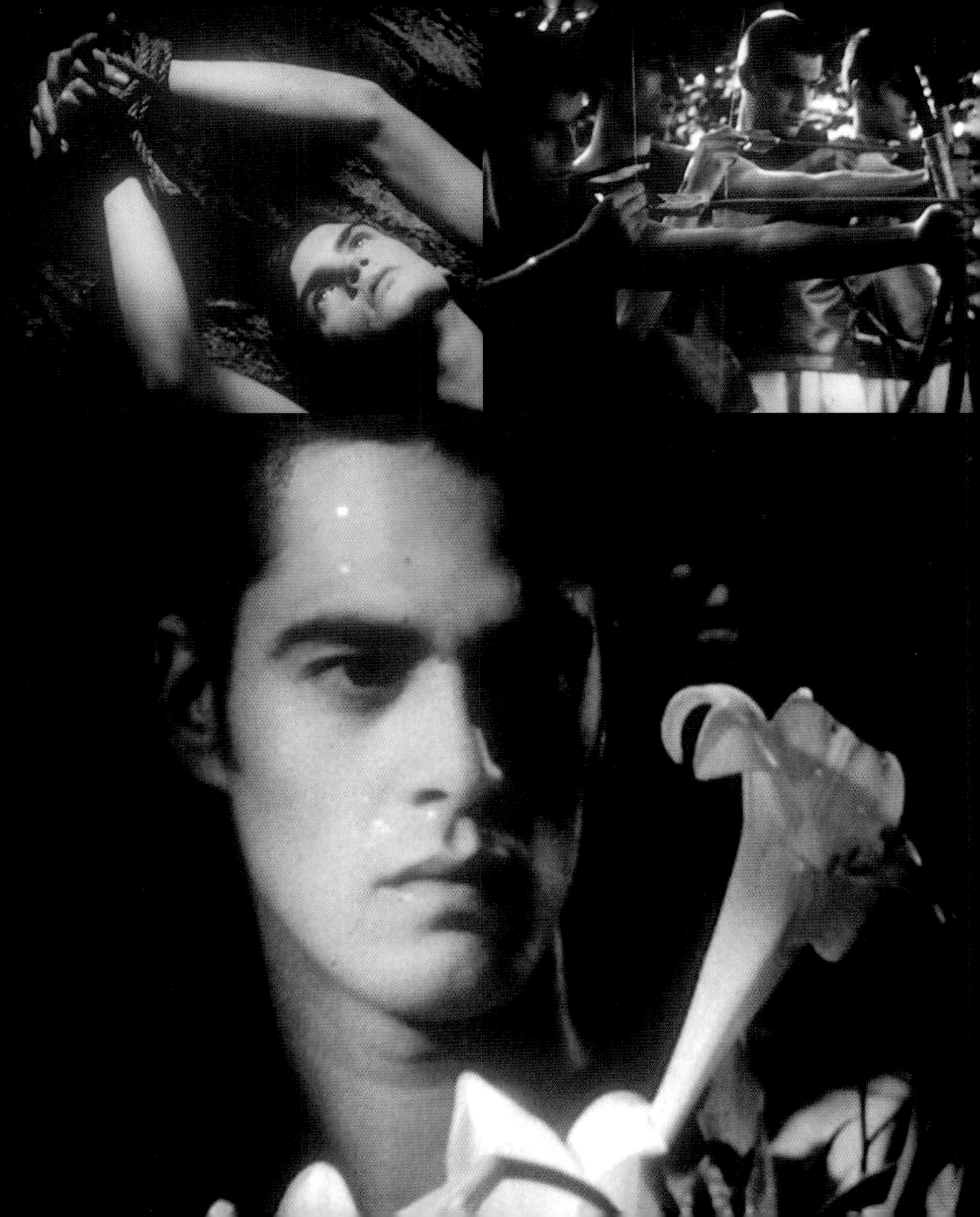

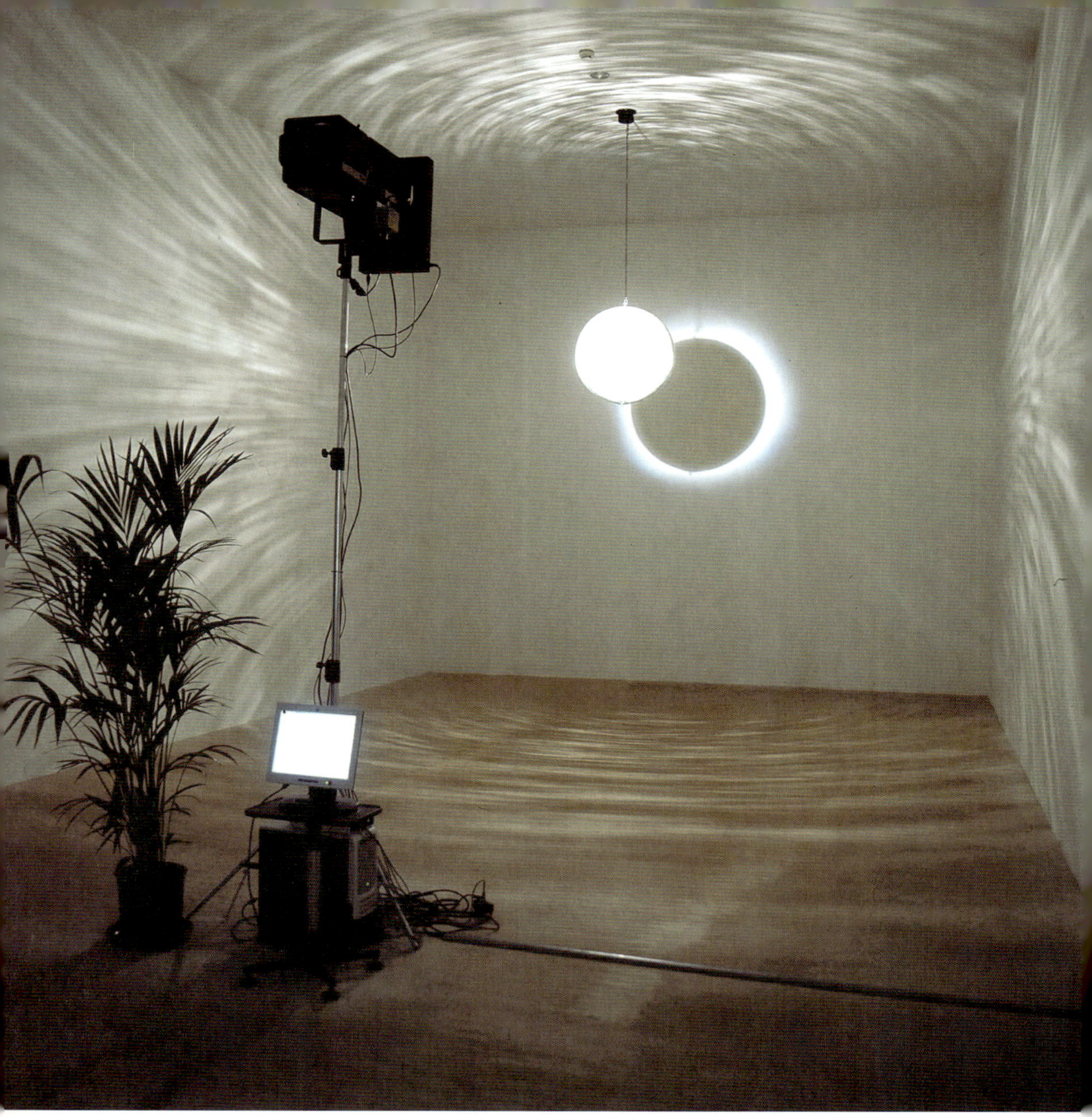

CERITH WYN EVANS
Installation View: *Cleave 02 (The Accursed Share)*, 2002
Installation View: *Cleave 00* , 2000

Cerith Wyn Evans

Yukio Mishima was born in 1925 in Tokyo. Actor, narcissist, fanatical body-builder and self-styled samurai, he wrote plays as well as novels and his work has been published internationally. His public death by hara-kiri in 1970, combined with an abortive attempt at a coup d'etat, caused a world-wide sensation. His suicide – his "final work of art" - has been regarded as the ultimate realisation of his fantasies of pain and death. "Confessions of a Mask" is a haunting story of a Japanese boy's growth towards a homosexual identity during and after the Second World War. It is a classic account of fantasy, obsession, despair and alienation.

"I began turning a page toward the end of the volume. Suddenly there came into view from one corner of the next page a picture that I had to believe had been lying in wait there for me, for my sake.

It was a reproduction of Guido Reni's *St. Sebastian*, which hangs in the collection of the Palazzo Rosso at Genoa.

The black and slightly oblique trunk of the tree of execution was seen against a Titian-like background of gloomy forest and evening sky, somber and distant. A remarkably handsome youth was bound naked to the trunk of the tree. His crossed hands were raised high, and the thongs binding his wrists were tied to the tree. No other bonds were visible, and the only covering for the youth's nakedness was a course white cloth knotted loosely about his lions.

I guessed it must be a depiction of a Christian martyrdom. But, as it was painted by an esthetic painter of the eclectic school that derived from the Renaissance, even this painting of the death of a Christian saint has about it a strong flavor of paganism. The youth's body- it might even be likened to that of Antinous, beloved of Hadrian, whose beauty has been so often immortalized in sculpture- shows none of the traces of missionary hardship or decrepitude that are to be found in depictions of other saints; instead, there is only the springtime of youth, only light and beauty and pleasure.

His white and matchless nudity gleams against a background of dusk. His muscular arms, the arms of a praetorian guard accustomed to bending of bow and wielding of sword, are raised at a graceful angle, and his bound wrists are crossed directly over his head. His face is turned slightly upward and his eyes are opened wide, gazing with profound tranquility upon the glory of heaven. It is not pain that hovers about his straining

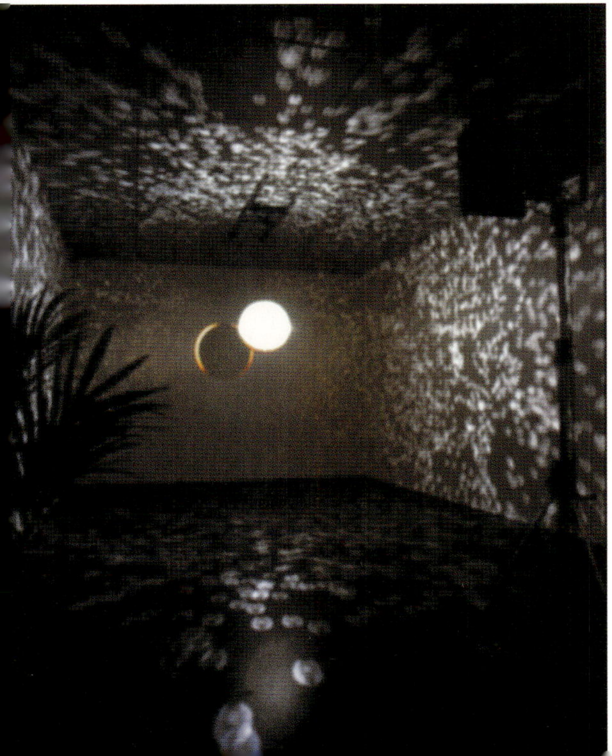

chest, his tense abdomen, his slightly contorted hips, but some flicker of melancholy pleasure like music. Were it not for the arrows with their shafts deeply sunk into his left armpit and right side, he would seem more a Roman athlete resting from fatigue, leaning against a dusky tree in a garden.

The arrows have eaten into the tense, fragrant, youthful flesh and are about to consume his body from within with flames of supreme agony and ecstasy. But there is no flowing blood, nor yet the host of arrows seen in other pictures of Sebastian's martyrdom. Instead, two lone arrows cast their tranquil and graceful shadows upon the smoothness of his skin, like the shadows of a bough falling upon a marble stairway."

Excerpt from: Yukio Mishima, *Confessions of a Mask*, New York: New Directions, 1958

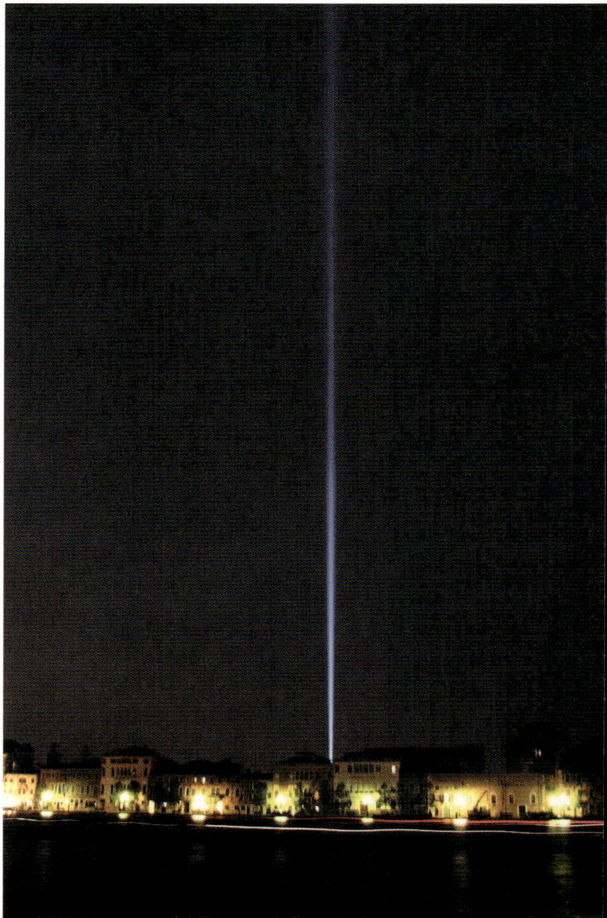

CERITH WYN EVANS
Installation View: *Cleave 03 (Visions of the Sleeping Poet)*, 2003
Installation View: *Cleave 01*, 2001

Morse Code

A cryptographic code invented in the 1830's by Samuel Morse for transmitting telegraph messages. Each letter of the alphabet and number has a characteristic sequence of dots and dashes (short and long pulses), a dash being three times as long as a dot. The code has been used widely for transmitting messages by sound and by light flashes. The signal SOS - 'SAVE OUR SOULS' - (three short pulses, three long pulses, and three short Pulses) was for some 150 years the universal distress signal. However, from 1993 satellite technology made the tapping out of distress signals unnecessary and by the late 1990s Morse code was rarely used at sea, except occasionally for flashing lights between ships. Morse code continues to be used for identifying aeronautical navigation beacons.

International Morse Code

Letters

A	·–	N	–·
B	–···	O	–––
C	–·–·	P	·––·
D	–··	Q	––·–
E	·	R	·–·
F	··–·	S	···
G	––·	T	–
H	····	U	··–
I	··	V	···–
J	·–––	W	·––
K	–·–	X	–··–
L	·–··	Y	–·––
M	––	Z	––··

Numbers and Punctuation

1	·––––
2	··–––
3	···––
4	····–
5	·····
6	–····
7	––···
8	–––··
9	––––·
0	–––––
Period	·–·–·–
Comma	––··––

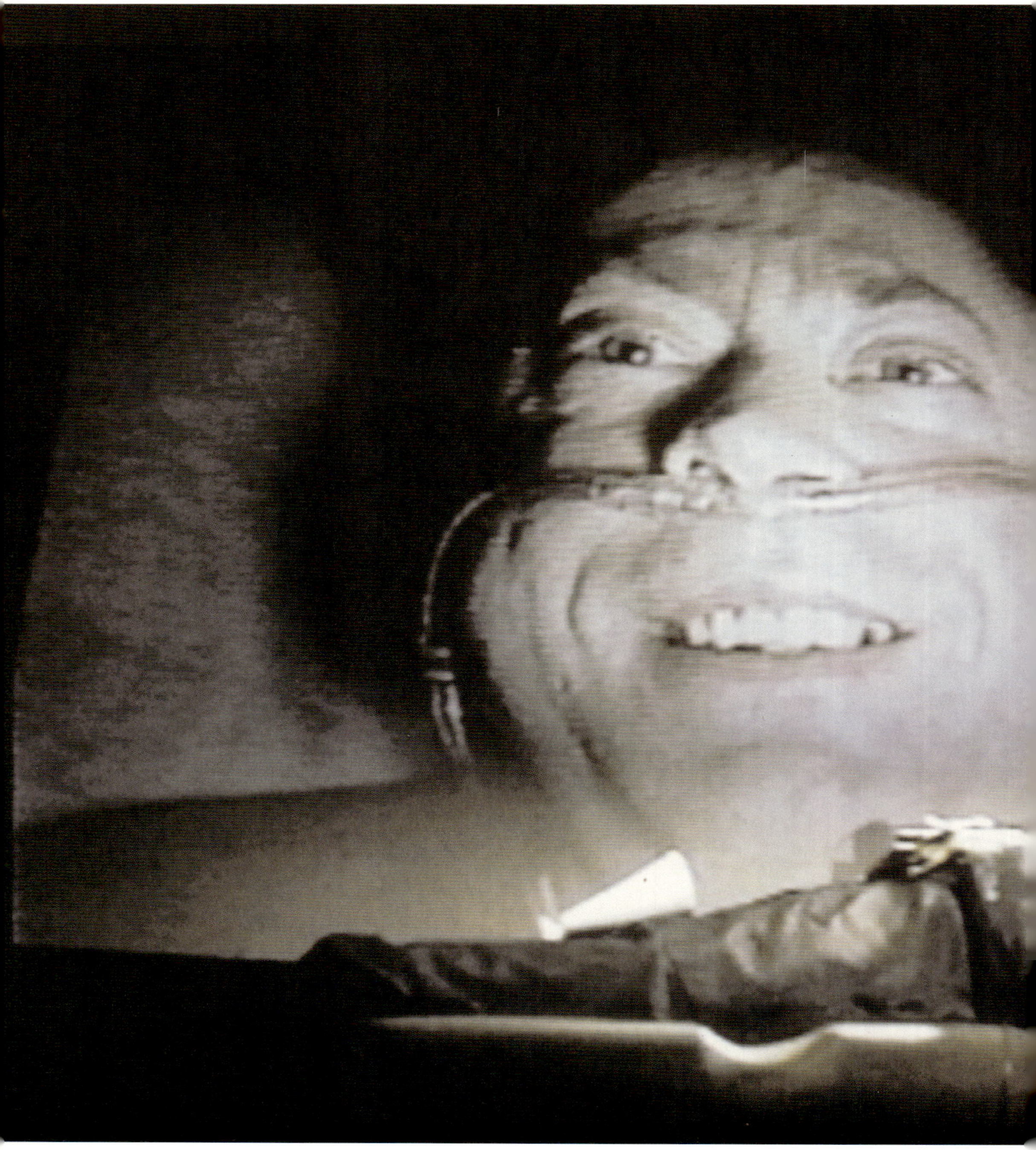

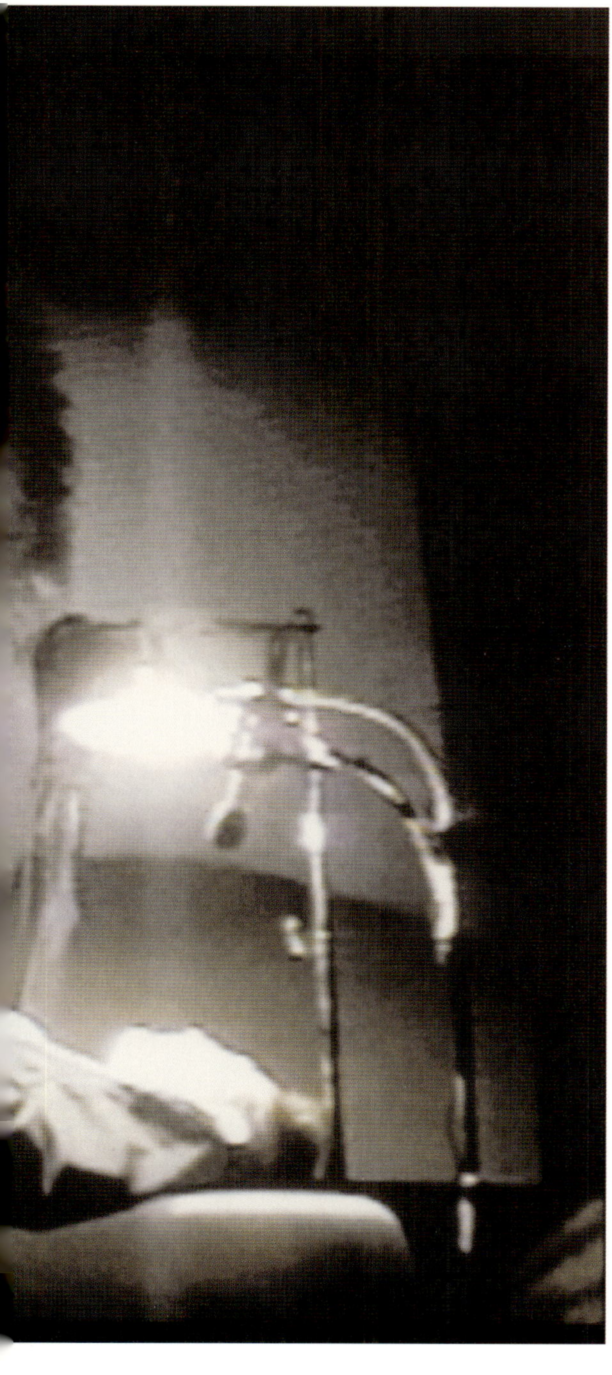

Bob Flanagan

Bob Flanagan was born with mucoviscidosis, a hereditary disease commonly known as cystic fibrosis, which is present from birth and does not permit people to have long lives. As he says himself, he developed a survival strategy, fighting the illness with illness, the physical with the mental. And so he became a "supermasochist". In his poem *Why*, which was very often played in the background during Flanagan's performances, the artist justifies his masochism as follows: "Because it feels good; because it gives me an erection; because it makes me come; because I'm sick; because there was so much sickness; because I say fuck the sickness; because I like the attention; because I was alone a lot; because I was different; because beat me up kids beat me up on the way to school; because I was humilated by nuns; because of Christ and the crucfixion".

The creative work of Flanagan as a performance artist, musician and poet is documented in Kirby Dick's film, which shows his life and that of his partner and torturer Sheree Rose. The couple is shown both in loving intimacy and in their radical sexual practices. The film opens up a view of the drama of dying and surviving, and ends with the death of Bob Flanagan, which he was nevertheless able to hold back so long.

Angela Stief

Stills from: Kirby Dick,
Sick: The Life and Death of Bob Flanagan, Supermasochist, 1997

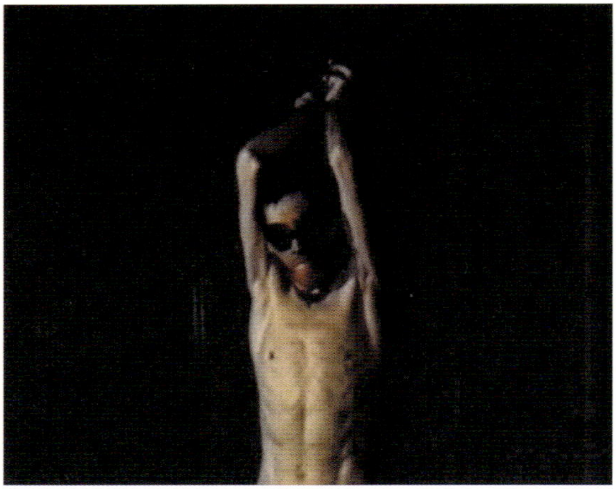
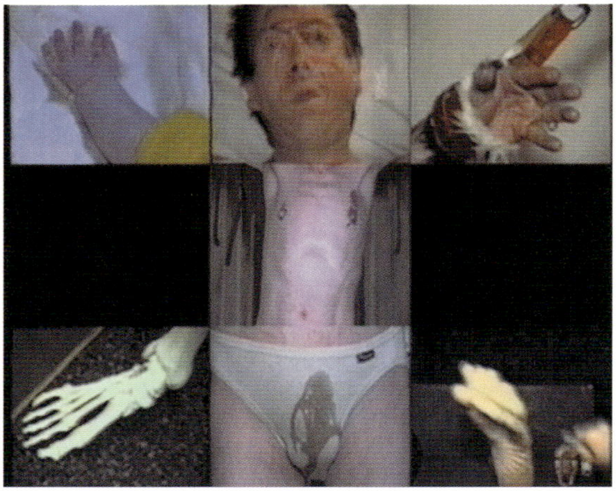
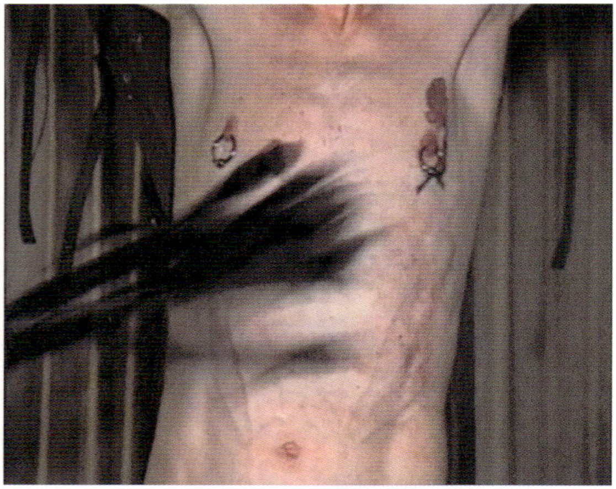
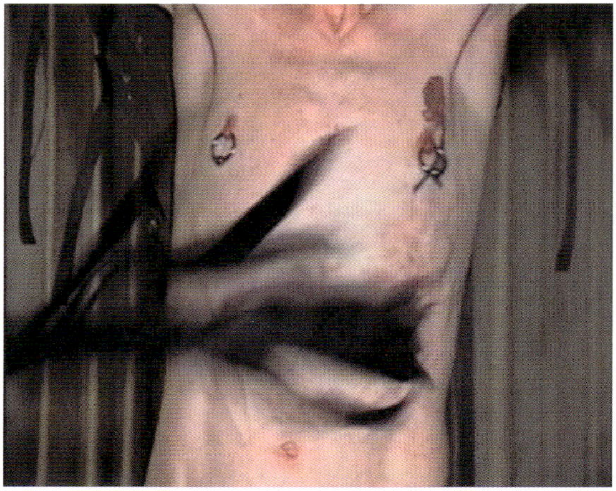
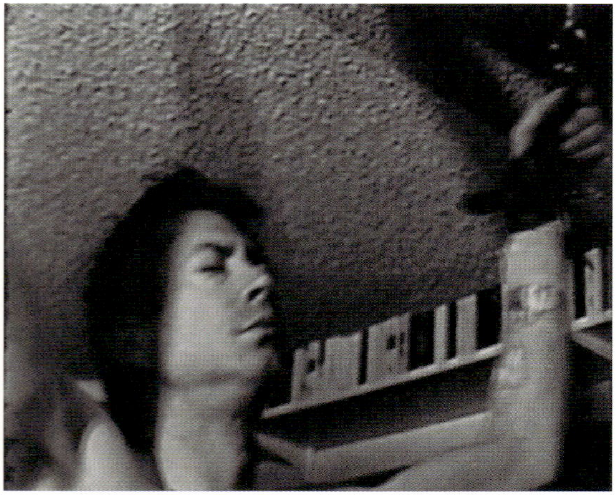
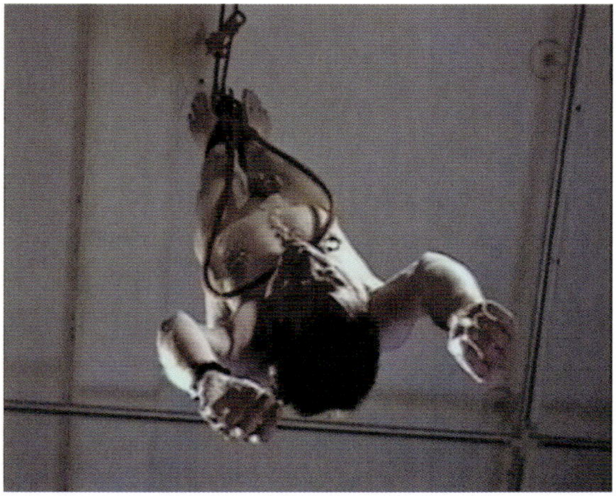

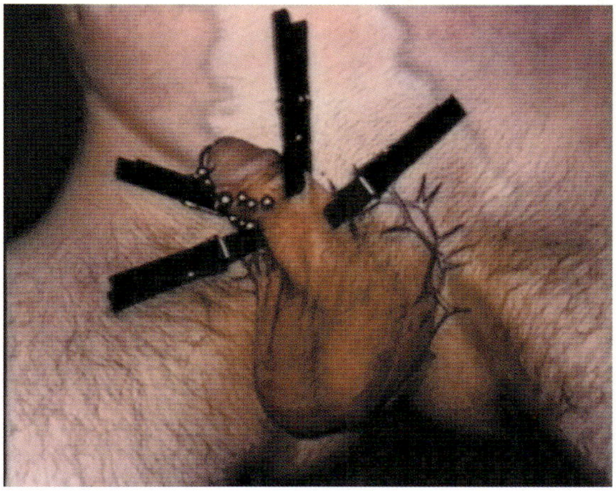
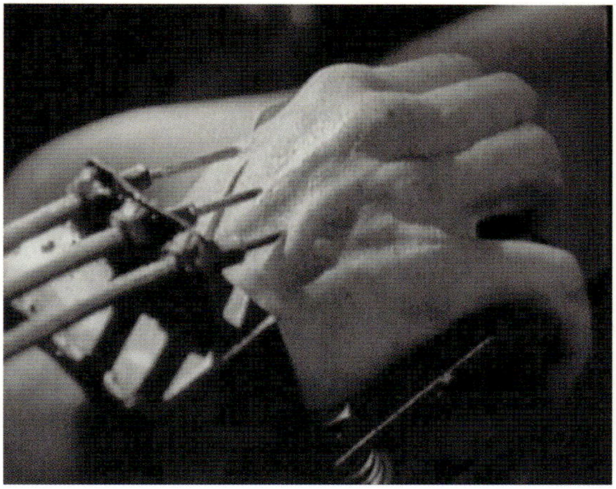
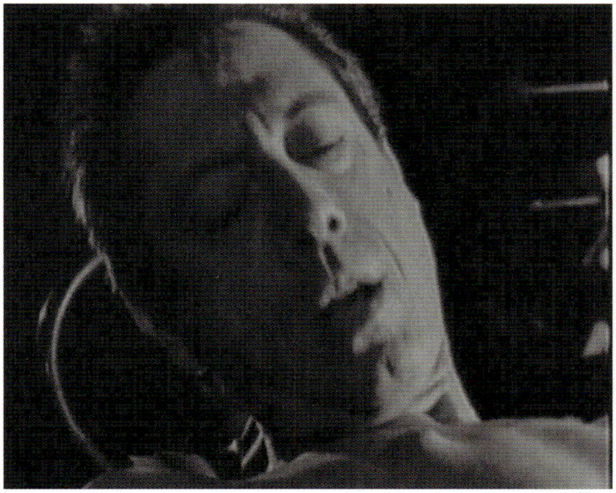
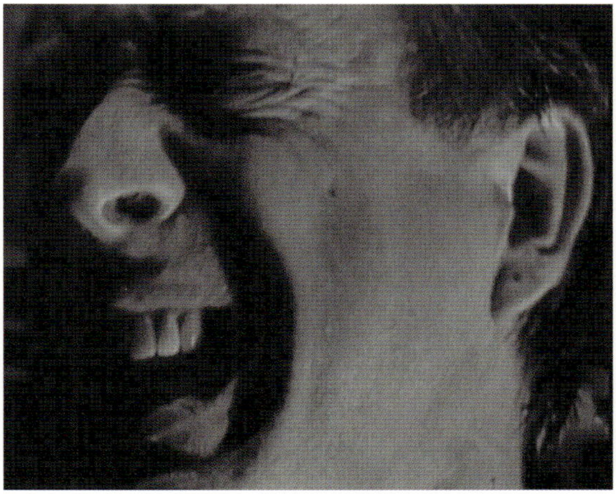
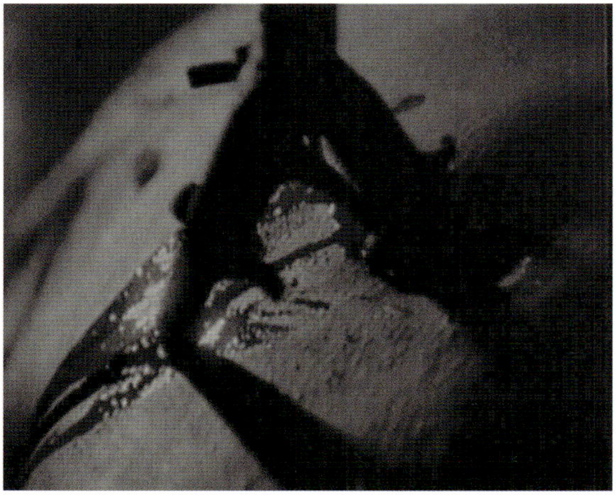

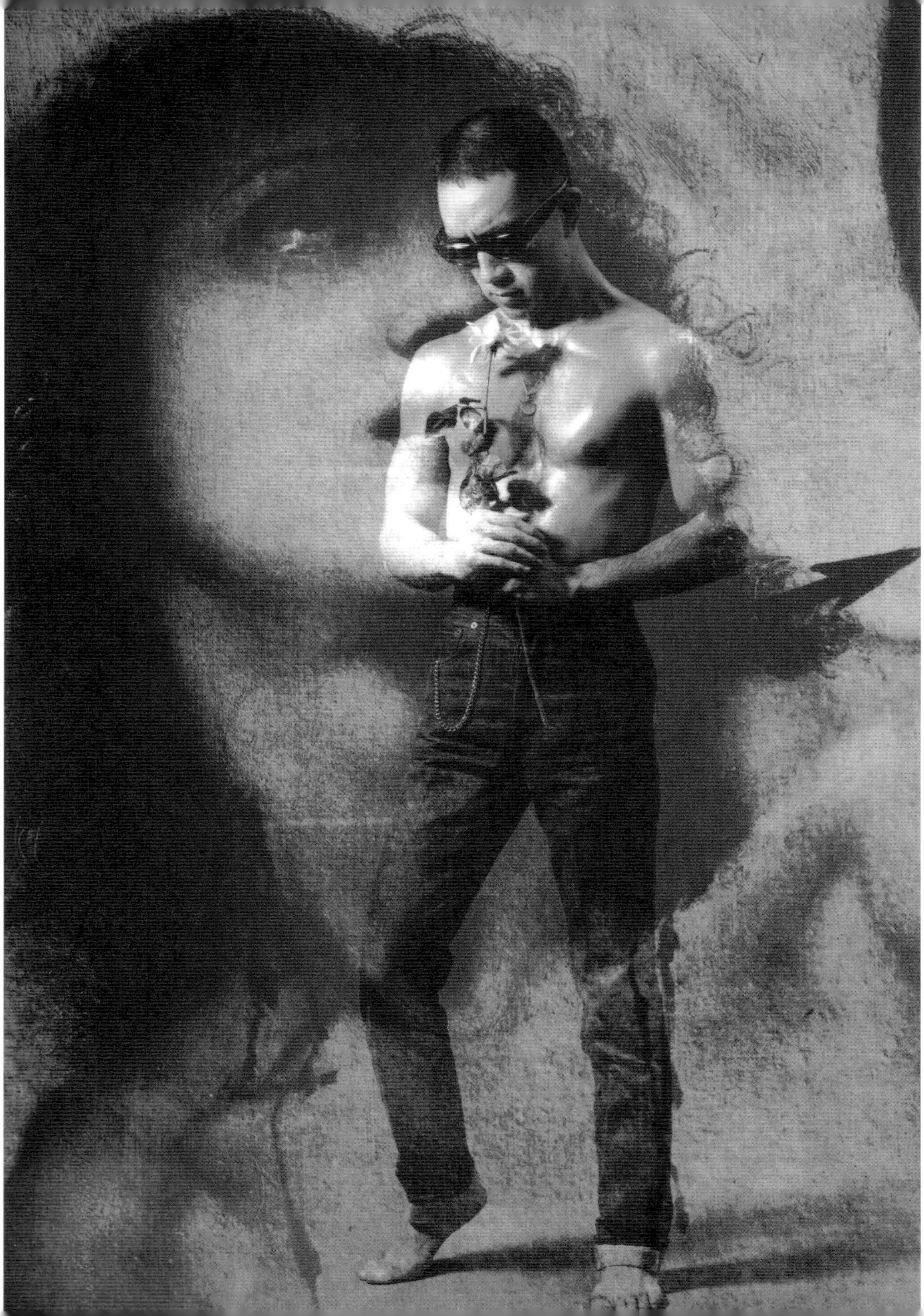

Eikoh Hosoe

The series *Ordeal by Roses (BA RA KEI)*, is a collection of subjective documentary photographs evolving from my own imagination. It is I, therefore, who must take the whole responsibility for everything that is presented in them. *Ordeal By Roses* is also an unrepeatable event – for it is Yukio Mishima who served as my model.

As Mishima confirms in his preface to *Ordeal By Roses*, he never asked me how he was to be photographed or depicted. "Before (Hosoe's) camera," he wrote, "I soon realized that my own spirit, the workings of my mind, had become totally redundant. It was an exhilarating experience, a state of affairs I had long dreamed of."

The main theme of *Ordeal By Roses* is "life and death". This was a theme, I thought, that I would be able to depict only through Mishima's flesh. Mishima was most generous in allowing this young photographer to pursue his ambition.

I dedicated these platinum prints to Yukio Mishima, a man who never allowed his own physical decline. Today they serve as a permanent record of his immortal beauty, gorgeous at its peak at age thirty-eight.

EIKOH HOSOE

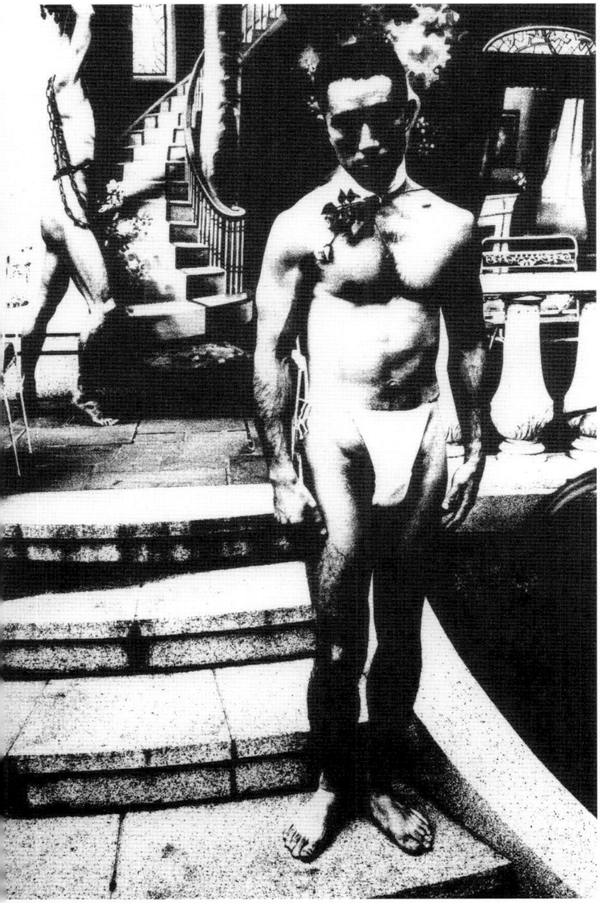

EIKOH HOSOE
Ordeal by Roses (BA RA KEI) # 25, 1962
Ordeal by Roses (BA RA KEI) # 1, 1961

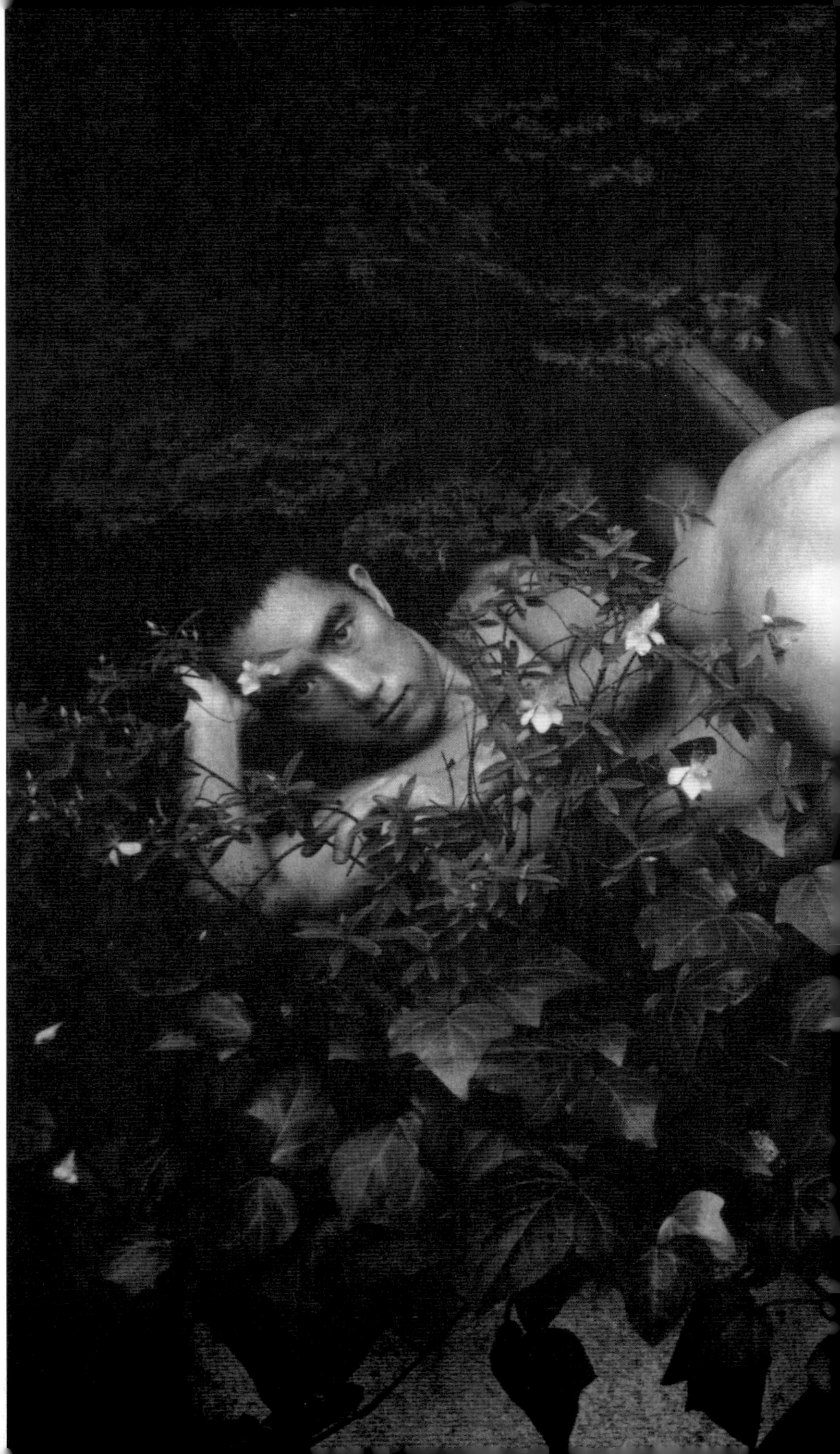

EIKOH HOSOE

Ordeal by Roses
(BA RA KEI) # 15, 1961

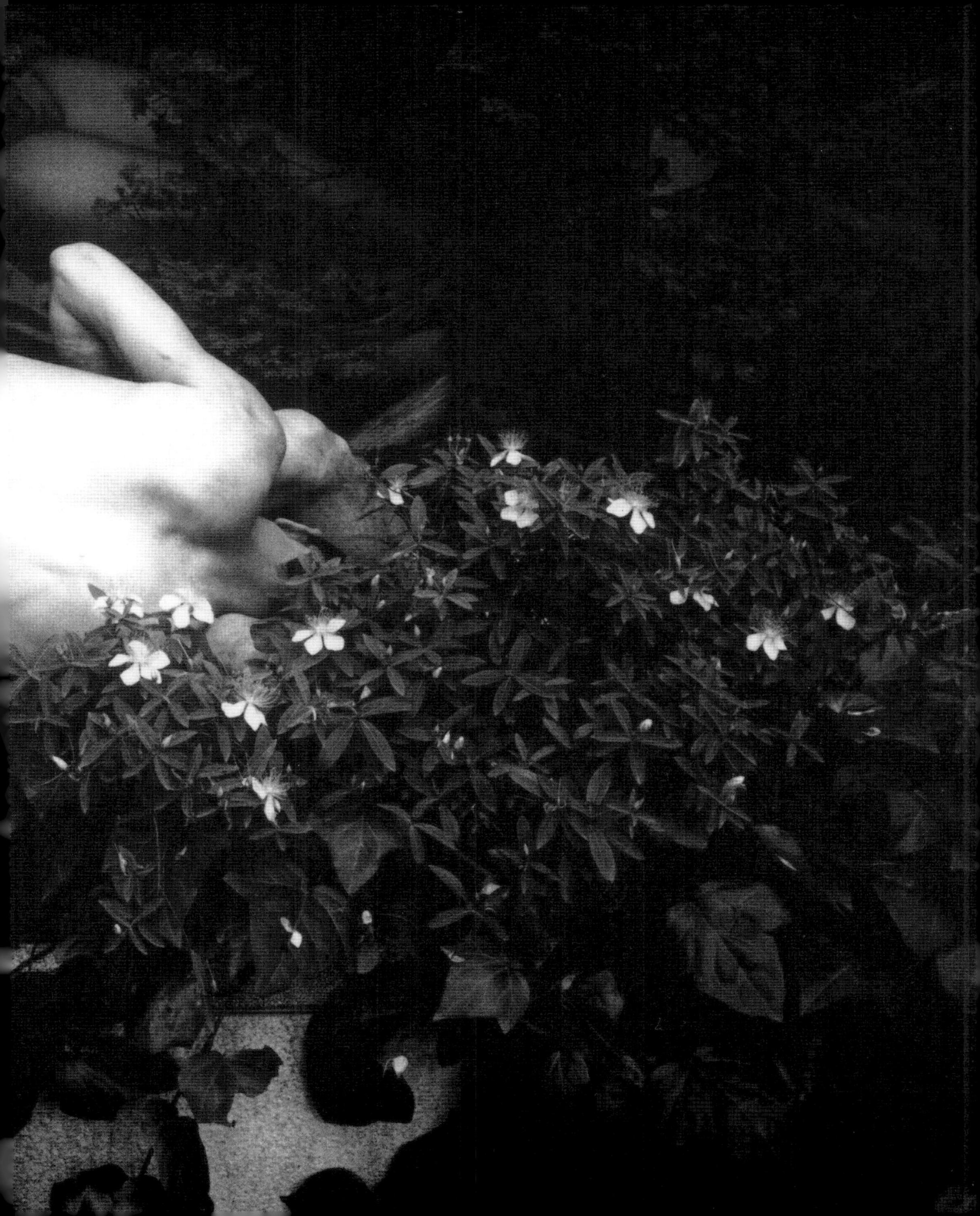

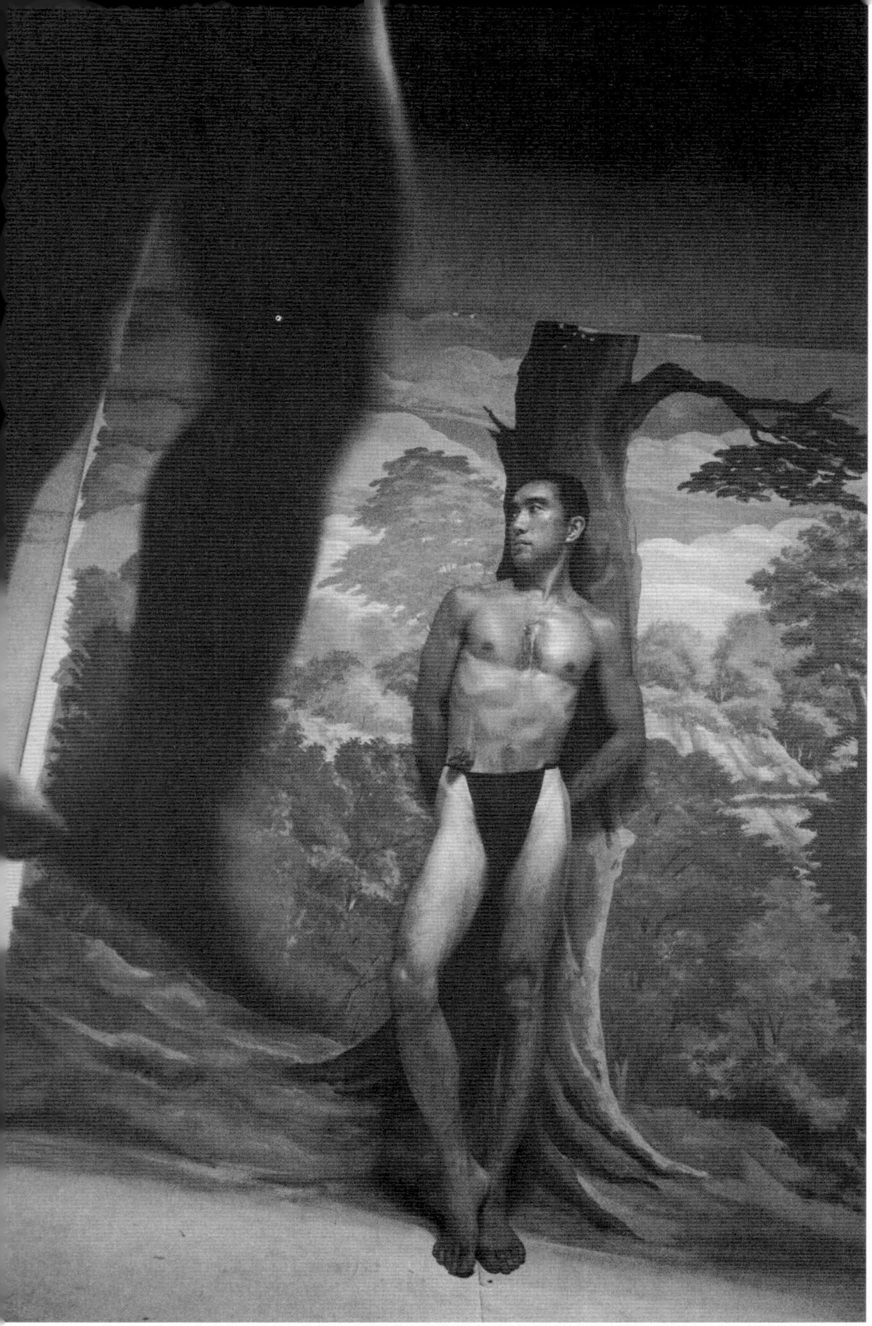

EIKOH HOSOE
Ordeal by Roses (BA RA KEI) # 34, 1961
Ordeal by Roses (BA RA KEI) # 29, 1962

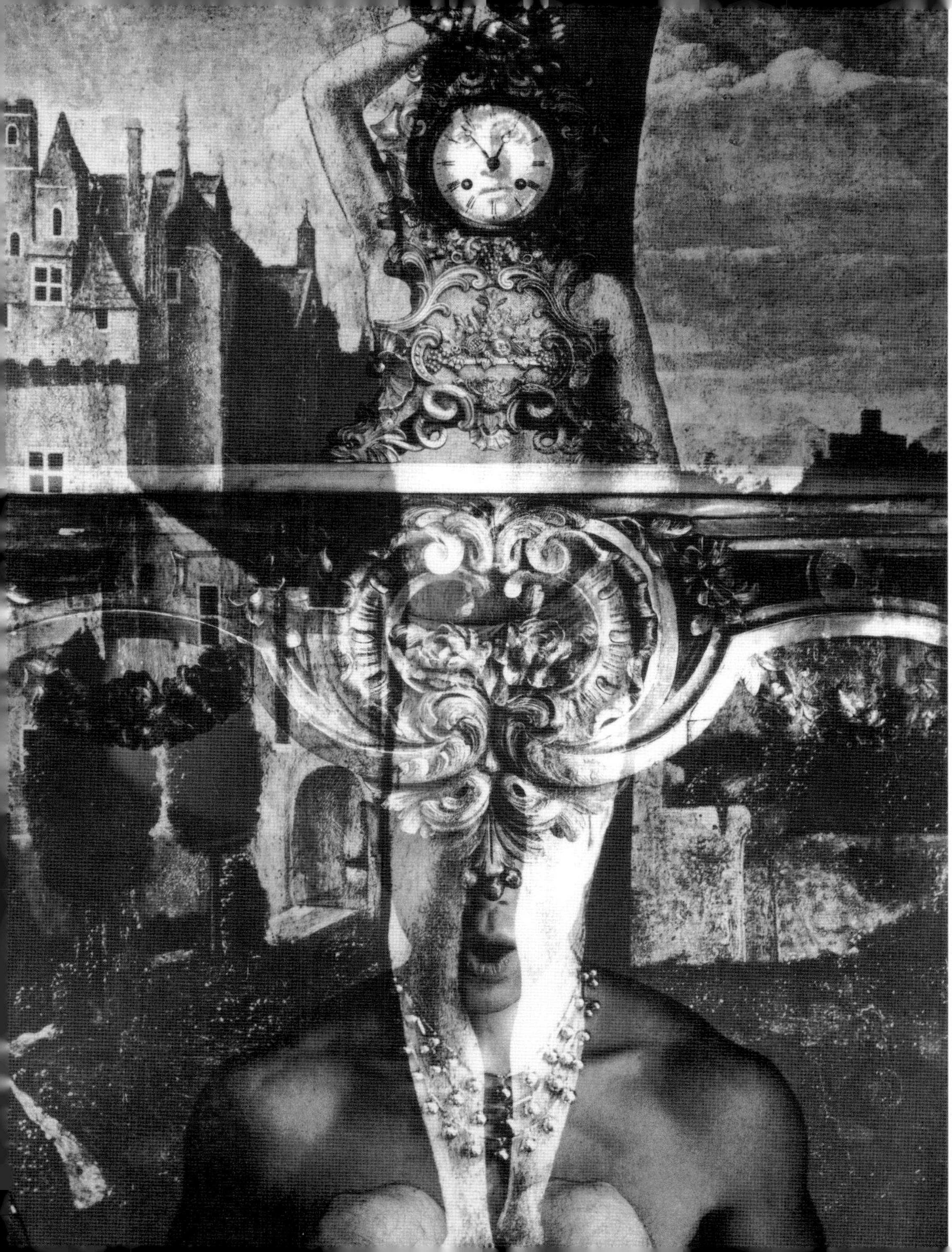

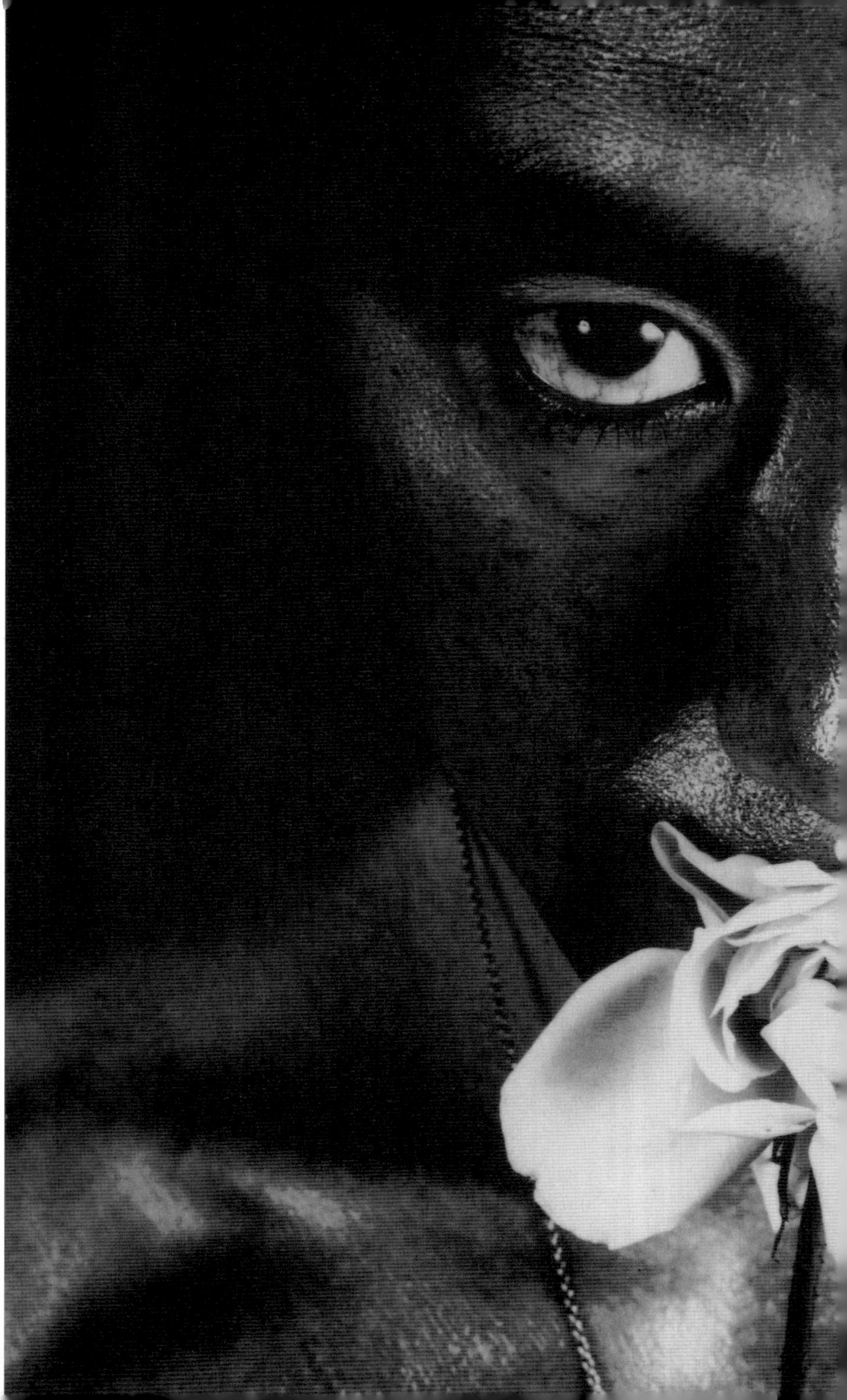

EIKOH HOSOE

Ordeal by Roses (BA RA KEI) # 32, 1961

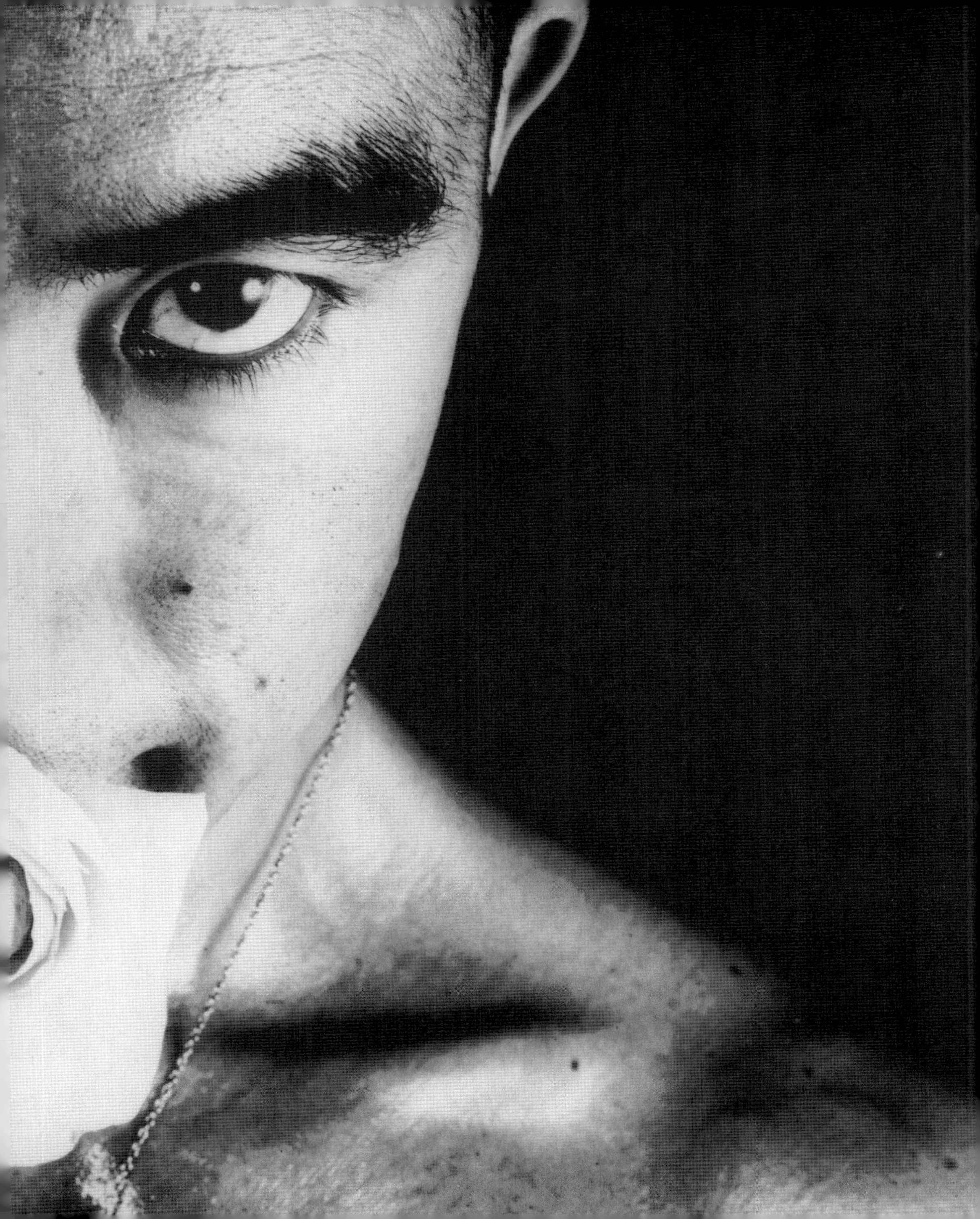

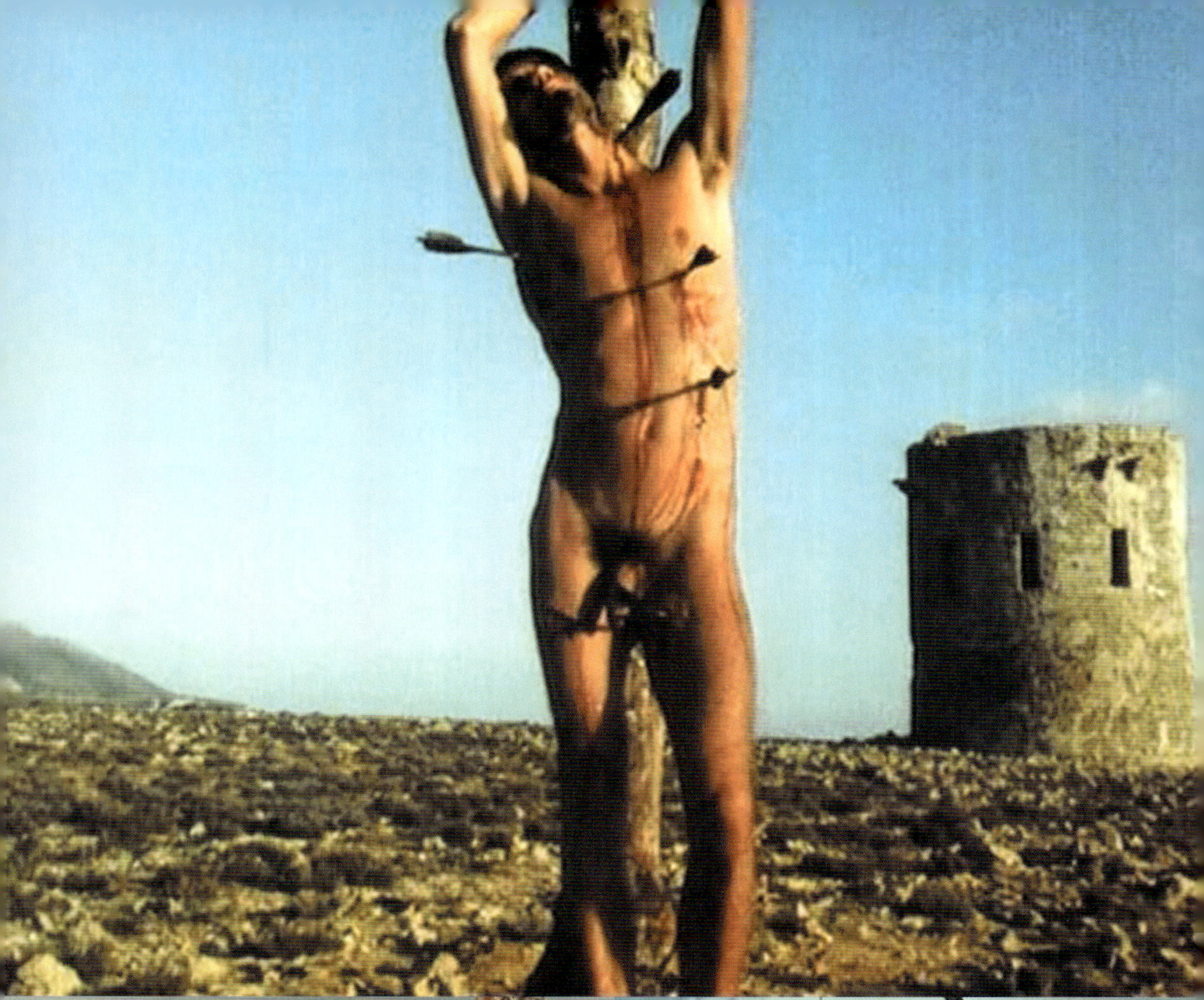

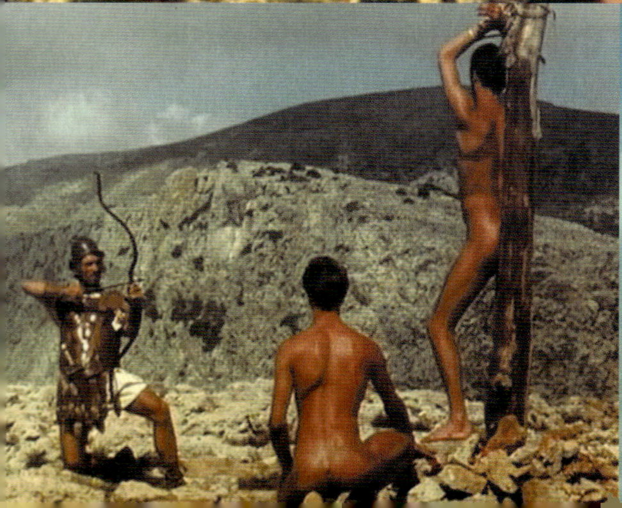

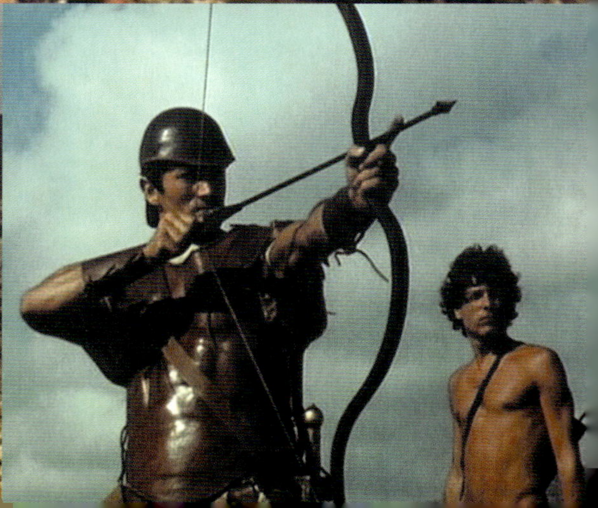

Derek Jarman

It started with sweats in the night and swollen glands. Then the black cancer spread across their faces – as they fought for breath, TB and pneumonia hammered their lungs, and Toxo at the brain. Reflexes scrambled – sweat poured through hair matted like lianas in the tropical forest. Voices slurred – and then were lost forever. My pen chased this story across the page, tossed this way and that in the storm.

My sight failed a little more in the night.
H.B. offers me his blood.
It will kill everything he says.

Impatient youths of the sun
Burning with many colours
Flick combs through hair
In bathroom mirrors
Fucking with fusion and fashion
Dance in the beams of emerald lasers
Mating on suburban duvets
Cum splattered nuclear breeders
What a time that was.

Excerpts from: DEREK JARMAN, *Blue*, 1993, Film, 75 mins.

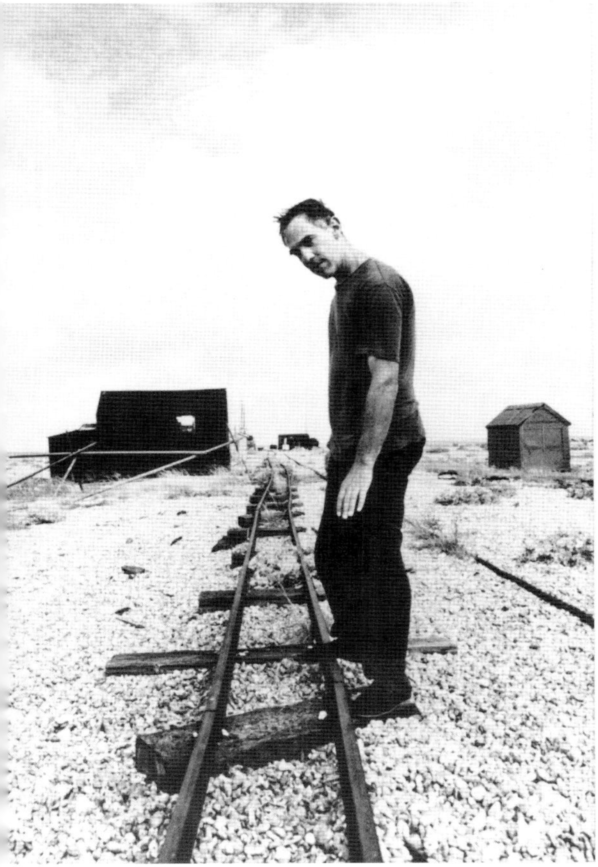

DEREK JARMAN

Stills from: DEREK JARMAN, *Sebastiane*, 1975

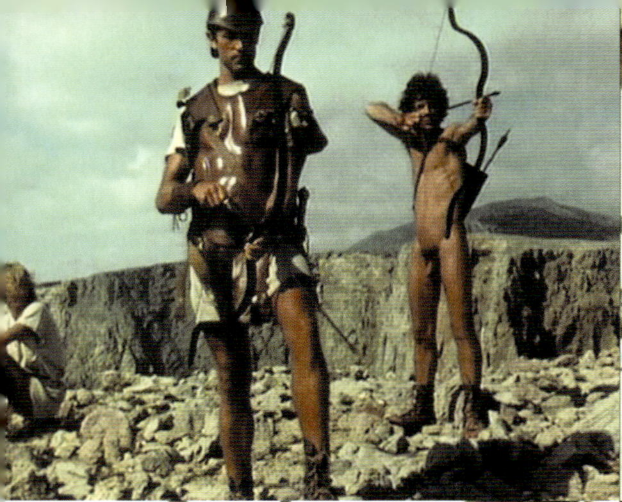
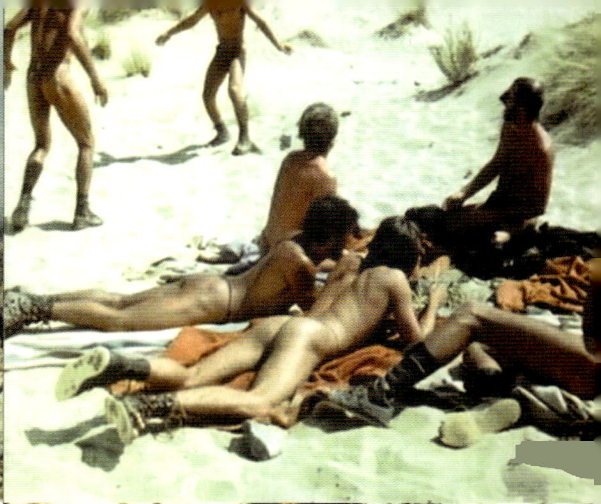
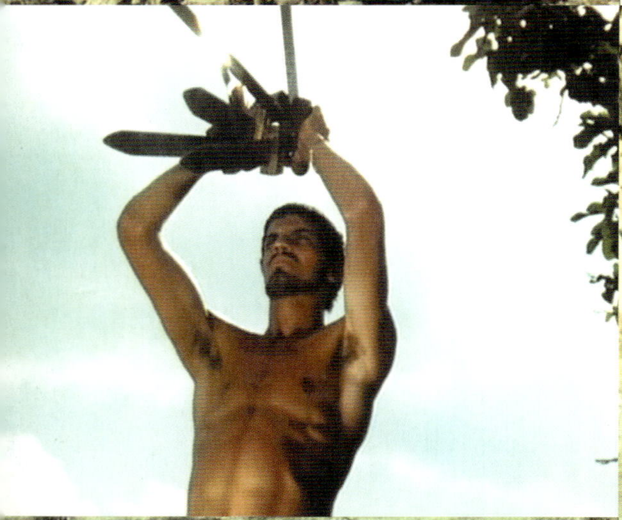
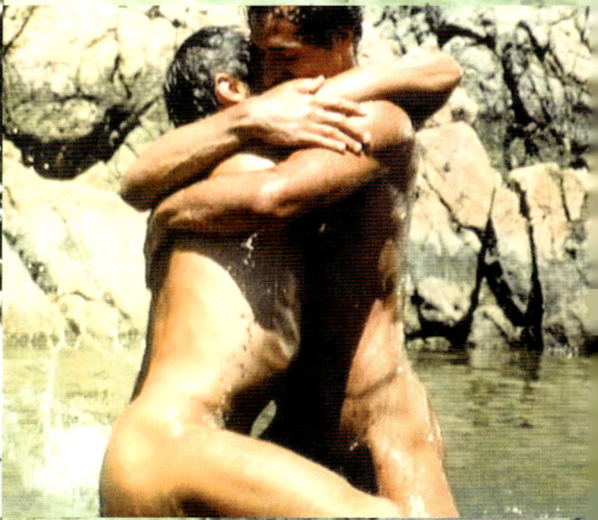
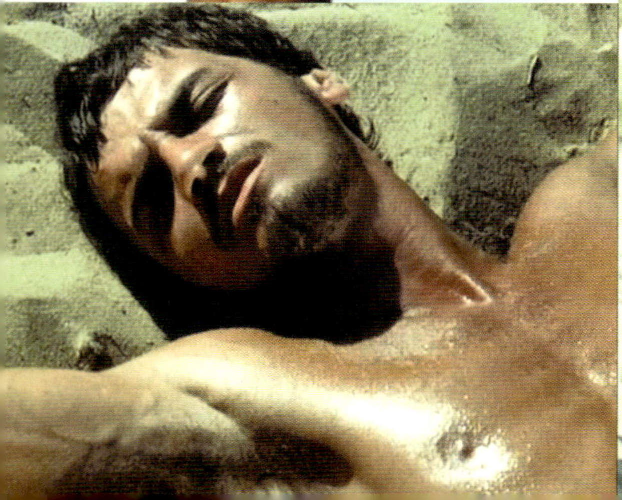
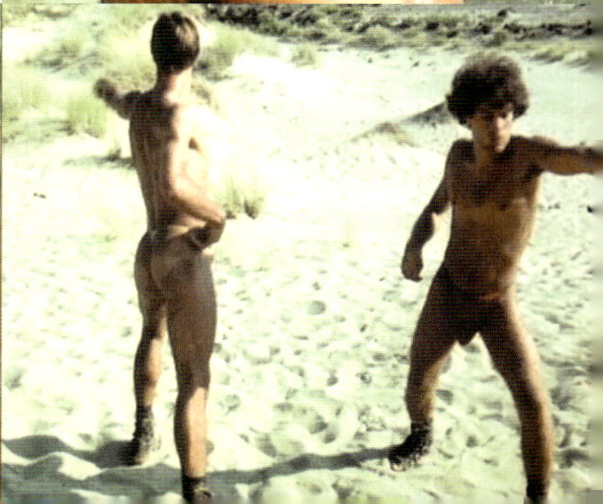

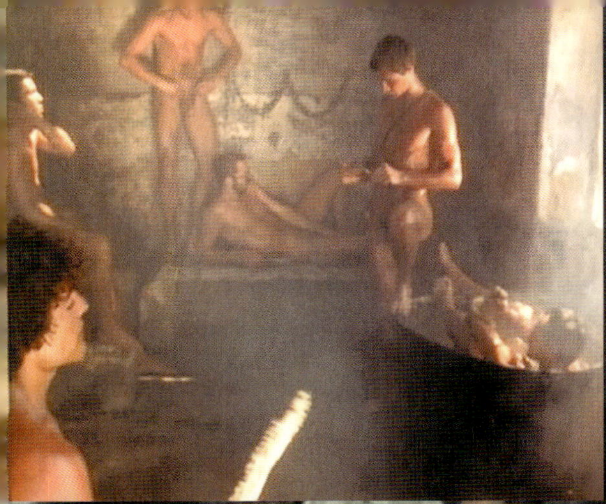
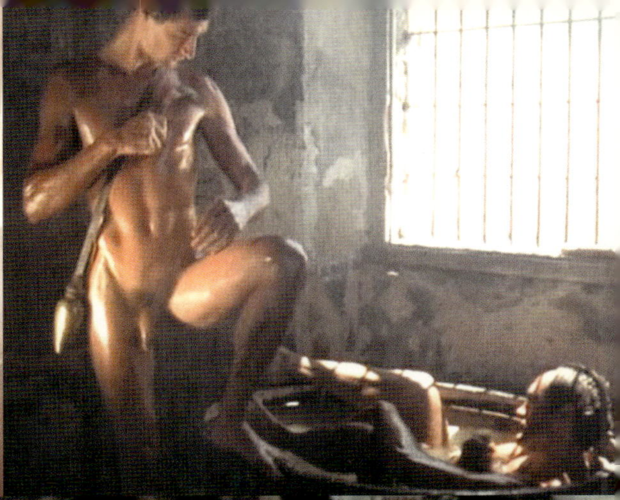
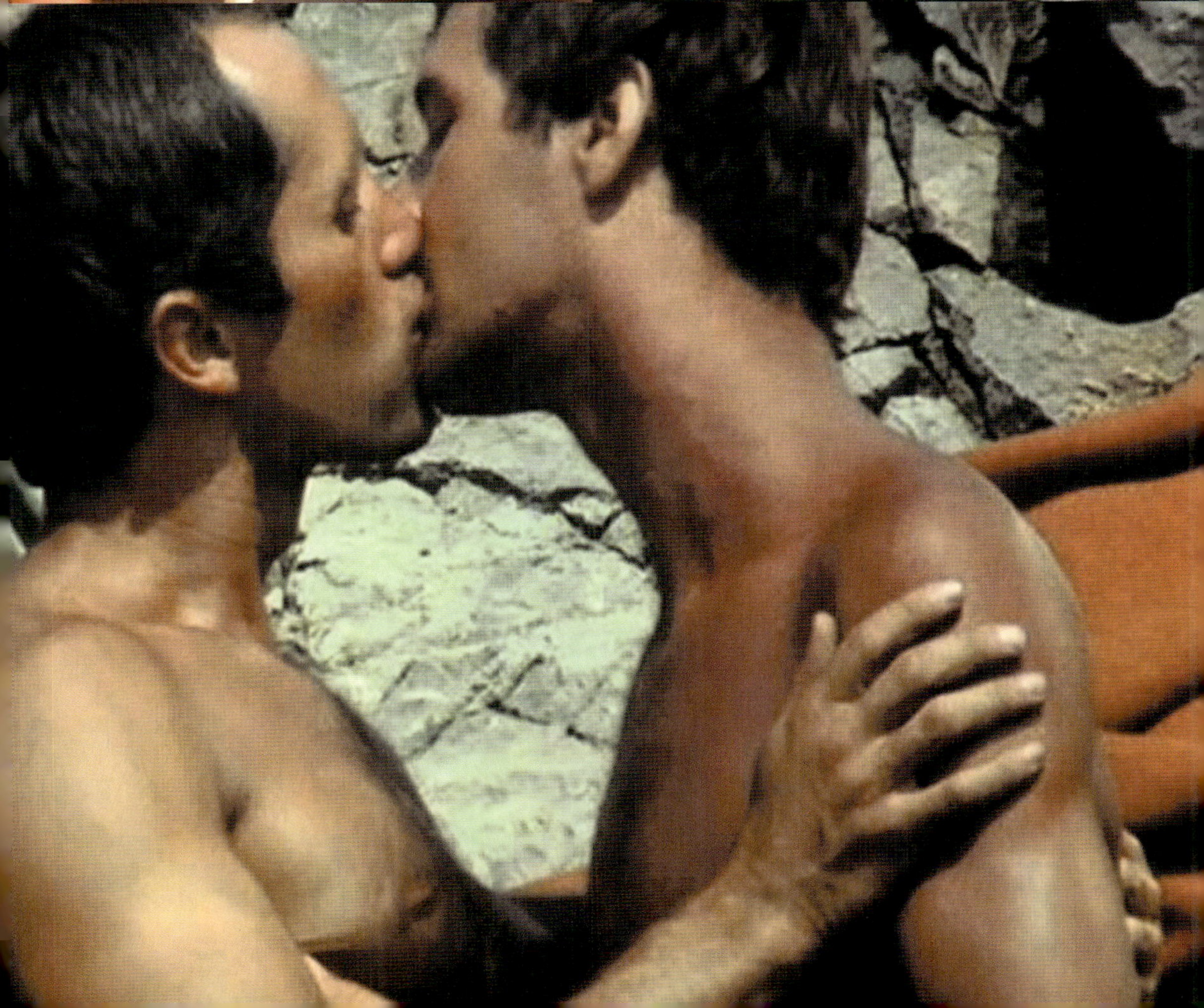

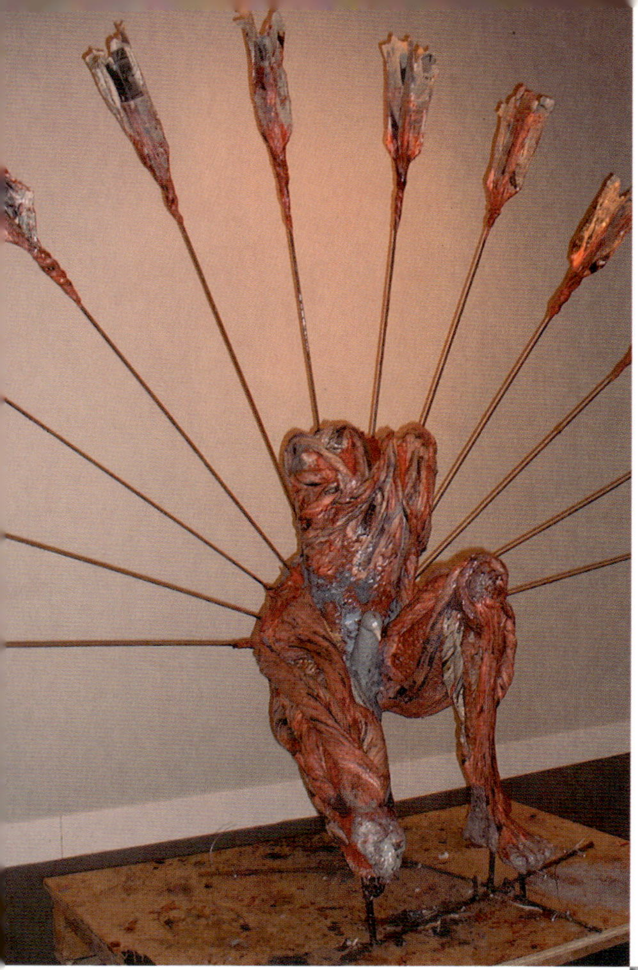

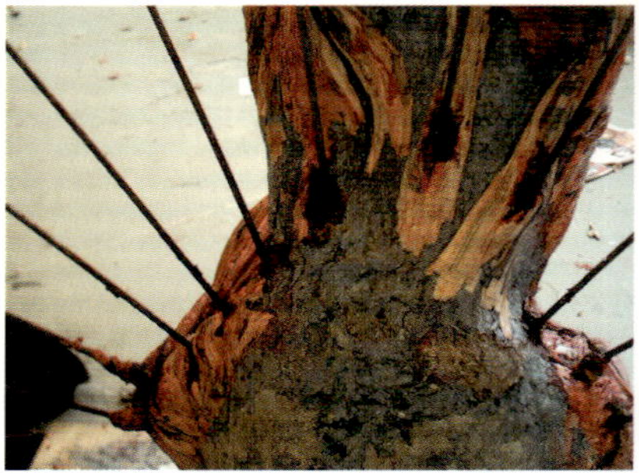

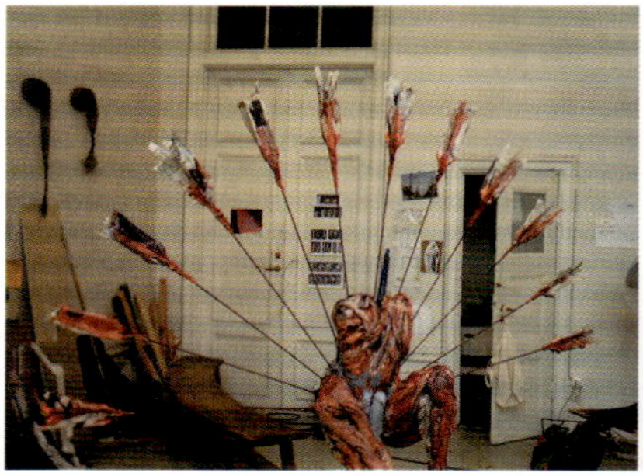

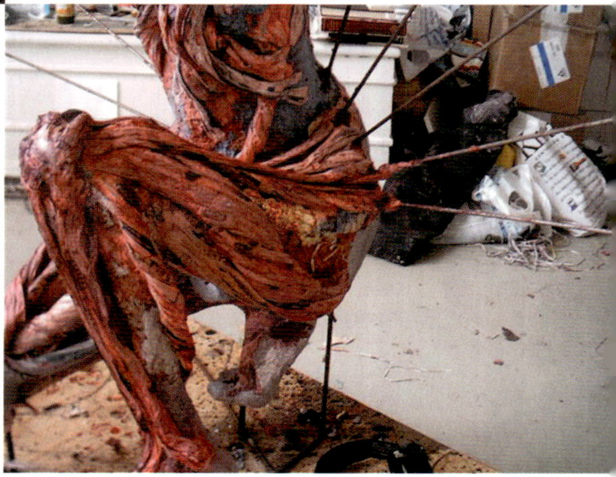

Sigalit Landau

Man with arrows adorning-penetrating his waste.

Half peacock with spears for feathers. The seductive deadly fan spreads open. The human erected-blue penis is the birds body-head-beak.

"I think with my heart and feel with my brain" someone once said to someone else.

Within Christian imagery – like the *barbed hula* video, in which a woman torso (me) is an apex to a centrefugal barbed hula hoop dance – pain for passion. A spectecualr encounter at the *victimological gardens.*

SIGALIT LANDAU

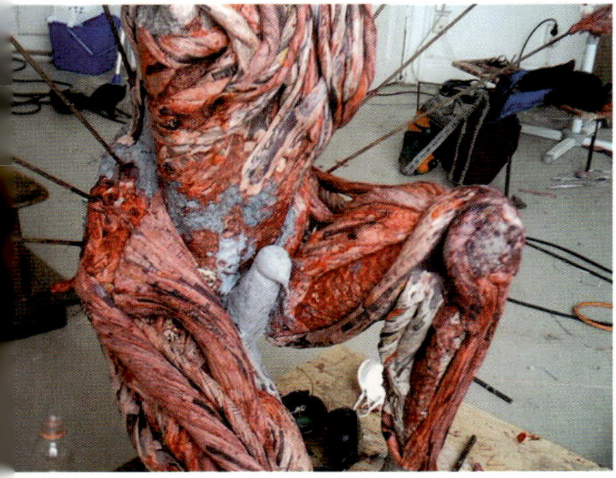

Installation View: SIGALIT LANDAU, *Passion Victim, the Peacock*, 2003

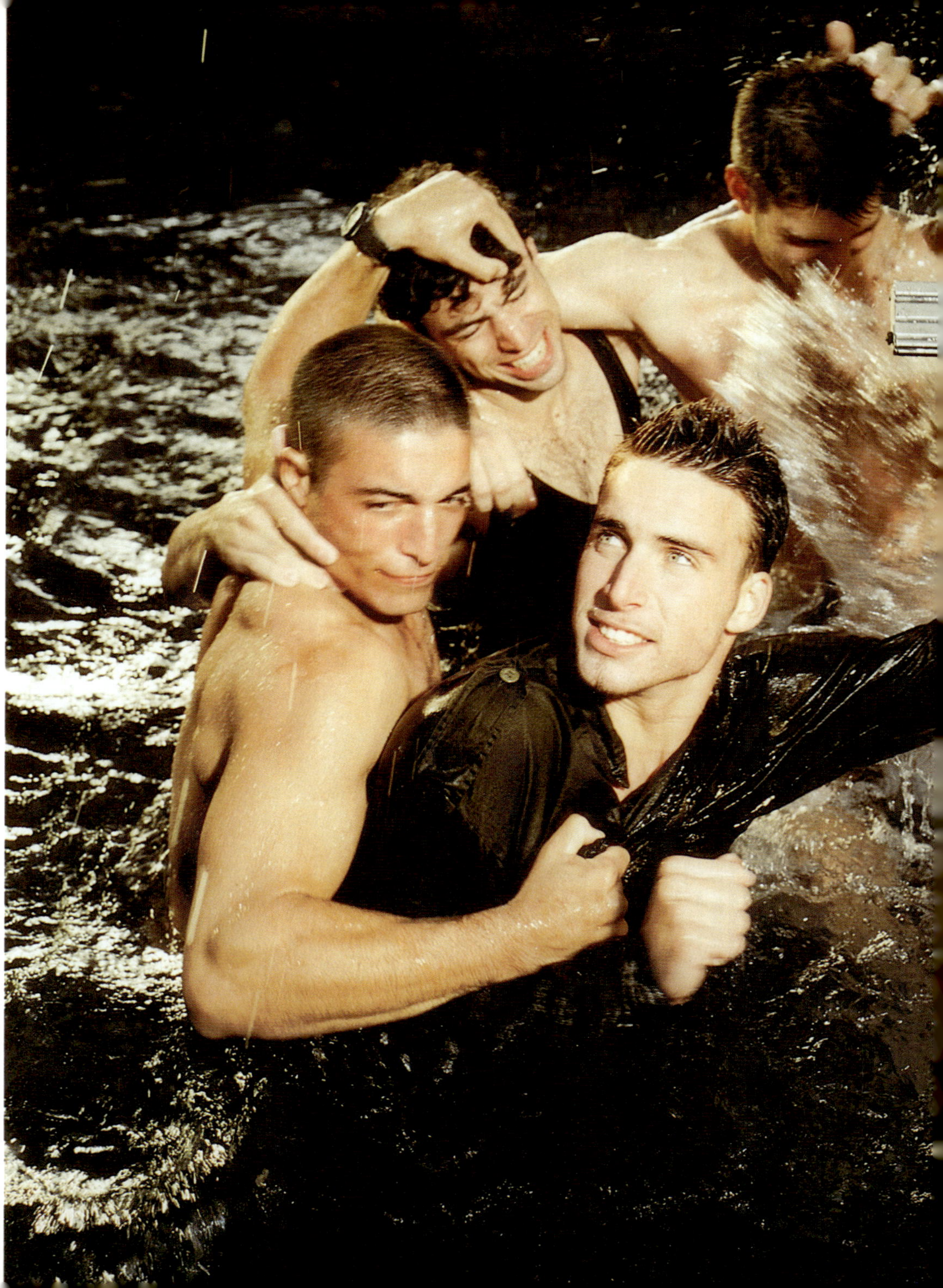

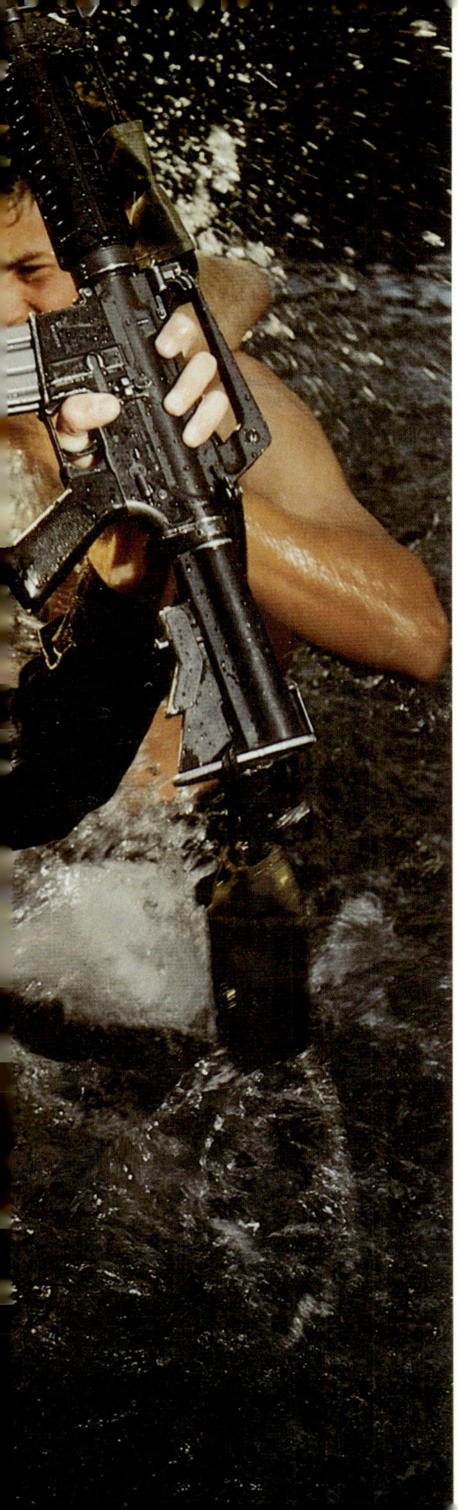

ADI NES
n. t., 1999

Adi Nes

Private Sebastian

At midday on the last day of the Six-Day War, a Life magazine photographer snapped an Israeli soldier in the waters of the Suez Canal, a smile in his eyes and a Kalashnikov automatic rifle in his hands – spoils of the extolled war. Printed on the cover of the June 1967 edition, this famous picture became the symbol of the strong, victorious Israeli conqueror.

Thirty years later, an Israeli photographer born in that same war, has returned to the famous snapshot. In Adi Nes's *photo-quote*, the scene is nocturnal and dramatic, like in Gericault's *Le Radeau de la Méduse*. And alongside the handsome paratrooper, other paratroopers burst from the water into a theatrical light that falls on their nude muscular forms, while the soldier's smile is brushed by terror in the male fraternity closing in on him. The alter ego of today's soldier peeps from the image of his comrades-in-arms in a turbulent crescendo of male homosexuality. Whereas the original photo was the success symbol of the small and daring State of Israel, this new version divulges the state's motives and difficulties.

Like Sebastian, the patron saint of archers, Nes's soldiers and their wars integrate elements of mysticism and lust, ecstasy and eros, victory and defeat – a homoerotic masculinity in an atmosphere of martyrdom. Nes gazes at his soldiers with both admiration and compassion.

Nes's work may be deceptive at first glance. This is no casual portrayal of the soldierly experience. Much energy goes into the production and meticulous staging of every detail in scenes that often draw on the history of art or well-known photos etched in collective memory. His photos revolve around a single main theme, the question of identity. St. Sebastian's mythological image enabled Renaissance artists to treat the male figure at a time that most artists dealt with female nudity. In the same way, the subject of Israeli soldiers allows Adi Nes, an Israeli gay artist, to probe both Israeli and homosexual identity at one and the same time. In so doing, he permits us to look into the private world of one who is part of Israeli reality, a reality that is constantly scrutinizing its identity.

Israeli reality of incessant war and terror attacks in restaurants and on buses appears below the surface in Nes's work. His figures are depicted in an air of sadness and compassion. The picture of the soldiers napping on the bus is not innocent, the strong shadows hinting at death. As in the first act of a dramatic play, only parts of guns invade the frame edges while the soldiers's necks tilt sideways as if waiting for the hangman, and all are being conveyed like sheep to the slaughter.

The sacrifice of Sebastian recalls Christ's crucifixion; both are symbols of tortured martyrs. Adi Nes, in his work, employs a blatant manipulation. At first glance, the pair of soldiers photographed seem to be caught up in a heroic situation – the one supporting and succoring a wounded comrade. But a closer look shows that Nes has staged the Pieta (the dead Christ mourned by Mary). Mary's place, however, is taken by a soldier holding a make-up brush, while the wounds of the soldier in Christ's pose seem to emanate from an open make-up kit reminiscent of an artist's palette. Manhood is portrayed here as a designer product in a religious context (man's self-sacrifice to save the world), while touching on the homosexual context and male fraternity.

Christianity, like all religions and cultures, requires mythical heroes such as Sebastian. "Israeli-ness", too, in its formative stages needed heroes – male models of self-sacrifice for the general good. Adi Nes, like all Israelis, served in the army and may, perhaps, be viewed as one of the soldiers he photographed. Sebastian, in Adi Nes's photographs, is the self-aware, self-sacrificing artist, coercing and coerced by the arrows of those he is meant to protect, seducing and seduced, instigating and insurgent.

Ilan Sheinfeld

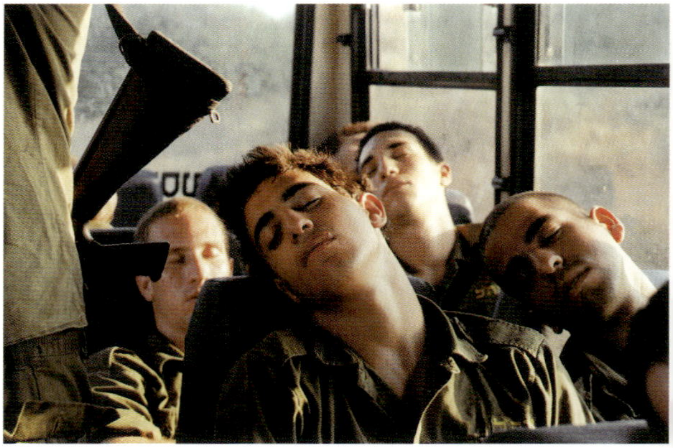

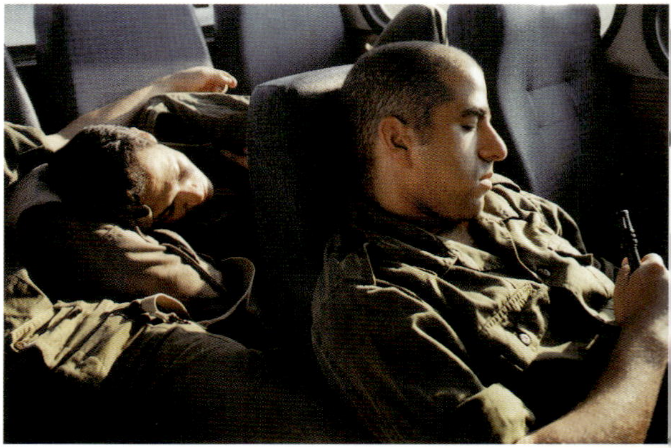

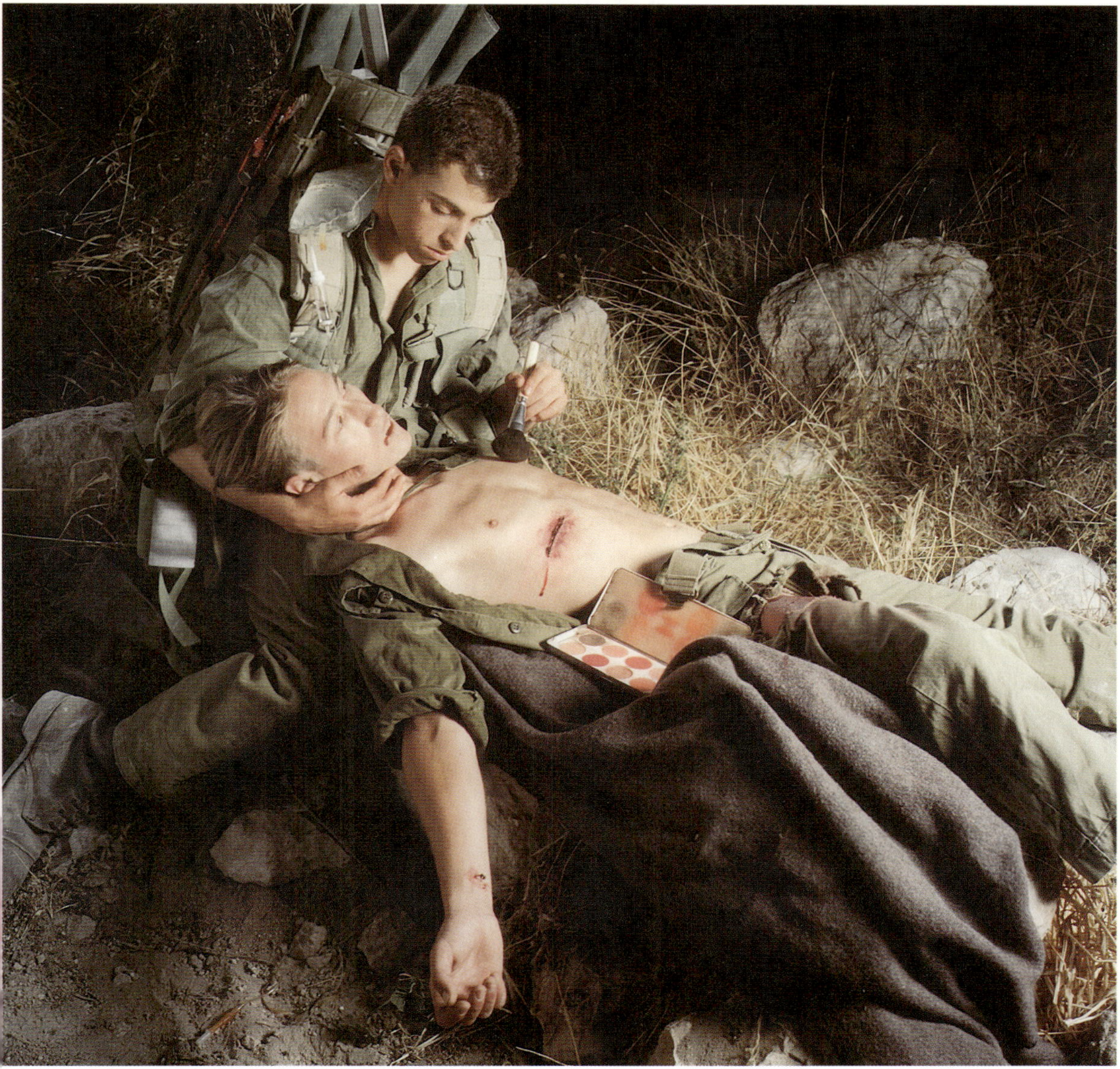

ADI NES
n. t., 1999
n. t., 1999
n. t., 1995

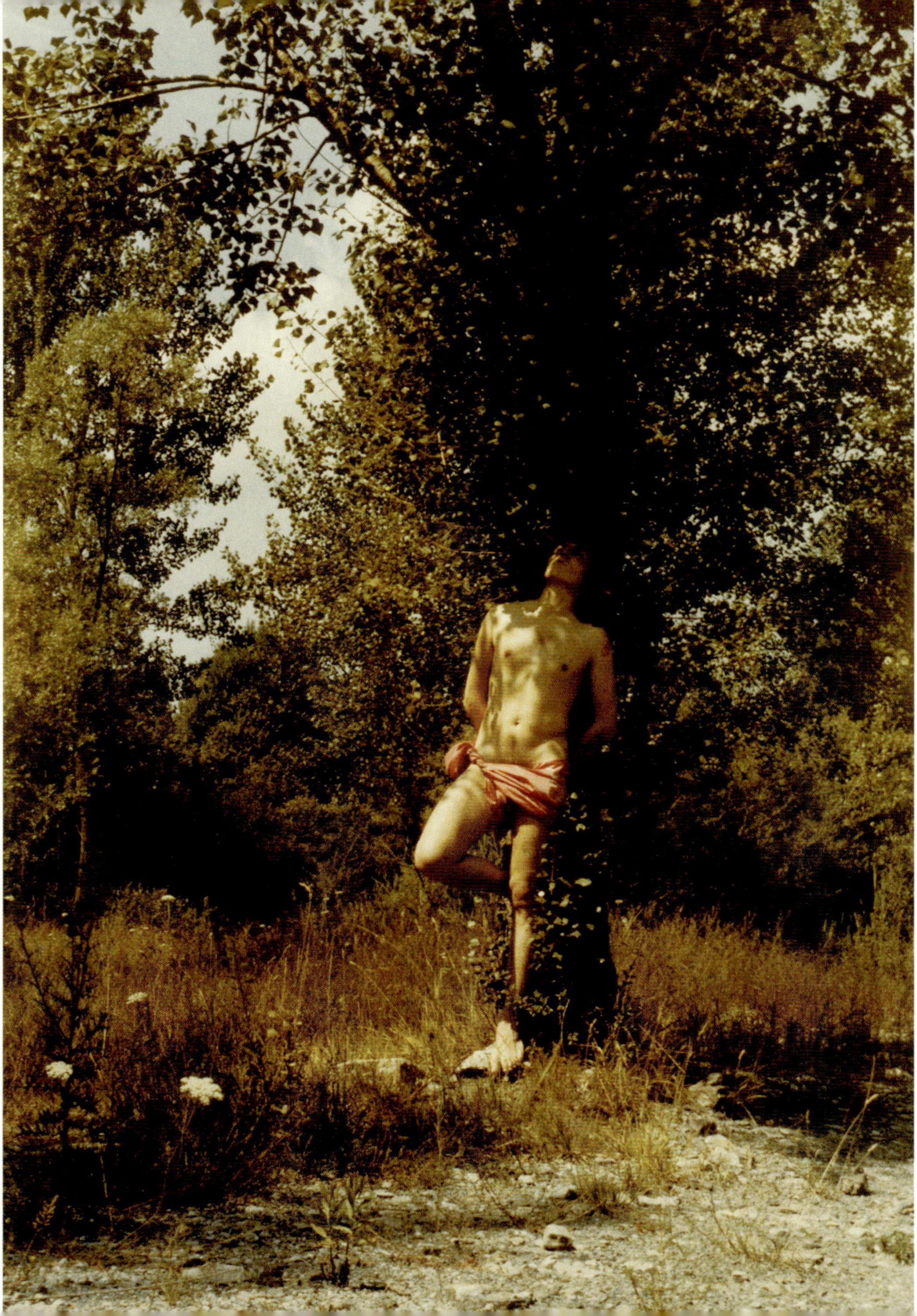

Luigi Ontani

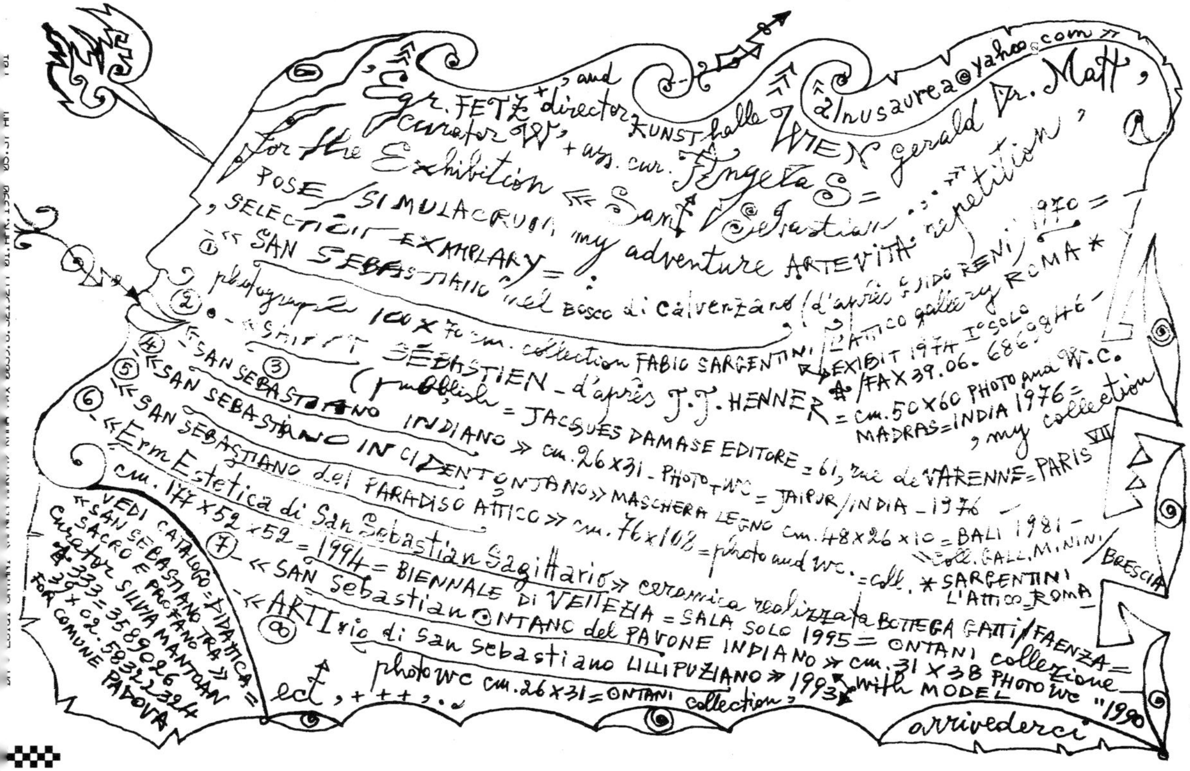

Fax compiled for Kunsthalle Wien on the exhibition theme by Luigi Ontani.

LUIGI ONTANI
San Sebastiano nel bosco di Calvenzano, 1970

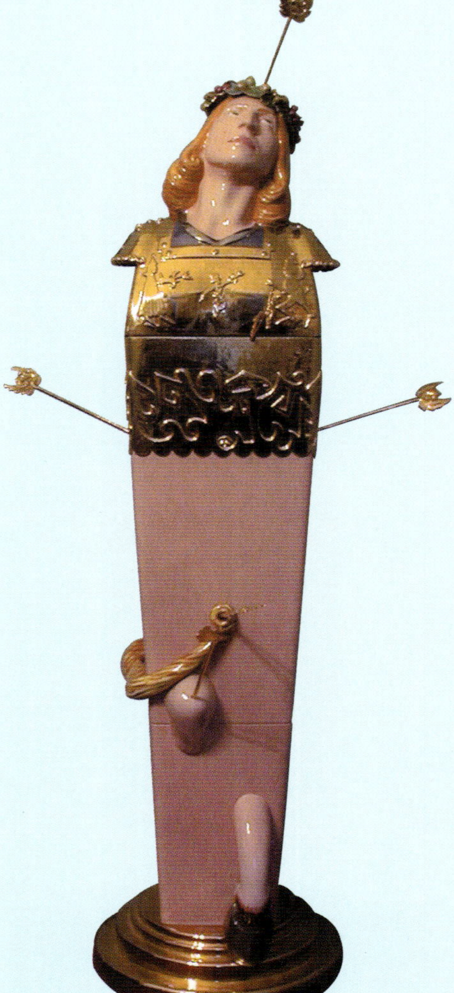

LUIGI ONTANI
ErmEstetica di San Sebastian Sagittario, 1994
S. Sebastianello al Paradiso Attico, 1982

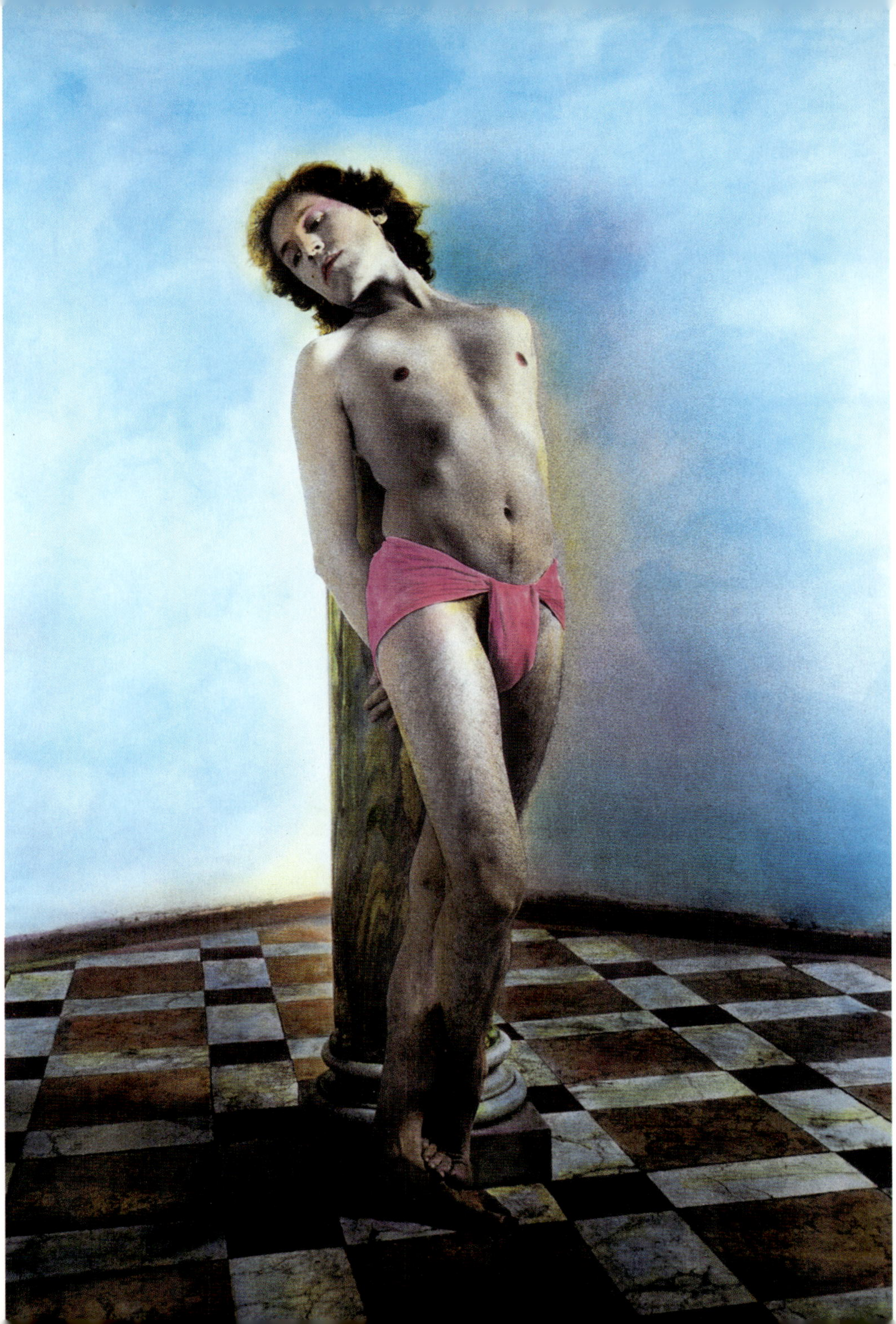

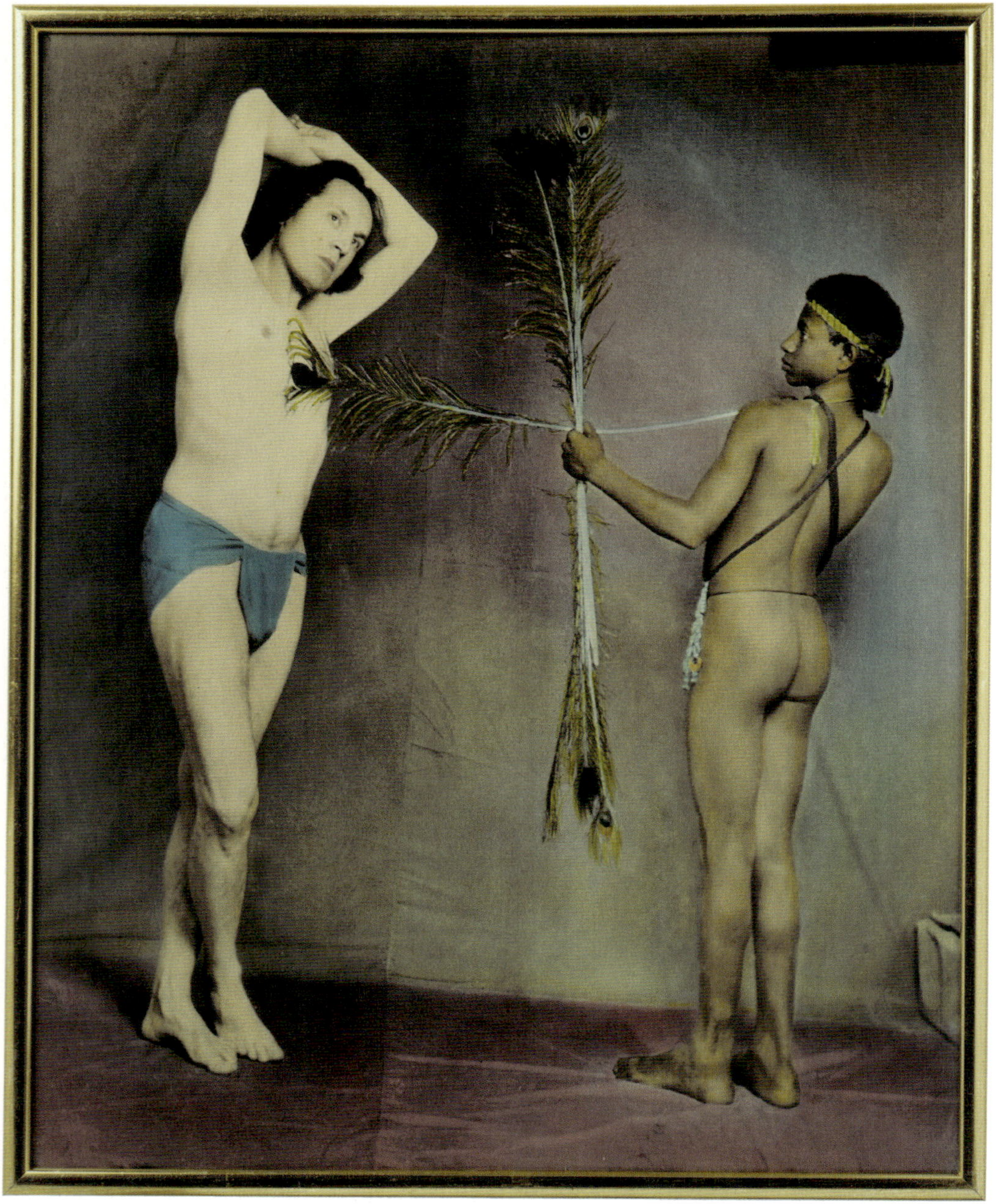

LUIGI ONTANI

San SebastianOntano del Pavone Indiano, Dehli/Indien, 1990

San Sebastiano of BroOKlyn, New York/USA, 1985

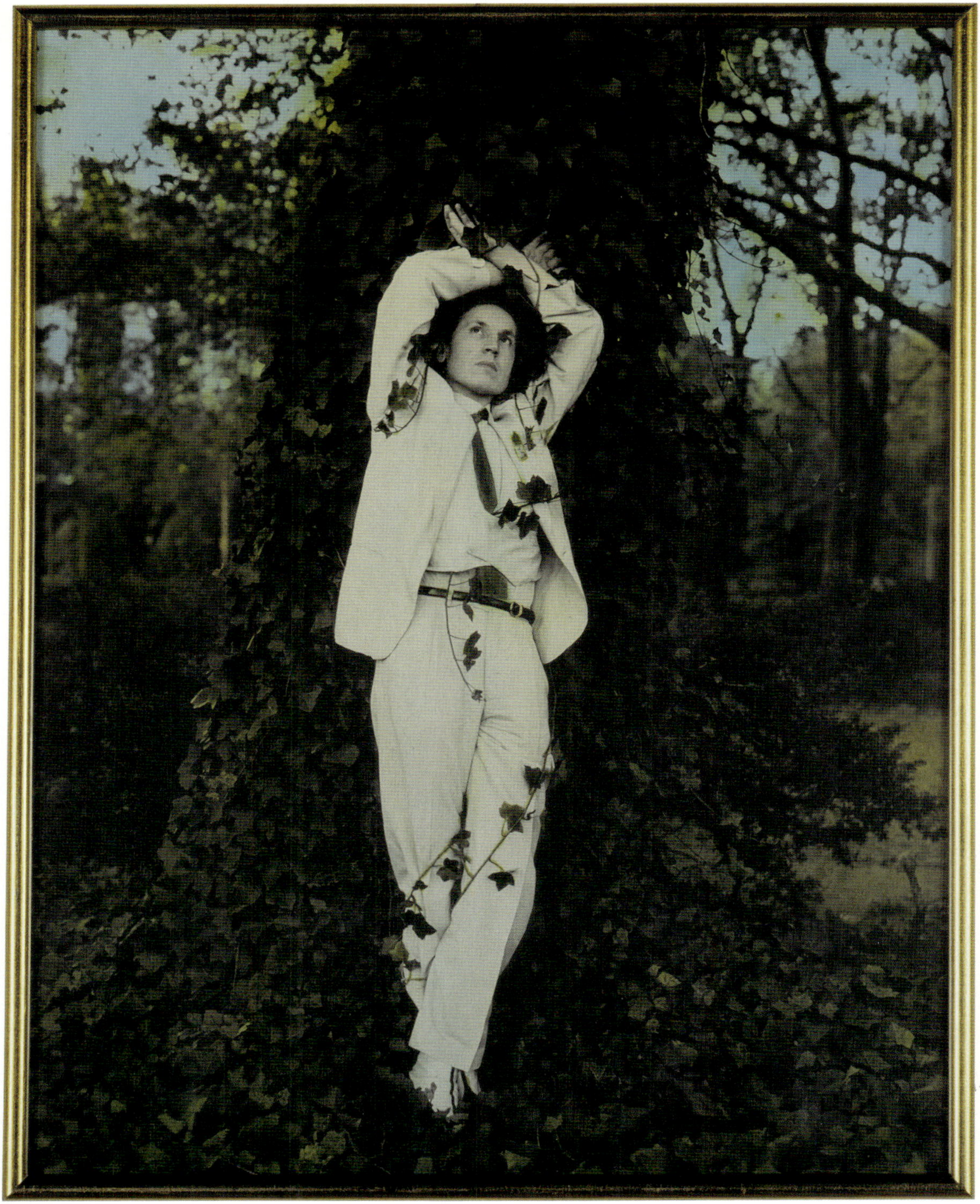

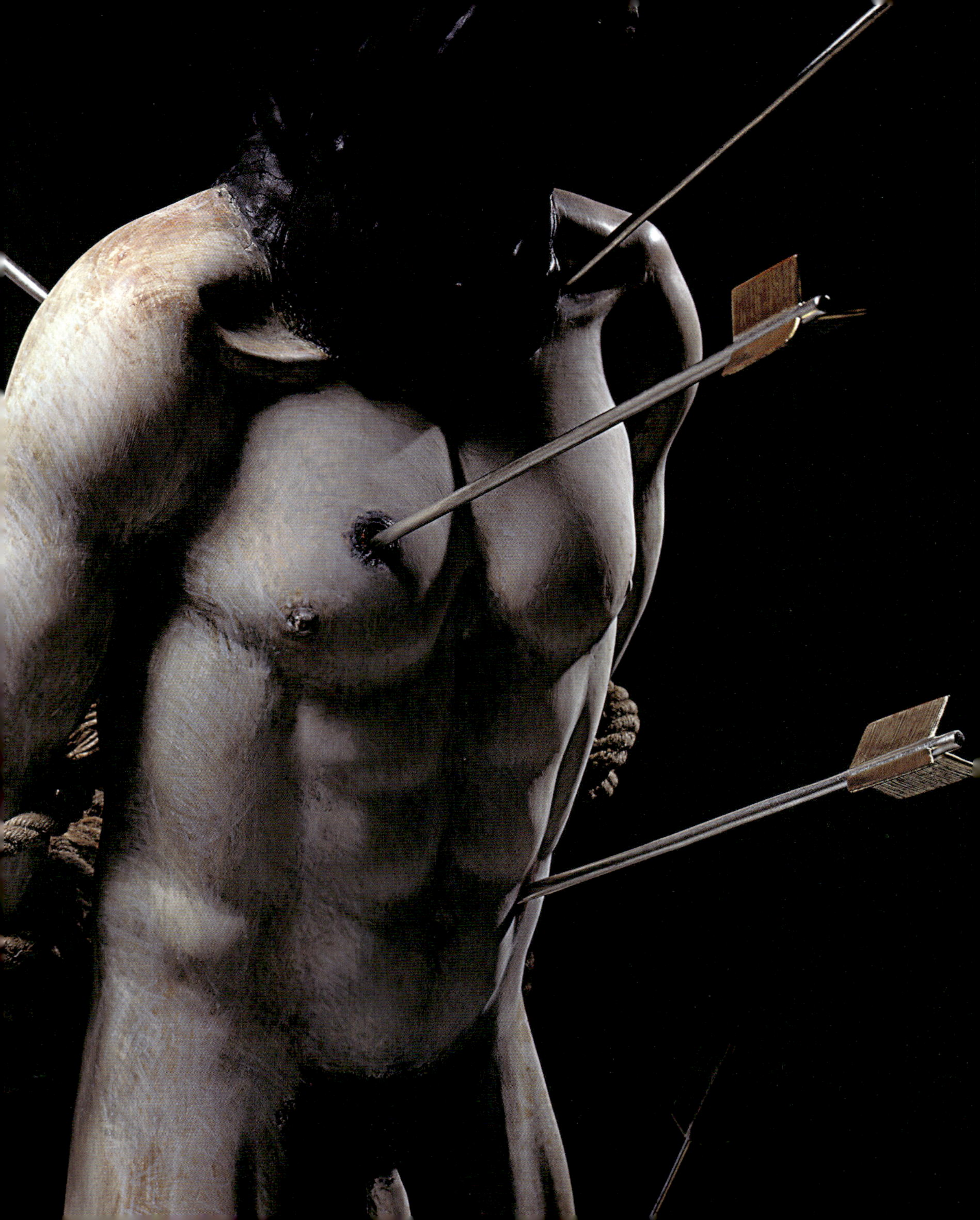

Ana Maria Pacheco

The image of the arrow-man was initially inspired by the legend of the early Christian Saint Sebastian, who was punished for his faith by being shot with arrows. However, Pacheco's title of the piece, *Dark Night of the Soul*, omits his name. Therefore, we are free to see this victim-figure as Sebastian if we want to, but other readings are also possible.

Pacheco's piece, however, is no traditional representation. By adding the hood, she immediately wrenches the old story from the safety of the past and drops it firmly in our own time. The artist is keen to distance herself from what she calls a "pamphlet kind of art" but the political implications are none the less undeniable. One of her sources for *Dark Night of the Soul* was a photograph, originally published in a Brazilian newspaper, showing a victim of one of the many notorious South American death squads. The man in the picture is kneeling, virtually naked and bound by his neck to a wooden post. He has been garroted. Pacheco had a copy of this photograph, which she tore from a magazine, taped to the wall of her studio when she was working on her piece and the visual similarity is strong. Such images are now so commonplace that we hardly notice them as they flash on our television screens. When the image is frozen, though, as in a news photograph, we can study it at our leisure. Our horror is compounded by the sense that we have become voyeurs at a gruesome spectacle, consumers of a product that has its origin in the suffering of an unknown individual. We are powerless to intervene but we still stop to stare. We are glad that it is him, not us.

Pacheco adds her own female voice to the tradition of suspect Sebastians. Her muscular male victim is bound hard to the unambiguously upright pole. A further masculine symbol, the arrow, pierces his body in seven different places. The victim is punished for his maleness by symbols of that maleness. Furthermore, in traditional representations, Sebastian is never shown as completely naked. In the extremity of his agonies he successfully manages to retain his loin cloth, which, for decency's sake, even the cruelest of his torturers would never countenance removing. Pacheco's victim figure, however, is stripped of his sacred setting. He is also stripped of his loincloth, his prominent genitals echoing the form of the erect pole to which he is tied.

Colin Wiggins

Installation View:
ANA MARIA PACHECO
The Dark Night of the Soul, 1999

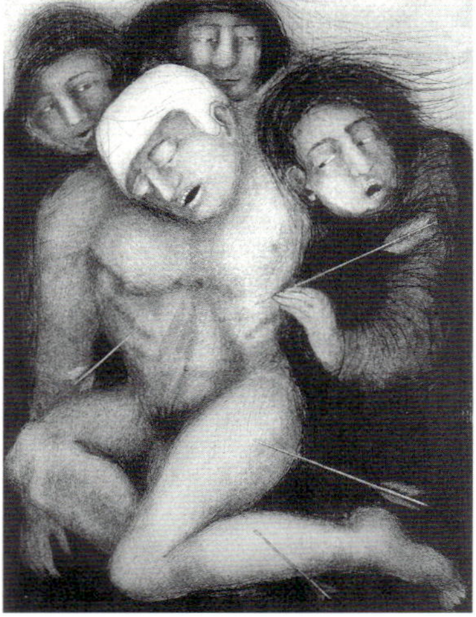

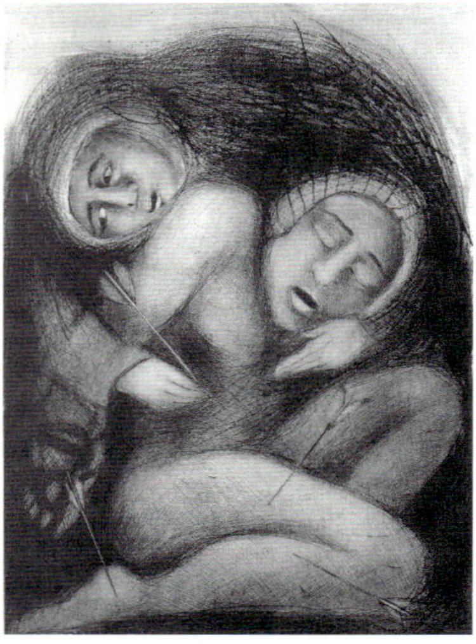

ANA MARIA PACHECO

Study for Saint Sebastian I, 1998

Study for Saint Sebastian II, 1998

Installation View:
The Dark Night of the Soul, 1999

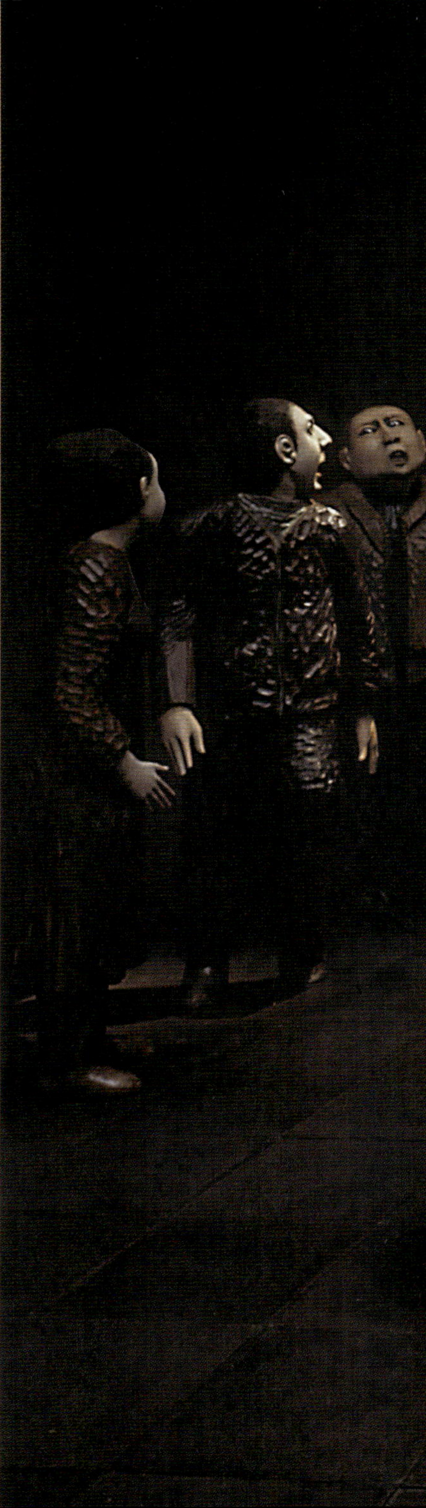

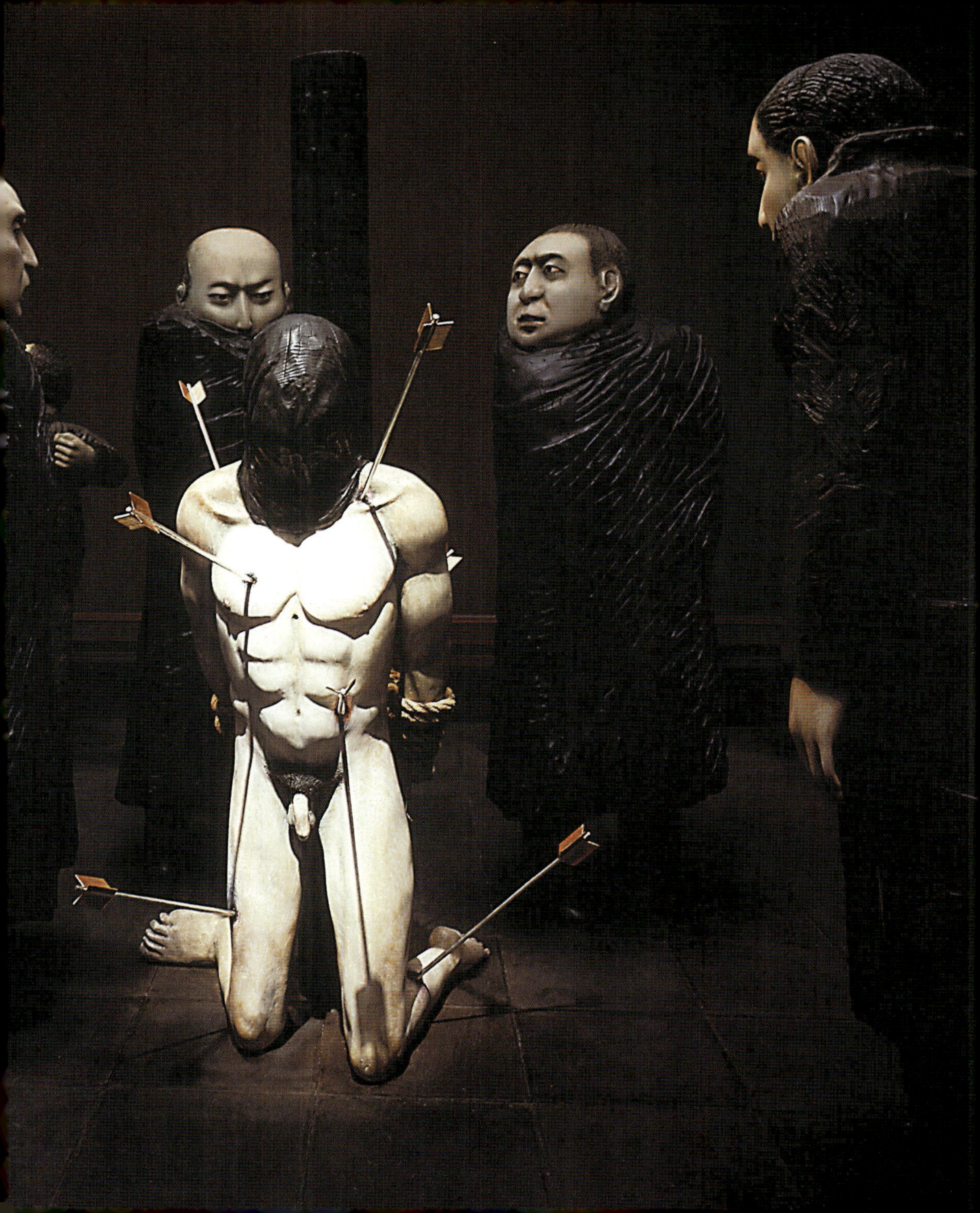

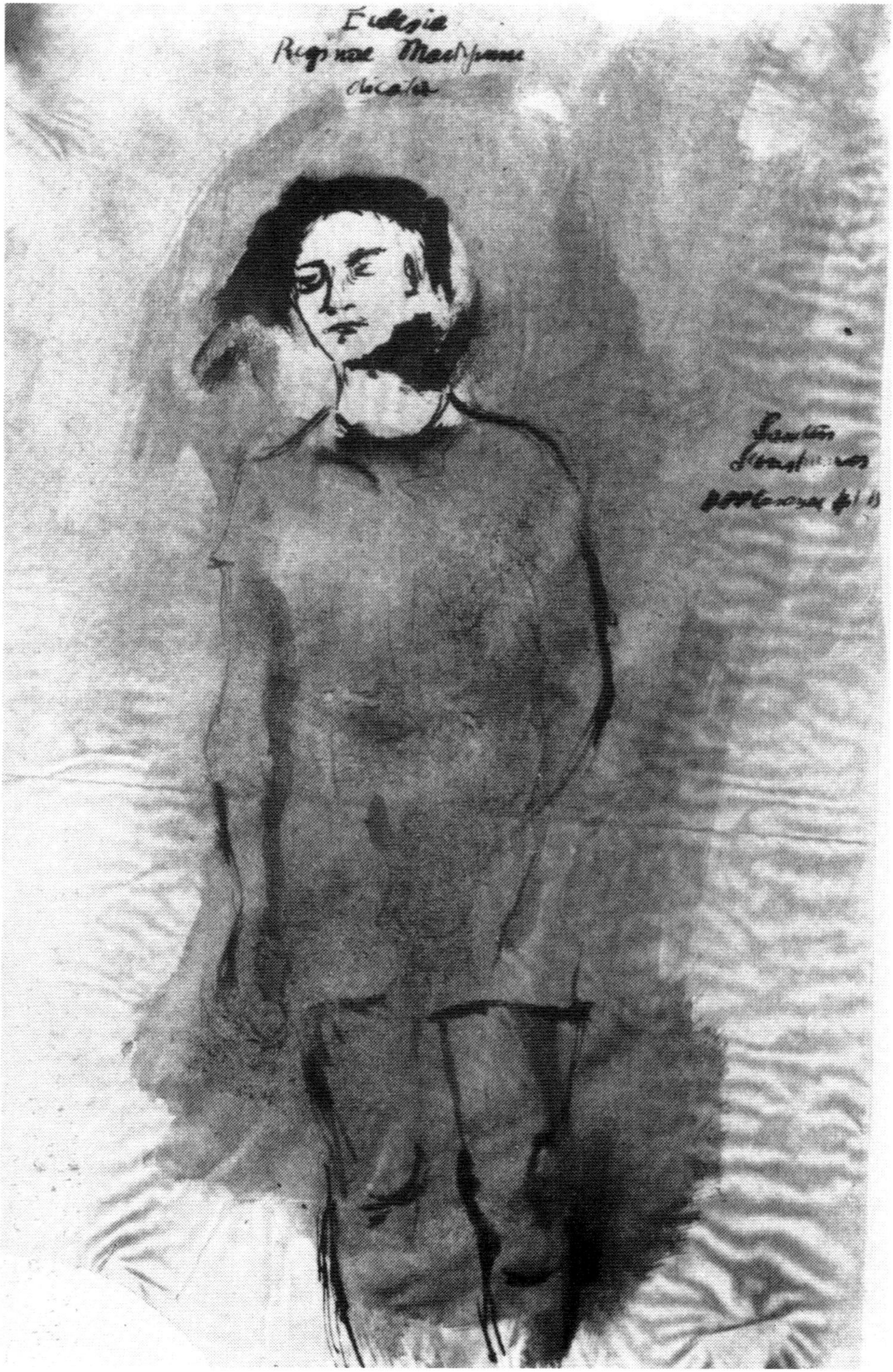

PIER PAOLO PASOLINI
Saint Sebastian, 1943

Pier Paolo Pasolini

Thirst for Death

I am destroyed or at least transformed,
so that I do not know myself, because in me
the law is destroyed which –
up to this moment –
had made me a brother of the others:
a normal boy, or at least not abnormal,
or abnormal like everyone else…even if
(need it be said) I was full
of all the errors that my class,
and my social level within it,
brings – and which privilege compensates for.
In spite of this,
before you entered my life –
putting it in doubt once more
and transforming it into a heap of rubble –
I was like all my companions.
So it is through the destruction of everything
that made me the same as the others
that I am becoming –
something unheard of and unacceptable – someone DIFFERENT.
This difference of mine reveals itself to me unexpectedly:
Up to this moment it had been hidden
by the unstable state of intoxication I had arrived at
(deceiving myself that I could be silent
about everything for ever), through your presence.
The one who made me different (a marvel!) has been near me.
And distracted me thus with the intensity and the unalterable
taste his sex had given my life.
The fear and the anxiety at not having you near me any more
to satisfy my desire, to see and touch you
when you are my comrade, but younger and fresher,
like a child, and more mature and powerful,
like a father, who does not know how divine
his simple member is –
that is very difficult from the consciousness
of having to lose you for so long – perhaps for ever.
It is the consciousness of the loss
that gives me consciousness of my difference.
What will happen from this night on?
The pain of farewell goes beyond
this tragic sense of a future
to be spent in the company of a new Pietro,
completely different from me.
And what do your serious eyes, friendly and obscurely pitiless
(or already distant?), reply in silence to all this?
Is your intention perhaps
to push me along the road of difference,
to the end and without compromise?
Do you mean that if this love has been born
it is useless to turn back,
it is useless to feel it as a pure and simple destruction?
That, as far as the pain of separation goes,
I could find someone who could replace you,
and recreate in me those feelings
of ridiculous tenderness and animal passivity
so recently born and so brusquely interrupted?
And if you were a father without wrinkles and without grey hair,
a father as he was when he was little more than my age,
could there not be a father like that
to replace you? Even if
that is inconceivable and terrifying,
indeed, precisely for that reason?

Excerpt from: Pier Paolo Pasolini: *Theorem*, translated by Stuart Hood, Quartett Books: London 1992, S. 81–82.

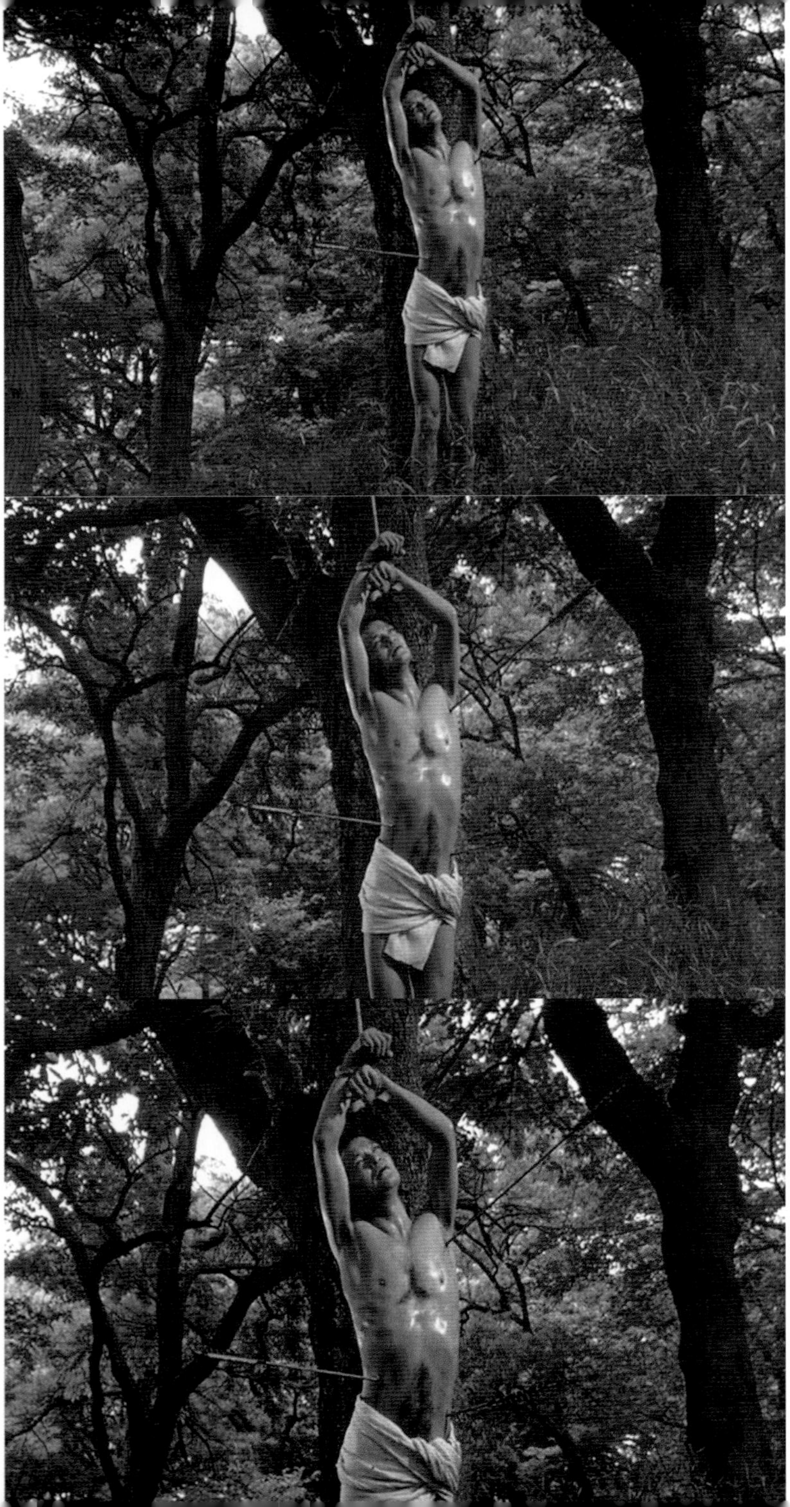

Paul Schrader

Mishima is a biographical film, one of the less likely areas for experimentation, one might think. The director Paul Schrader chooses to take an intellectual, almost literary approach to his subject. The film is divided into four chapters, *Beauty*, *Art*, *Action*, and *The Harmony of Pen and Sword*. Each chapter consists of intertwined threads of action. The last day of Mishima's life is presented in realistic color, in sequence. Mishima's past is treated, also sequentially, in a naturalistic fashion, but shot in black and white. The first three sections of the film also each contain a condensed version of one of Mishima's novels, *The Legend of the Golden Pavilion*, *Kyoko's House*, and *Runaway Horses*. These episodes are filmed in lush color using stylized sets. Bits and pieces of the three threads are woven together to make a surprisingly smooth whole, a thesis on the major motivating forces behind Mishima's life.

Yukio Mishima was perhaps the greatest author of post-World War II Japan. He wrote novels, plays, and short stories in great numbers. His works were very popular in Japan, and widely translated. But Mishima's life was not lived totally within his writings. Mishima believed in the ancient Japanese principle of the harmony of pen and sword, a creed which calls for a blending of art and action. Deeply traditional in many ways, Mishima saw much that he disliked in modern Japanese life, and he took action to change things in a uniquely Japanese way. When combined with a rather morbid attitude towards life and beauty, and a confused sexual identity embracing homosexuality and sado-masochism, Mishima lived a life and died a death that are unlike those of any other.

PETER WEIHER

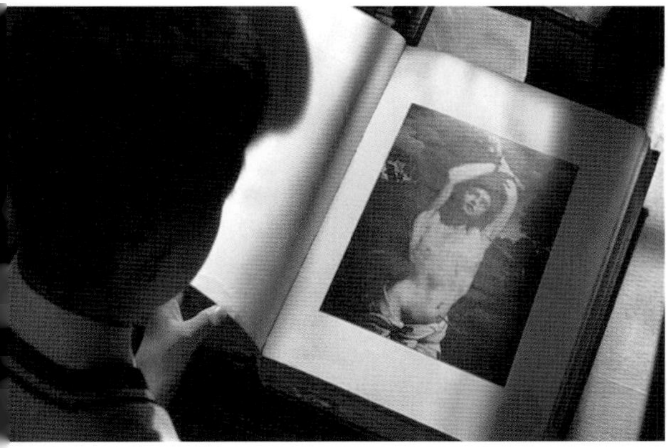

Stills from: PAUL SCHRADER, *Mishima*, 1985

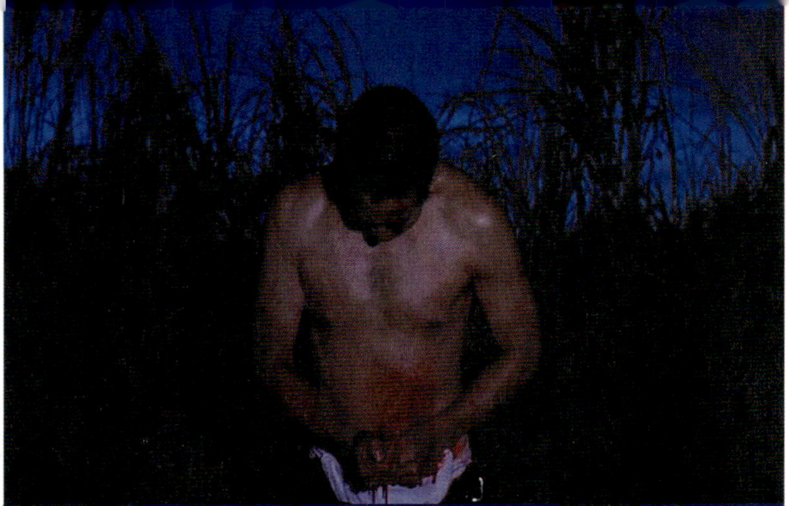
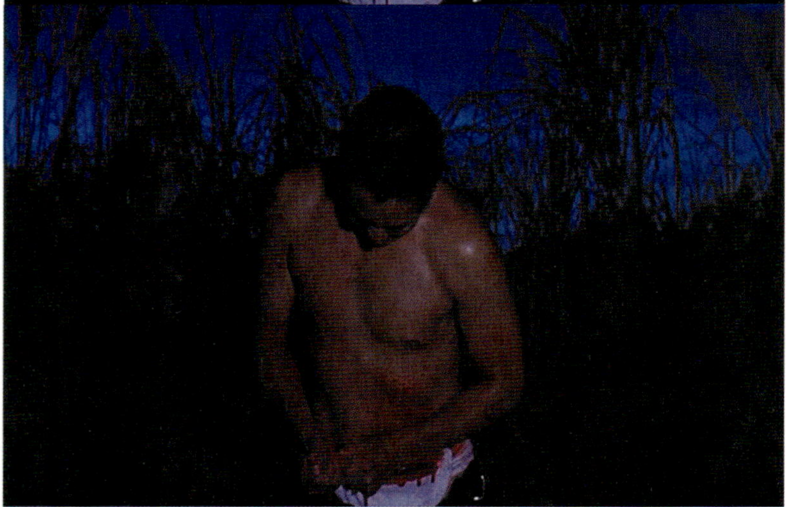
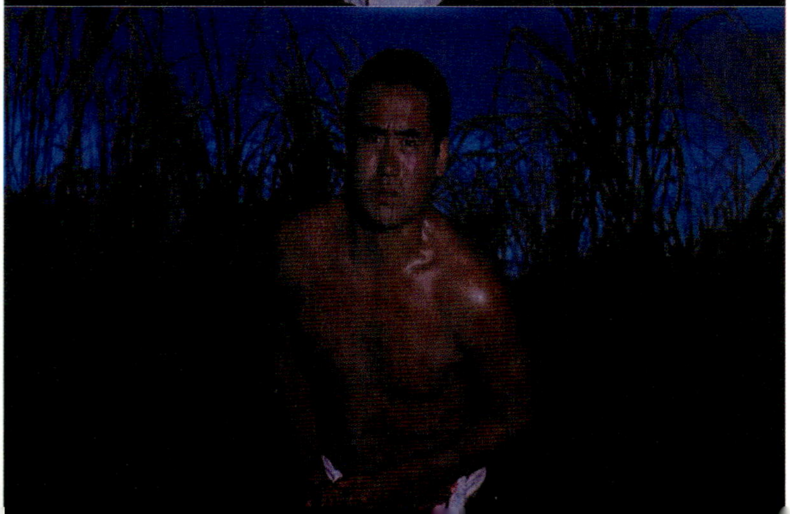
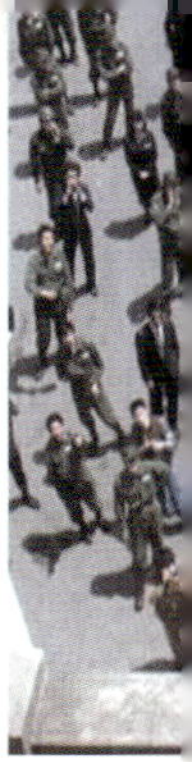
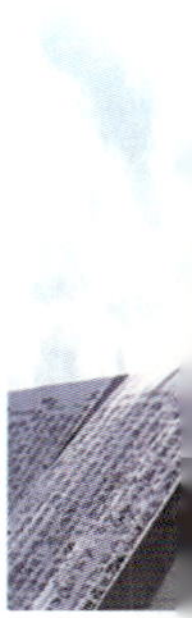

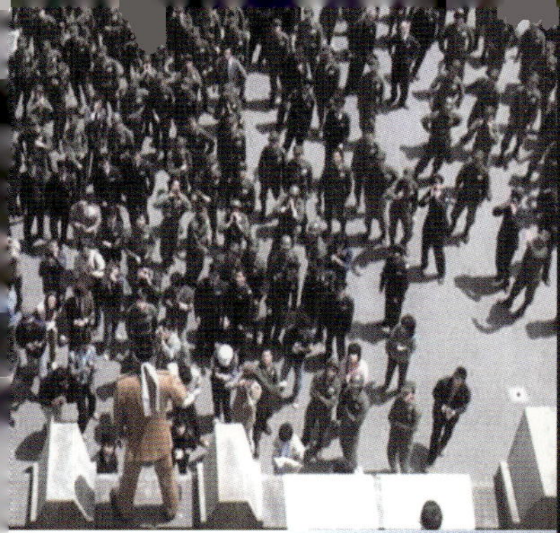

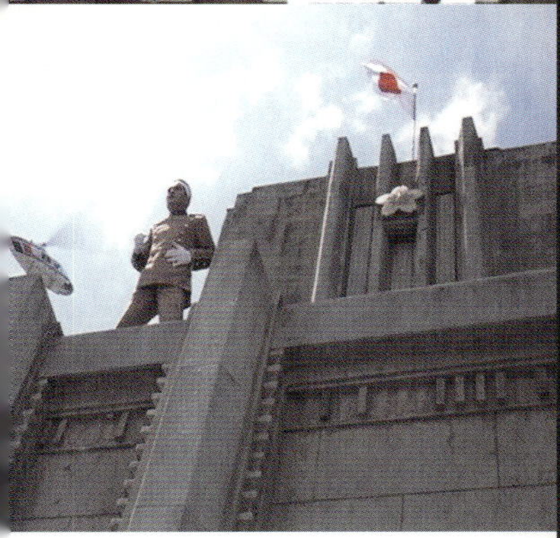

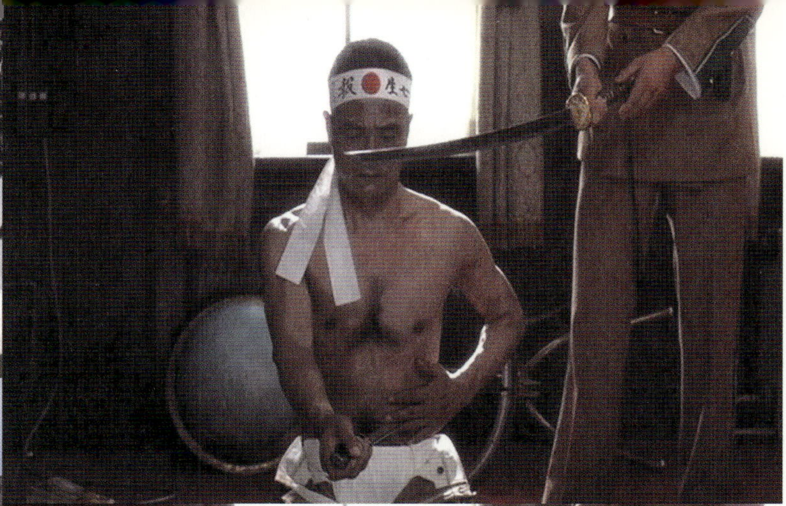

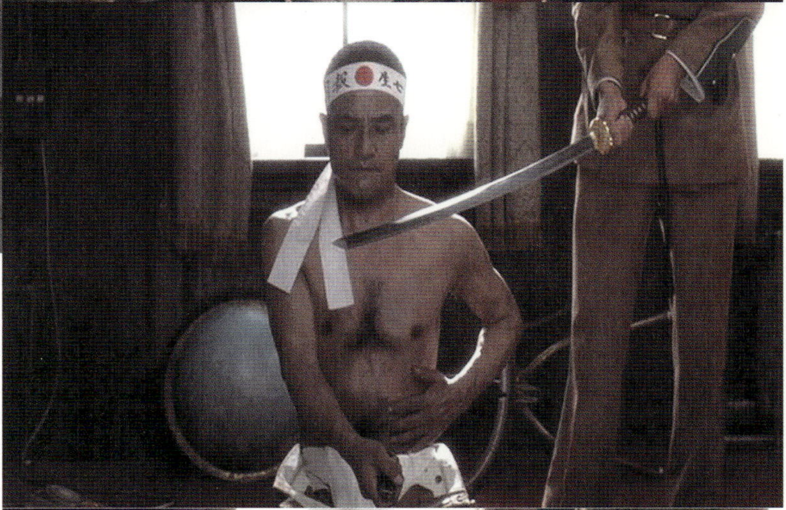

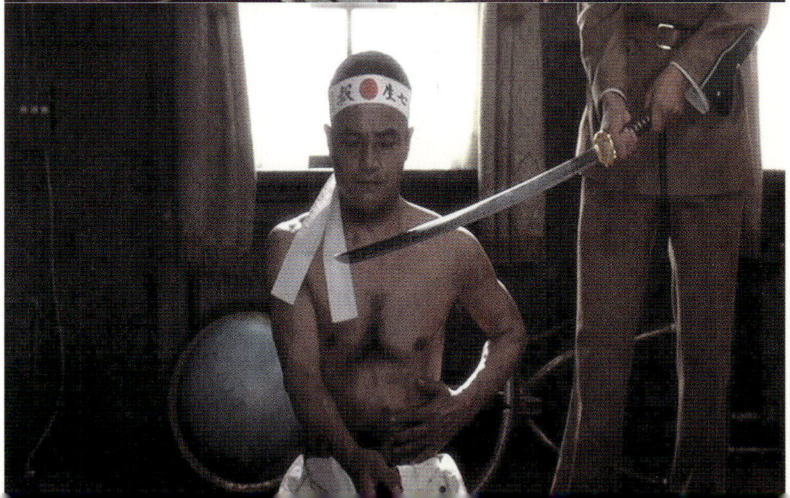

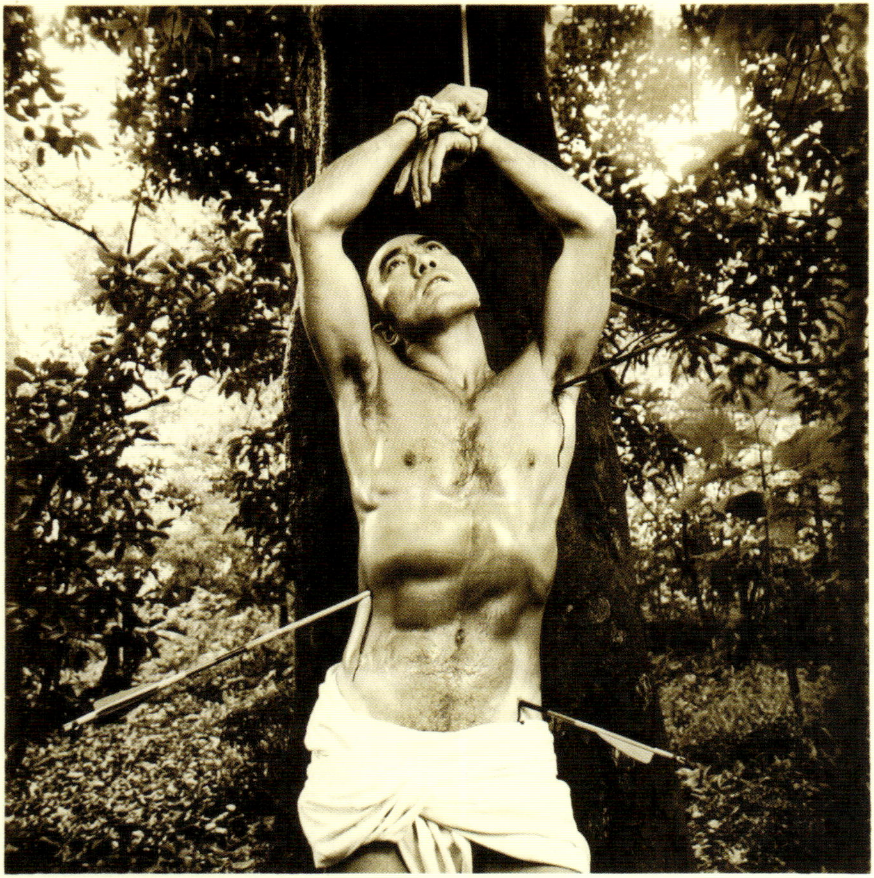

Kishin Shinoyama

For Mishima, ritual suicide was the cathartic moment of transcendence par excellence that he repeatedly rehearsed in his literary descriptions and cinematic enactments. But he also rehearsed them in his private orgasmic petites morts upon which such suicide is ultimately modeled. Shortly before his death, Mishima referred to harakiri as the "ultimate masturbation".

In his writing, Mishima adopted the idea of eroticized death and the form of ritualized sacrifice in his own characteristic way, most notably as the homoerotic motif of the excruciating death of a handsome youth. He describes his fascination with this subject in his autobiographical Confessions of a Mask, explaining that it originated in his discovery as a boy of a reproduction of Guido Reni's painting of Saint Sebastian …

Excerpt: Joel Black: *The Aesthetics of Murder. A Study in Romantic Literature and Contemporary Culture.* The Johns Hopkins University Press: Baltimore and London 1991, p. 205 f.

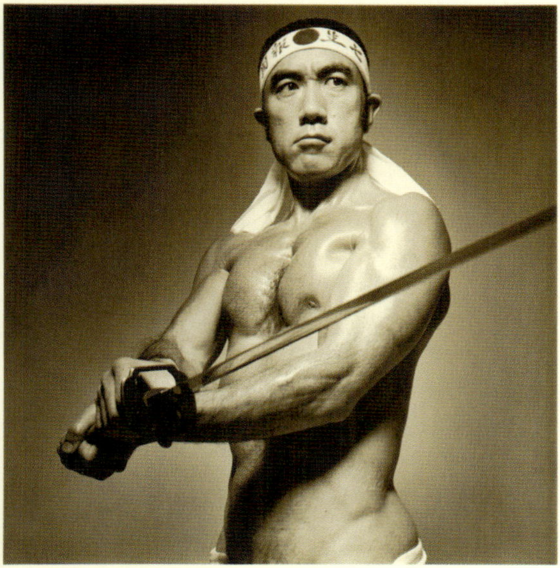

KISHIN SHINOYAMA
Mishima Yukio, 1968
Mishima Yukio, 1969

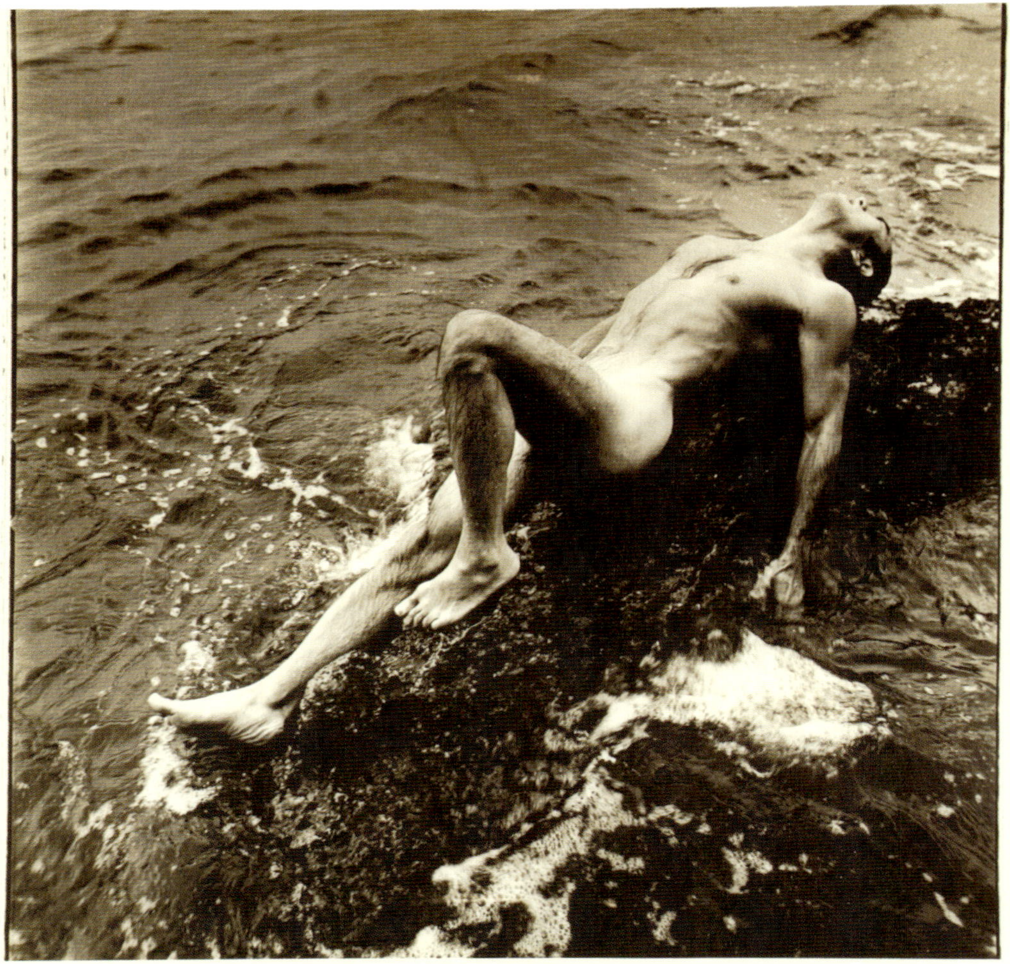

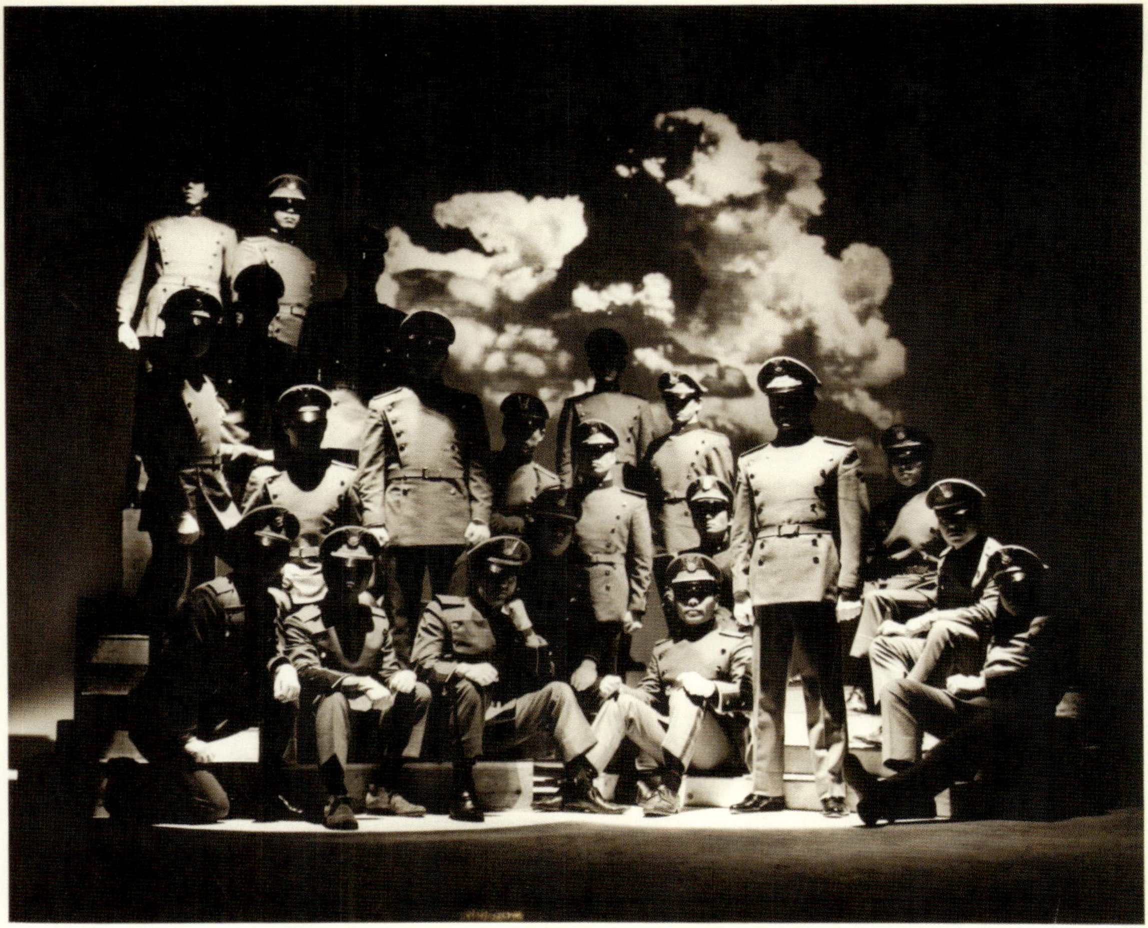

KISHIN SHINOYAMA
Mishima Yukio, 1970
Mishima Yukio + Tate No Kai, 1970

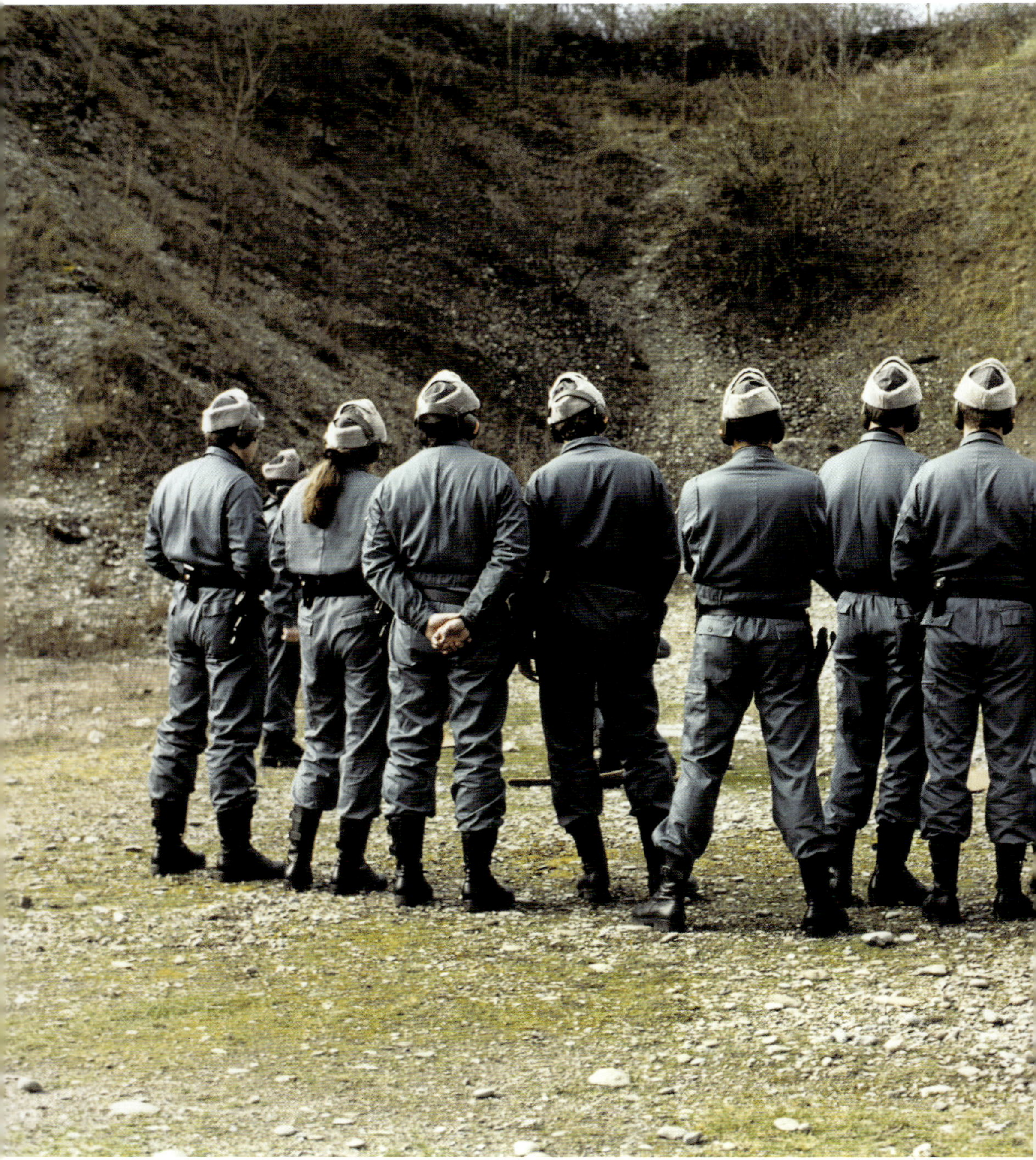

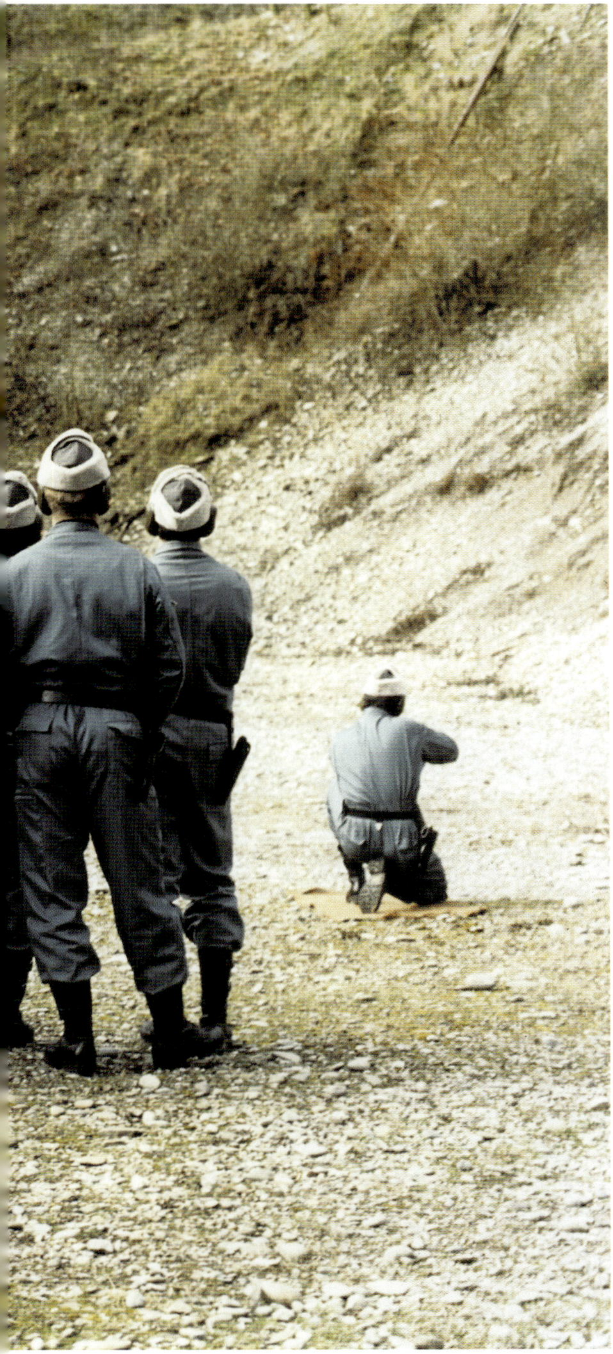

Wolfgang Tillmans

Swiss Police appears as a double page in the book where Wolfgang Tillmans has put together the series *Soldiers*. In the photograph the mass of soldiers is shown, made indistinguishable by their uniforms, which gives witness to their uniform point of view. The quiet, central composition of the image and the concentration of the soldiers on one place symbolises their targeted thoughts; their humanity is lost in the anonymity and facelessness that is conveyed to the viewer by the rear view of the protagonist's bodies. Their directed will, permitting no escape and only the single interest in fighting, is turned toward a centre that does not show itself. Precise ascription to a particular enemy is of no importance. The dichotomous structure of the image supports the very style of thought that is reduced to ascribing the roles of agent and victim. One might say that Wolfgang Tillmans's photograph reflects the mental attitude of the army, clarifying it.
In the third century AD Sebastian, a serving soldier, opposed his army and the will of the Emperor Diocletian. He turned away from heathen beliefs and decided to fight for Christianity. Sebastian was part of a group; one could imagine him a part of this group of soldiers shown by Tillmans, up to the moment when he begins to pursue his own ideas and his truth. From the fight against the common enemy, the individualist emerges, who would burst the frame of a picture like this. Christian propaganda or an early confession of subjectivity? An appeal to God or a call to the formation of identity?

Angela Stief

WOLFGANG TILLMANS
Swiss Police, 1994

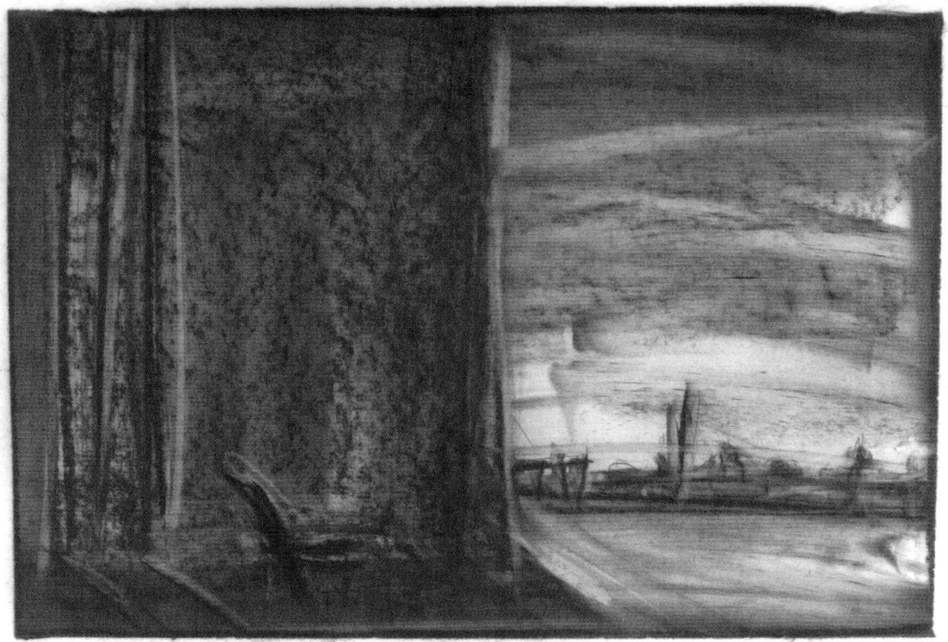

SAINT SEBASTIAN ACT III — '88

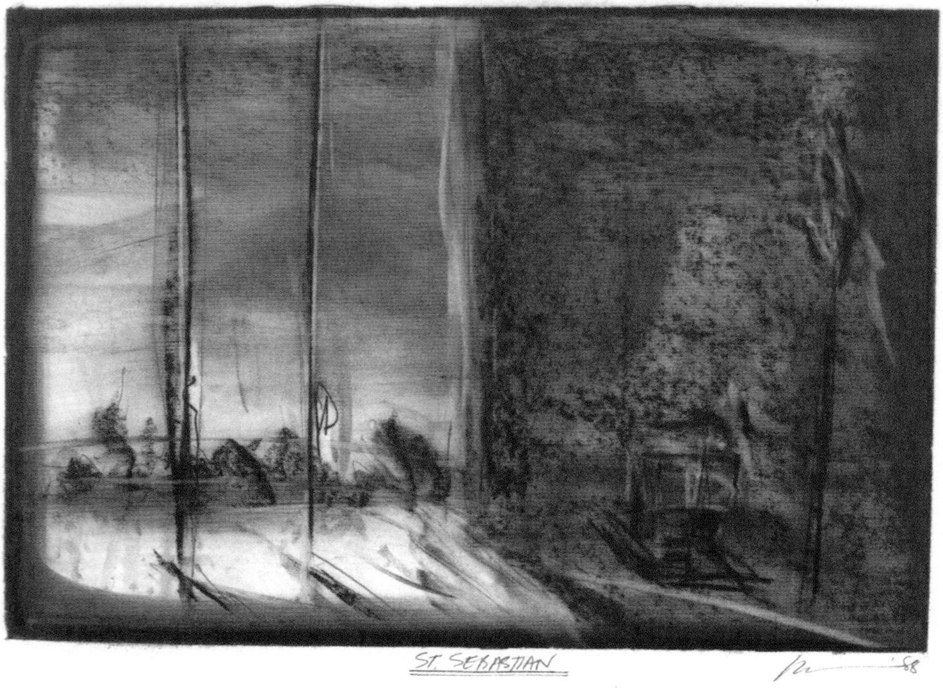

ST. SEBASTIAN — '88

Robert Wilson

Avec *Le Martyre de Saint Sébastien,* Robert Wilson approche – pour la première fois – le « ballet » : une interprétation gestuelle, à travers laquelle l'ambiguïté du personnage émanera, tantôt de Sylvie Guillem/Sébastien I, tantôt de Michaël Denard/Sébastien II (ce dernier, étant supposé avoir déjà subi son martyre, assiste en quelque sorte au spectacle de sa propre vie).

L'architecture des décors se découpe en lignes horizontales et verticales, recouvrant l'espace et le temps. Si, au prologue comme au paradis (La Dernière Mansion), l'horizontalité domine, La Deuxième Mansion est enfermée dans la verticalité. La Première et la Troisième Mansions présentent de hauts murs, avec pour l'une – à gauche – un jardin, et pour l'autre – à droite – une cité idéale : les arbres comme les édifices alternent formes arrondies et phalliques. Il y a aussi, pour symboliser l'élément masculin, la verticalité des colonnes, et celle des cordes de la cithare. Dans La Quatrième Mansion, l'élément féminin se retrouve dans Les Trois Pierres Rondes. Lignes et symboles ont également inspiré la forme des meubles.

Les costumes font référence à l'iconographie de tous les temps, ayant trait à Saint Sébastien (des corps dénudés de Mantegna au marin en support-chaussettes d'Alfred Courmes en passant par les bandelettes que Léon Bakst avait dessinées pour Ida Rubinstein.)

Précédant les larges fragments du texte de d'Annunzio, Wilson a conçu un prologue contemporain : sur un paquebot perdu en mer, un groupe de passagers semble attendre quelque catastrophe imminente (naufrage du Titanic ?), microcosme emblématique de la société à la veille de la Première Guerre Mondiale (le *Martyre de Saint-Sébastien* fut créé en 1911).

Scanned from: Programme of *Le Martyre de Saint Sébastien* by Gabriele D'Annunzio and Claude Debussy. Produced by Robert Wilson at Opéra National de Paris, Paris 1988, p. 78

ROBERT WILSON
Saint Sébastien, Act III, 1988
Saint Sébastien, Act I, 1988

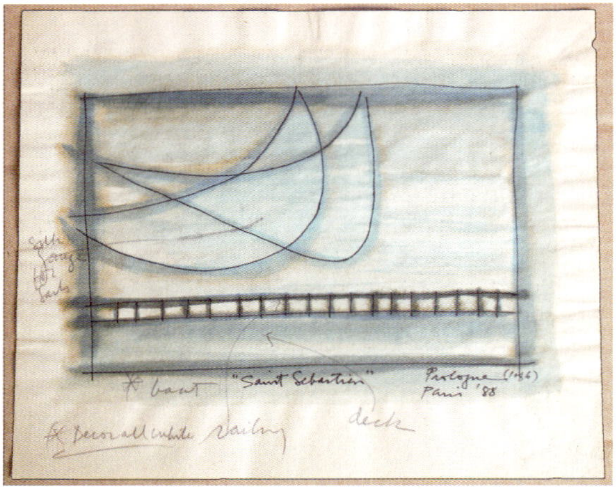

boat
"Saint Sebastien"
Prologue (1/6)
Paris '88
deck

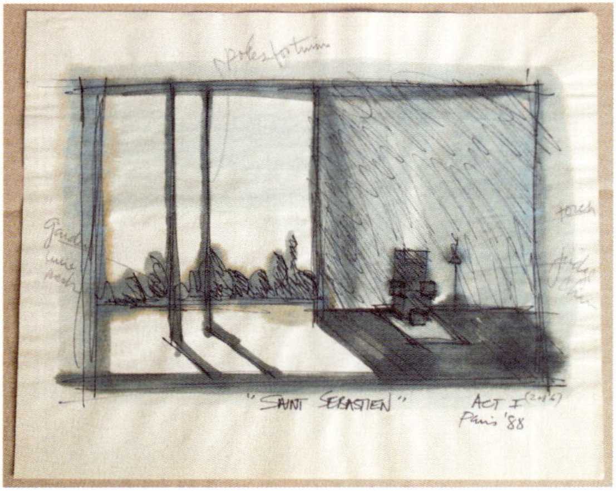

"SAINT SEBASTIEN"
ACT I (2/6)
Paris '88

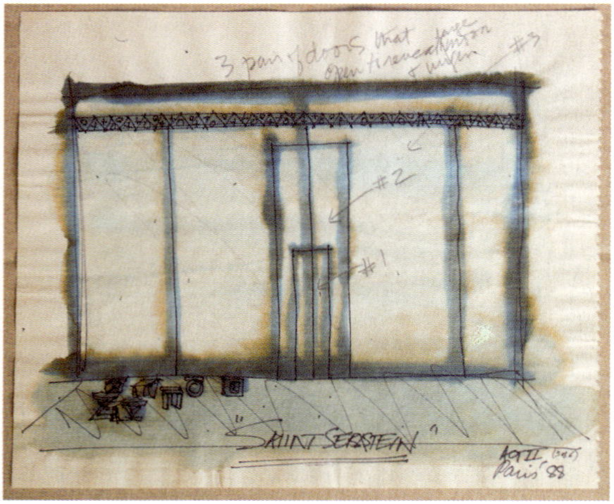

#3
#2
#1
"SAINT SEBASTIEN"
ACT II (3/6)
Paris '88

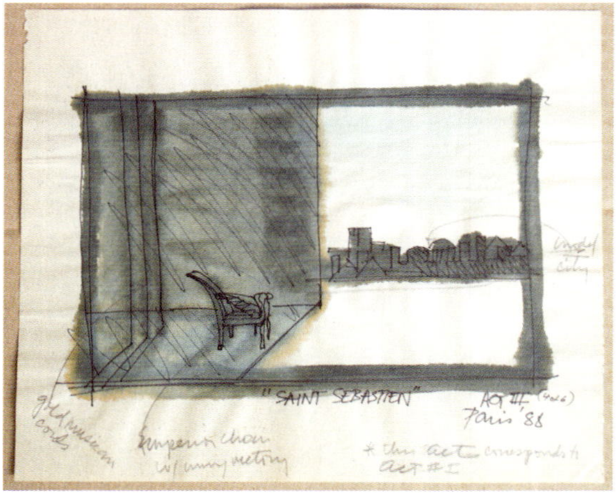

city
"SAINT SEBASTIEN"
ACT III (4/6)
Paris '88

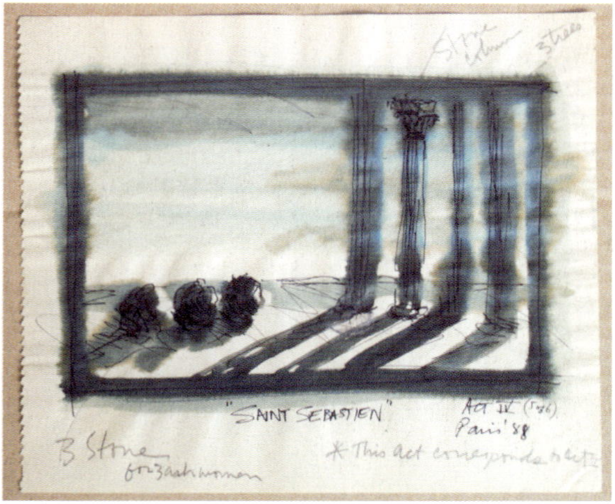

"SAINT SEBASTIEN"
ACT IV (5/6)
Paris '88

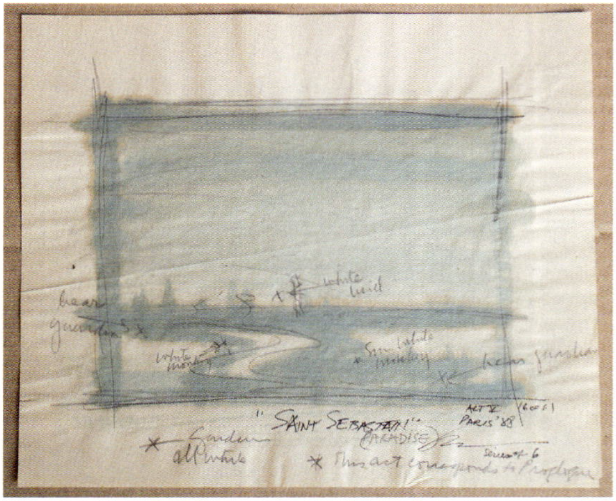

white bird
"SAINT SEBASTIEN"
(PARADISE)
Paris '88
* This act corresponds to Prologue

ROBERT WILSON

Le Martyre de Saint Sébastien, 1988

Act I, 1988

Act II, 1988

Act III, 1988

Act IV, 1988

Act V, 1988

MARC ENGUERAND

Le Martyre de Saint Sébastien,
staged by Robert Wilson, 1988

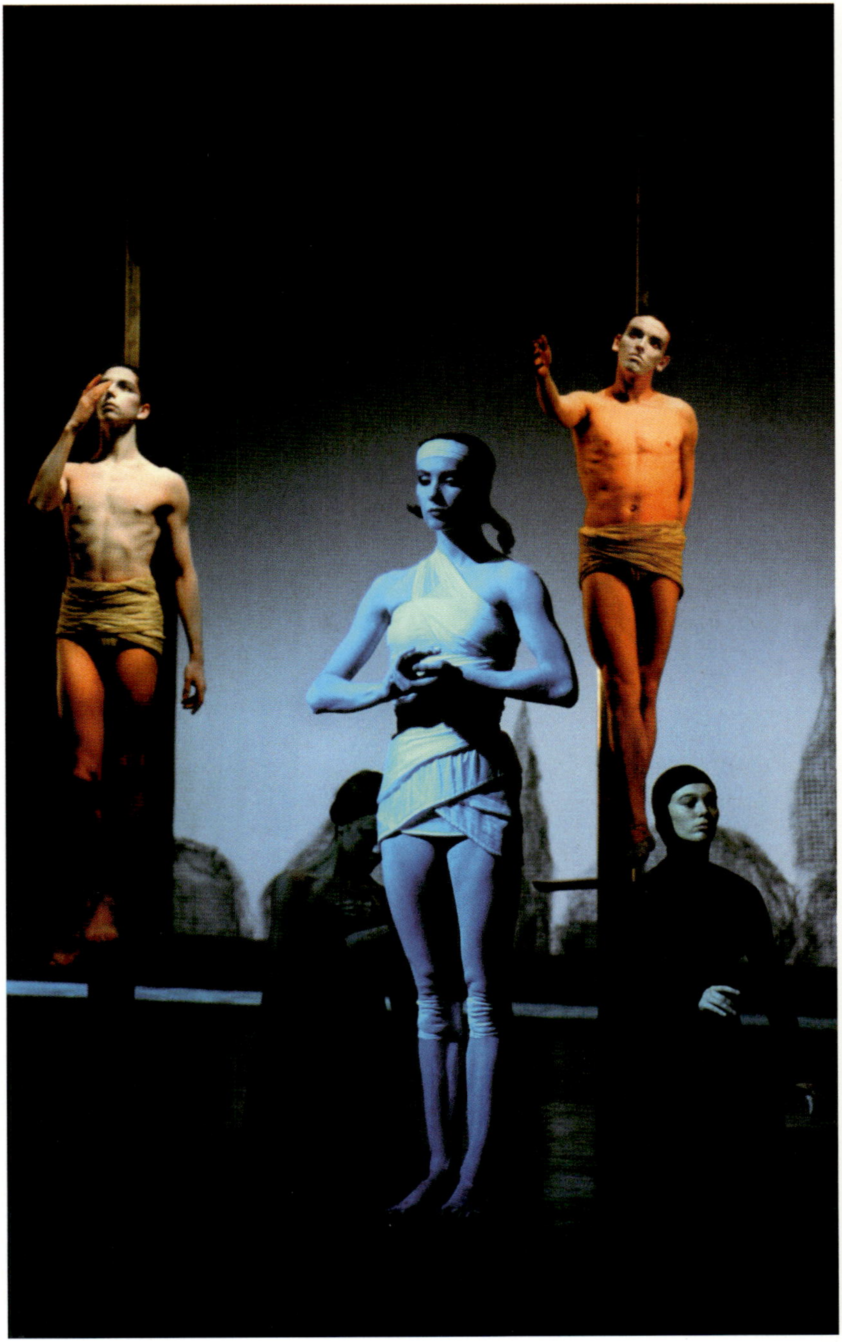

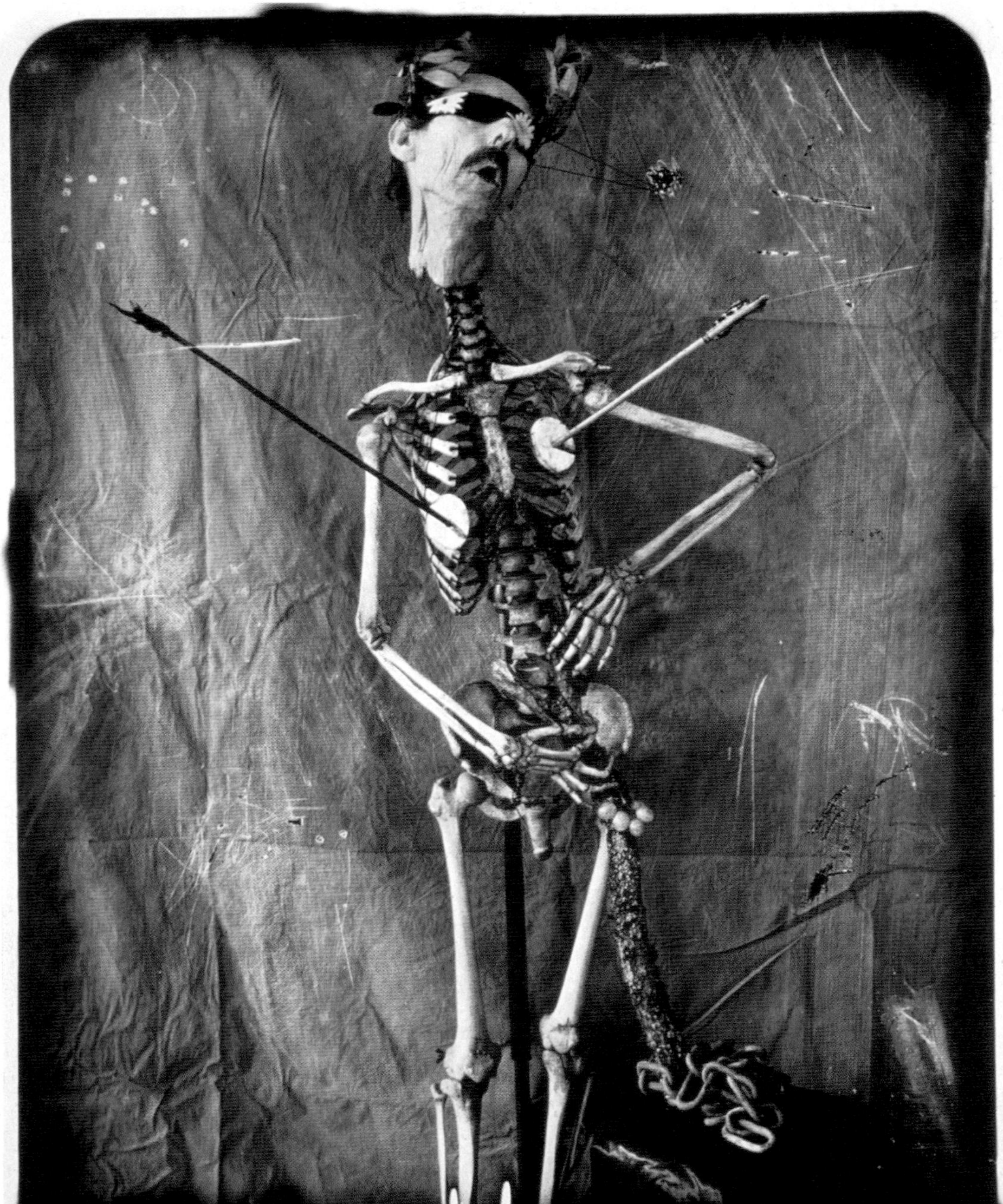

Joel-Peter Witkin

He was a member of the Praetorian Guard, yet secretly a Christian. For his faith he was bound to a stake and shot with many arrows. He lived, having been attended day and night by the wife of one of this converts. When he recovered his health, he chose not to flee but to confront the Emperor Diocletian. True to his reputation for cruelty, Diocletian had him clubbed to death in the Circus.

My Sebastian is broken and displaced. He is not the pretty boy of a homosexual fantasy aesthetic. Instead, I photographed him at the moment when the boredom of living is replaced by the suffering of being.

JOEL-PETER WITKIN

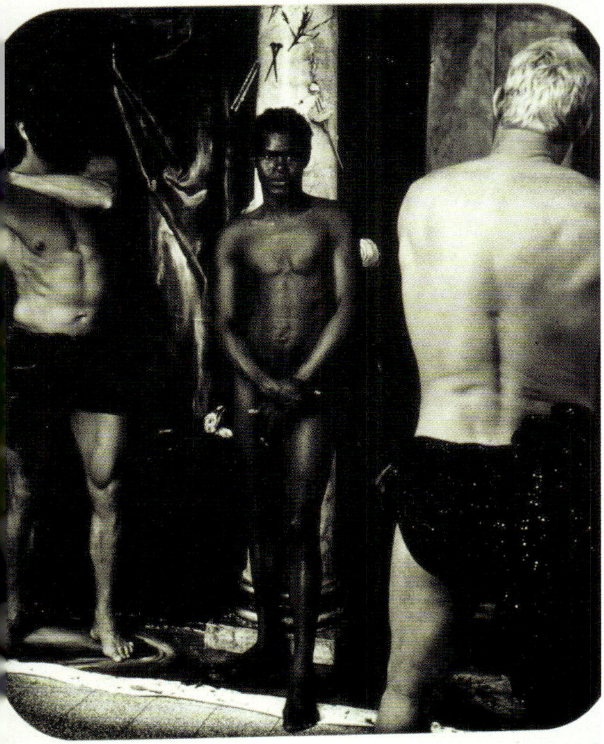

JOEL-PETER WITKIN
Queer Saint, Paris, 1999
Blackman Rome, 1996

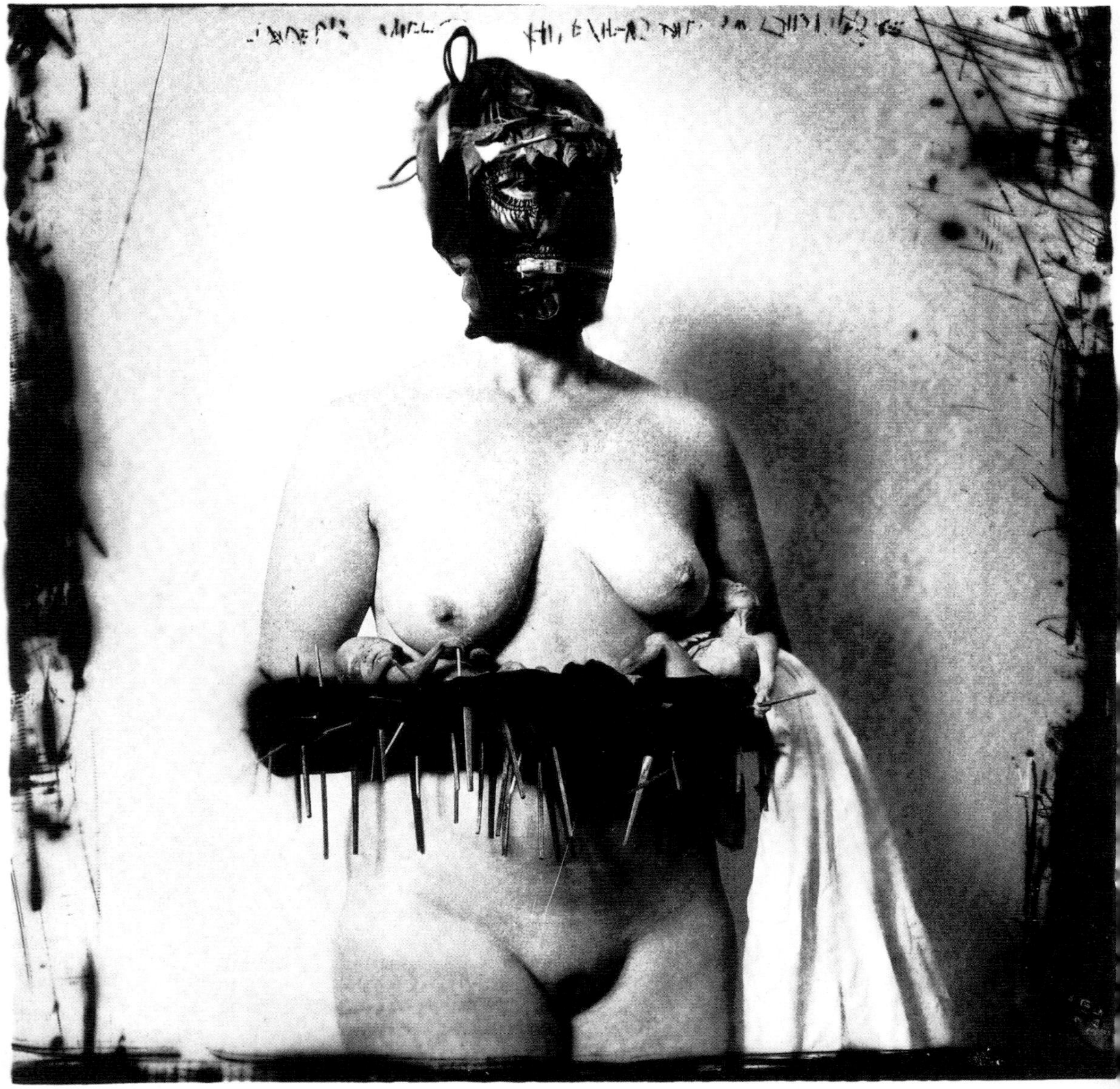

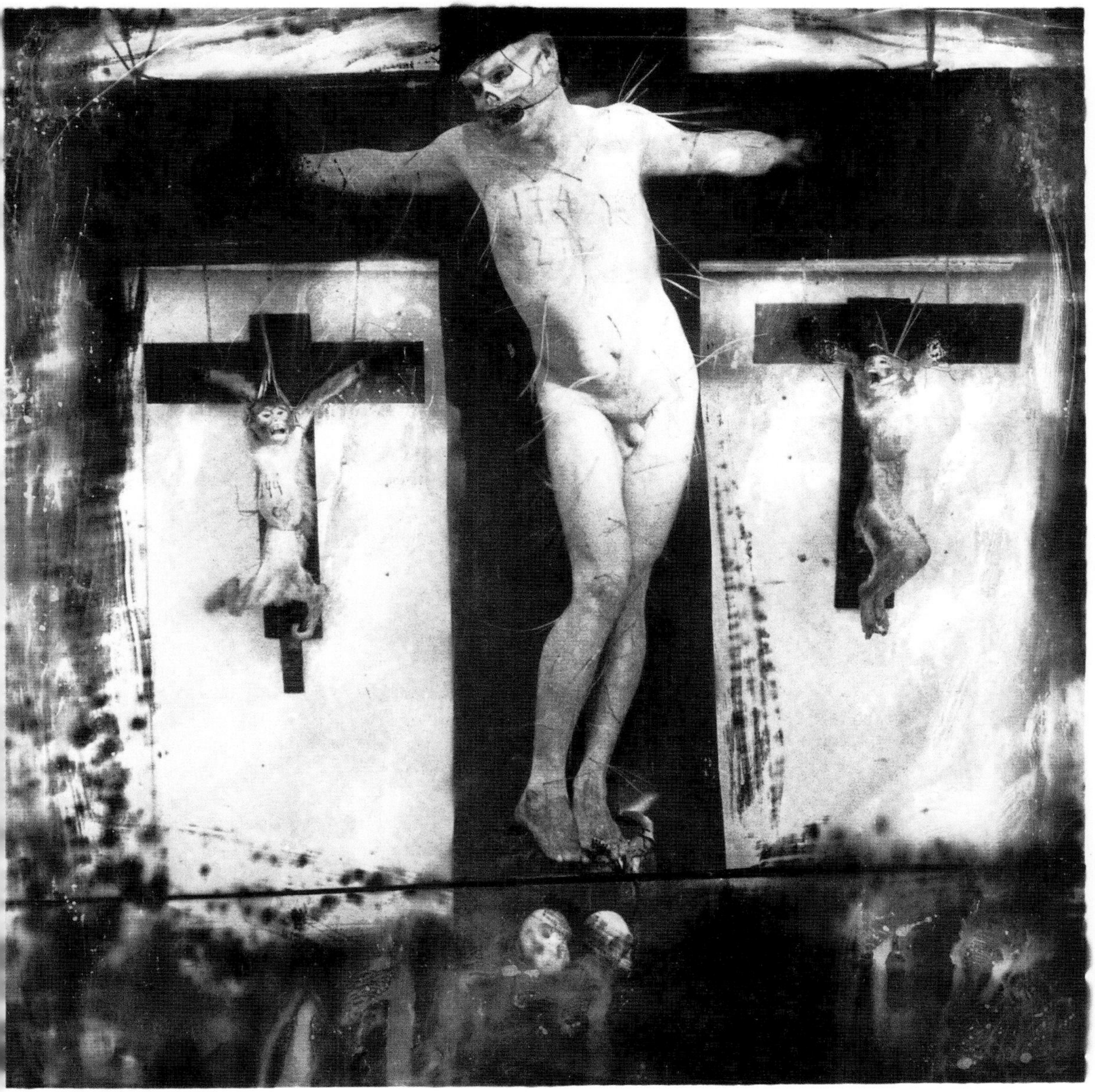

JOEL-PETER WITKIN
Sander's Wife, 1981
Penitente, New Mexico, 1982

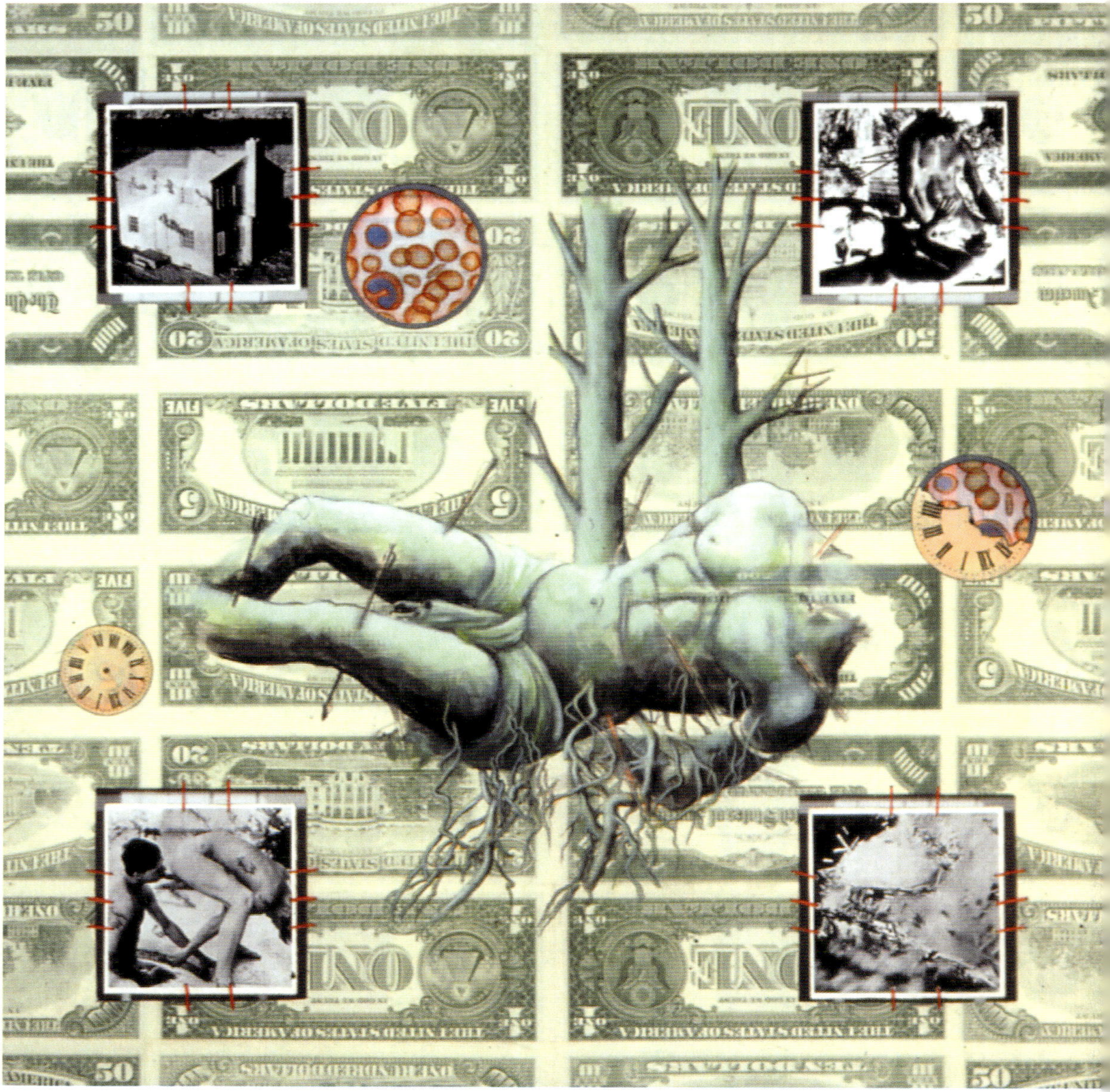

David Wojnarowicz

In various works of David Wojnarowicz his relationship to Saint Sebastian is condensed. Like the artists Kishin Shinoyama, Eikoh Hosoe and the filmmaker Paul Schrader, he refers to the Japanese writer Yukio Mishima. In Wojnarowicz's work *Peter Hujar Dreaming/Yukio Mishima: St. Sebastian* (1982) his friend and partner Peter merges with Sebastian and the masturbating Mishima. The scene with these three men is located in a space between the world – suggested by maps – and the stars, a world that is transfigured and sensual, like the men kissing each other in *Untitled* (1988) (see also the similar work: *Fuck You Faggot Fucker*, 1984). But the arrows that penetrate Sebastian in both works point to the brutal and cruel topicality of AIDS. As a saint who drew disaster onto himself in order to overcome it, Sebastian became the patron saint of sufferers of bubonic plague in the Middle Ages, and of those who suffer from AIDS in our days. In images and texts, Wojnarowicz, who is a friend of photographer Nan Goldin and has been portrayed by her, documents his own life and that of his friend Peter Hujar and those of innumerable people he knew, who died of the virus in the eighties.

In another work, *The Newspaper as National Voodoo: A Brief History of the U.S.A.* (1986), David Wojnarowicz translates the familiar motif of Sebastian penetrated by arrows into a Voodoo doll, pricked through with nails and a knife. On the margins of the collage, the world's evil becomes manifest. Both Saint Sebastian and the Voodoo doll are expressions of Wojnarowicz's apocalyptic visions of the world. They are motifs of overcoming his traumatic childhood and terrible youth between drugs and street-walking.

Angela Stief

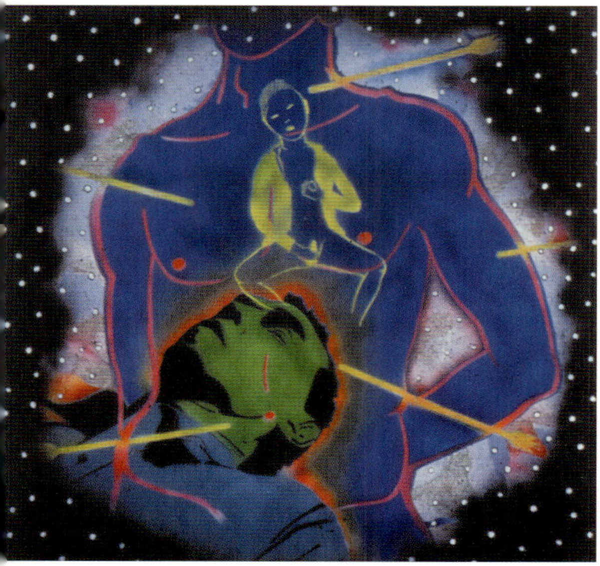

DAVID WOJNAROWICZ

Bad Moon Rising, 1989

Peter Hujar Dreaming/Yukio Mishima: St. Sebastian, 1982

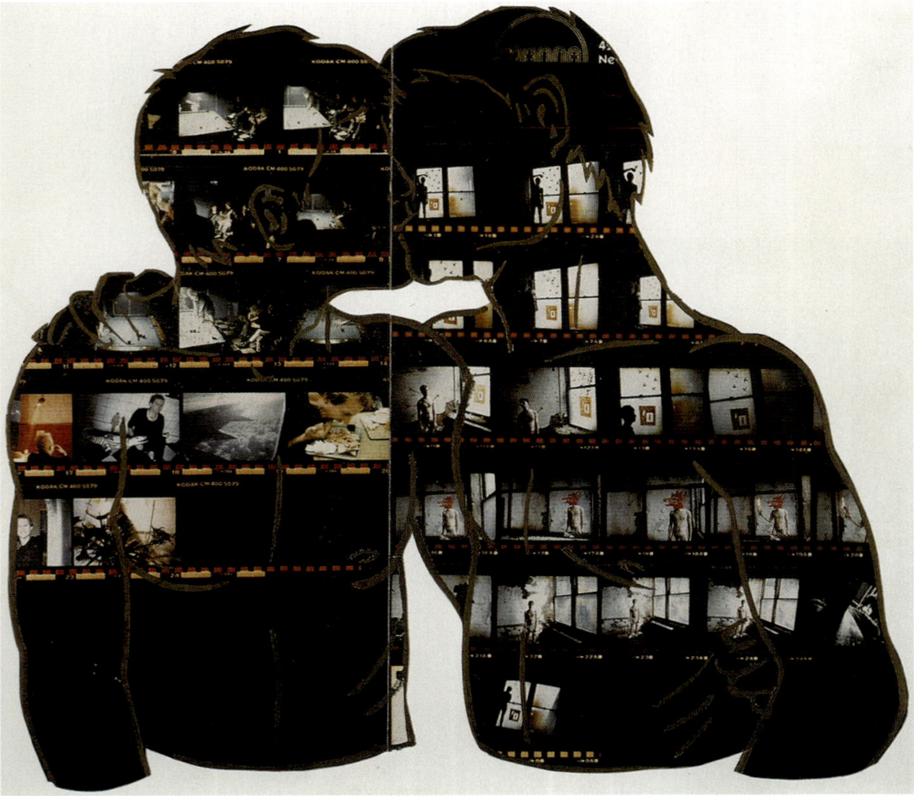

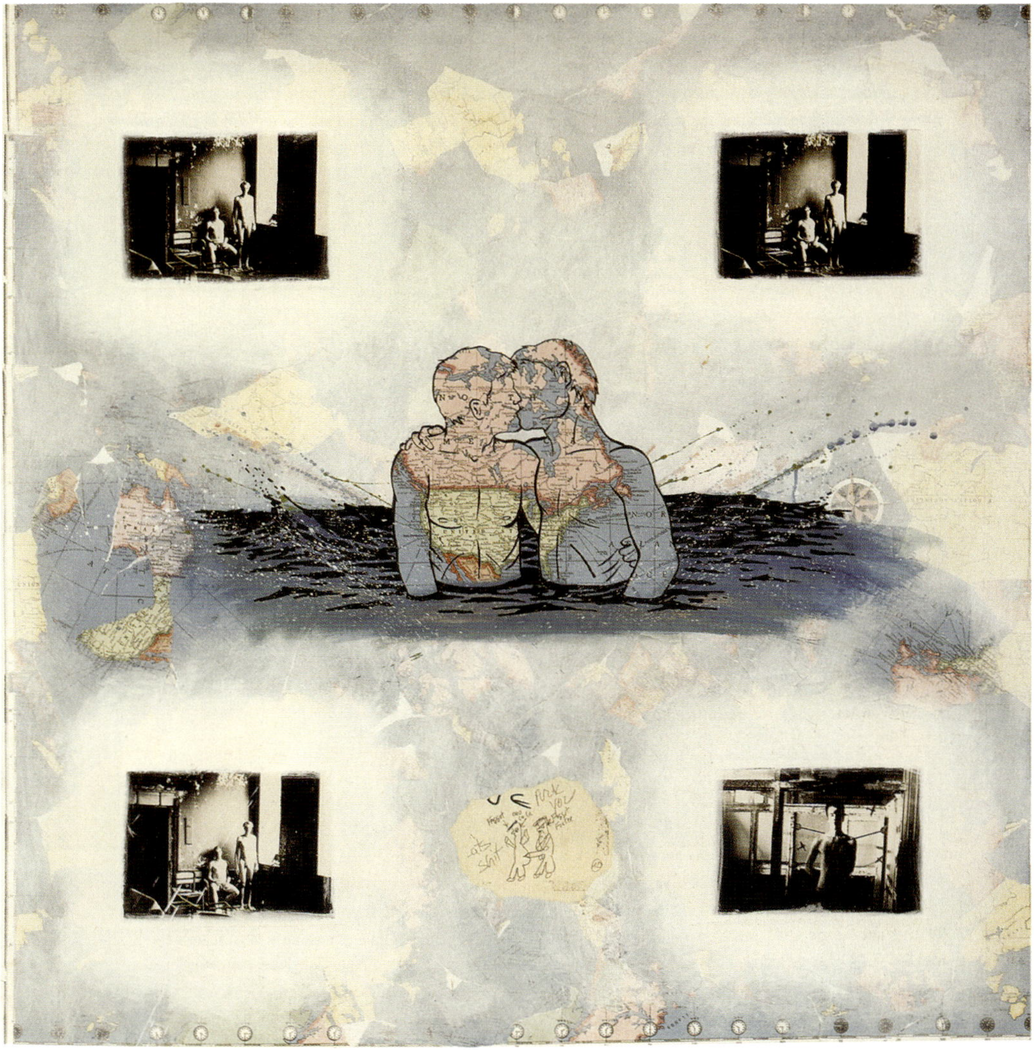

DAVID WOJNAROWICZ

Untitled, 1988

Fuck you Faggot Fucker, 1984

I feel a Vague Nausea, 1990

Arthur Rimbaud in New York (Shooting Up, Pier), 1978–79

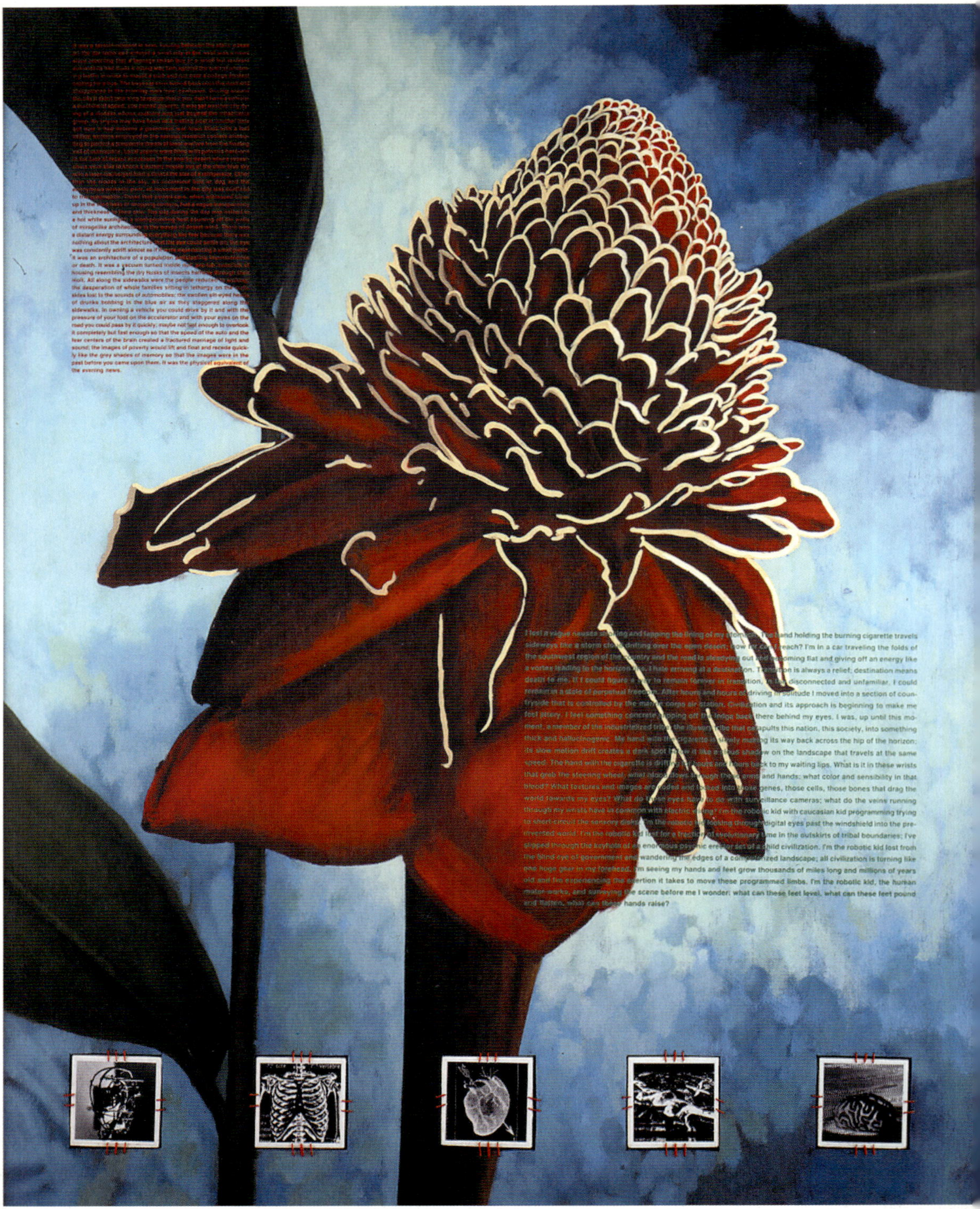
the desperation of whole families sitting in lethargy on the
of drunks bobbing in the blue air as they staggered along the
sidewalks. In owning a vehicle you could drive by it and with the
pressure of your foot on the accelerator and with your eyes on the
road you could pass by it quickly; maybe not fast enough to overlook
it completely but fast enough so that the speed of the auto and the
fear centers of the brain created a fractured marriage of light and
sound; the images of poverty would lift and float and recede quick-
ly like the grey shades of memory so that the images were in the
past before you came upon them. It was the physical equivalent of
the evening news.
hand holding the burning cigarette travels
reach? I'm in a car traveling the folds of
coming flat and giving off an energy like
is always a relief; destination means
disconnected and unfamiliar. I could
solitude I moved into a section of coun-
and its approach is beginning to make me
there behind my eyes. I was, up until this mo-
pults this nation, this society, into something
its way back across the hip of the horizon;
on the landscape that travels at the same
to my waiting lips. What is it in these wrists
and hands; what color and sensibility in that
genes, those cells, those bones that drag the
cameras; what do the veins running
kid with caucasian kid programming trying
digital eyes past the windshield into the pre-
in the outskirts of tribal boundaries; I've
child civilization. I'm the robotic kid lost from
landscape; all civilization is turning like
I'm seeing my hands and feet grow thousands of miles long and millions of years
ertion it takes to move these programmed limbs. I'm the robotic kid, the human
scene before me I wonder: what can these feet level, what can these feet pound
hands raise?

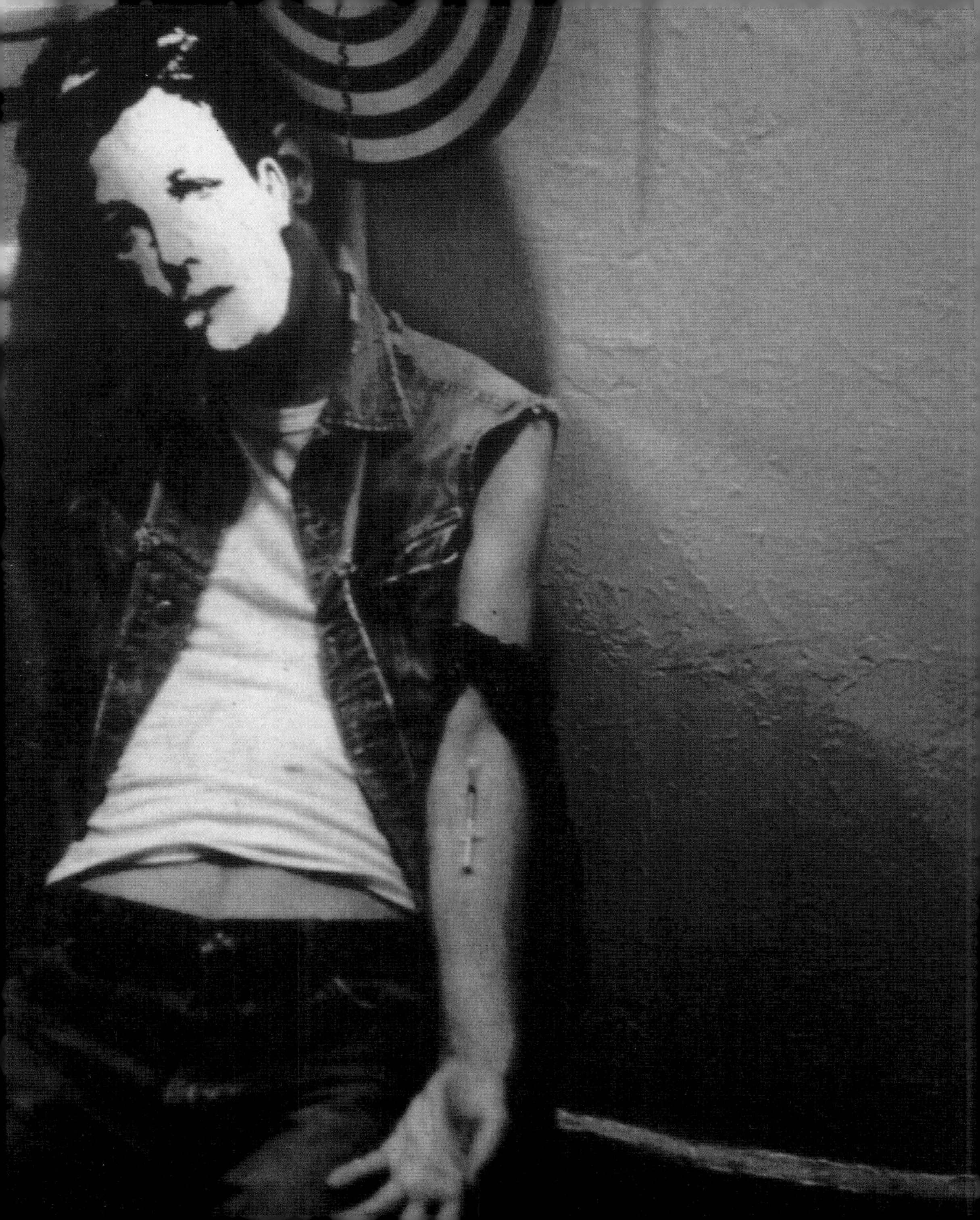

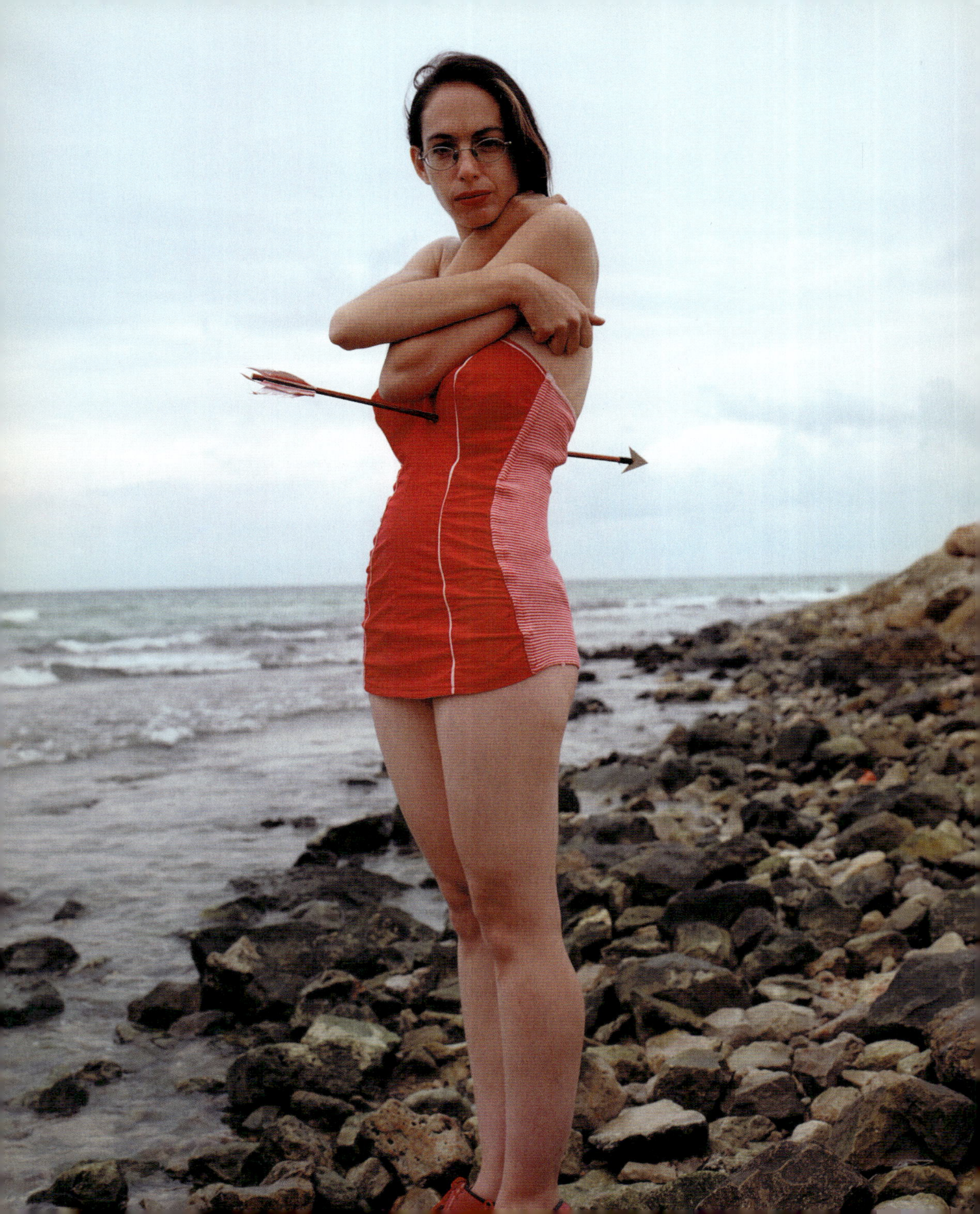

Rona Yefman

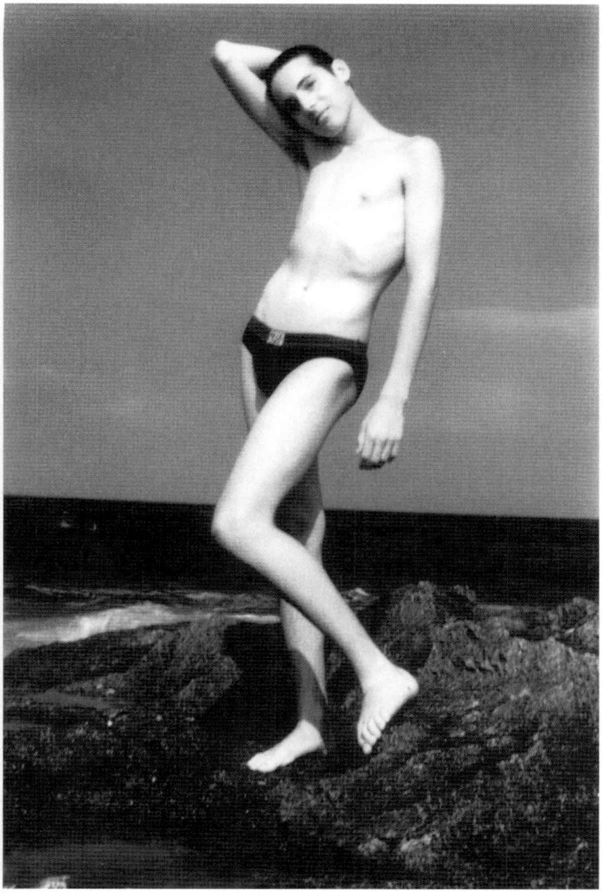

RONA YEFMAN
Gal with Arrows, 2003
Rocks, 2003

This set of works derives from a 'photo album' comprised of layers and segments from different stories. The collection of photographs attempts to open a window to a world of intimate stories about different characters – some of whom are real and some fictitious, as a metaphor for a different and colourful reality.

My aim is to try to tell the truth in some way about reality through different characters, situations and places, based on facts. Just as in a 'family album' it is only from the viewer's critical awareness and observation than one can begin to comprehend that the collection of photos is based on biographical details of my every day life developed out of living muses, with subjective compositions affected by passions, thoughts and fantasies.

The context in which this work connects work to the 'family album' came about by combining parts of documented stories based on my immediate family and close friends. The other characters relate in the sense that they add relevant details to help illustrate the personal and social identities that I am looking for.

In a documentary sense, the motives of time and place are used as a silent testimony to a condition, place and being of the characters, and to physiological changes such as aging, sex change and mood swings.

The central focus of the different layers that make up my work is the story of Gil, my brother/ sister who I began to photograph and document seven years ago, the deep identity crisis that she went through and with which I could identify. The collaborated work developed into a meaningful connection to a documented project about a joint journey of imagination and realism with hazy borders. One journey was to find an explanatory sexual identity, an inner place, as well as a social one, where we can function as beautiful and carefree characters without any worries, yet are still aware of eccentric situations which govern the dialogue with society, and spread clues to our secrets. The meaning of photographic language is impossible to separate from the dynamics of the work and life.

In order to describe reality in the most truthful sense, I didn't choose to use photography in a one-dimensional way. Instead, I decided to develop different languages and techniques, from black and white, colour photography, Polaroid slides and different format cameras, to using strategic ways and collecting different materials; snapshots, cinematically staged scenes – a language that is reminiscent of fashion photography and, equally so, anonymous materials.

The situations of 'dressing up' in my work are not allegories of reality, but the secret passion that becomes the reality itself. Photography allows me to validate reality in the same way that it wishes to be revealed.

RONA YEFMAN

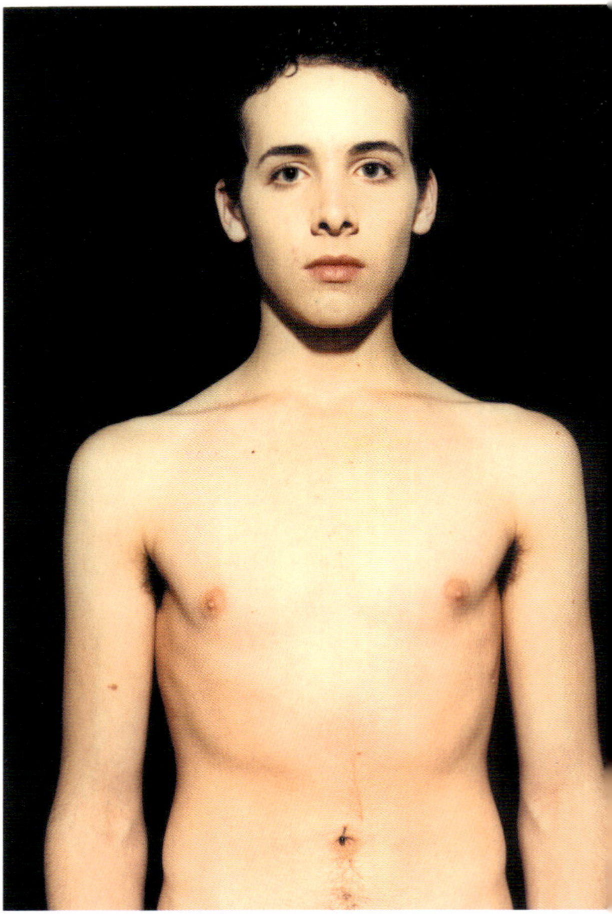

RONA YEFMAN
Young, 2003
Smoke, 2003

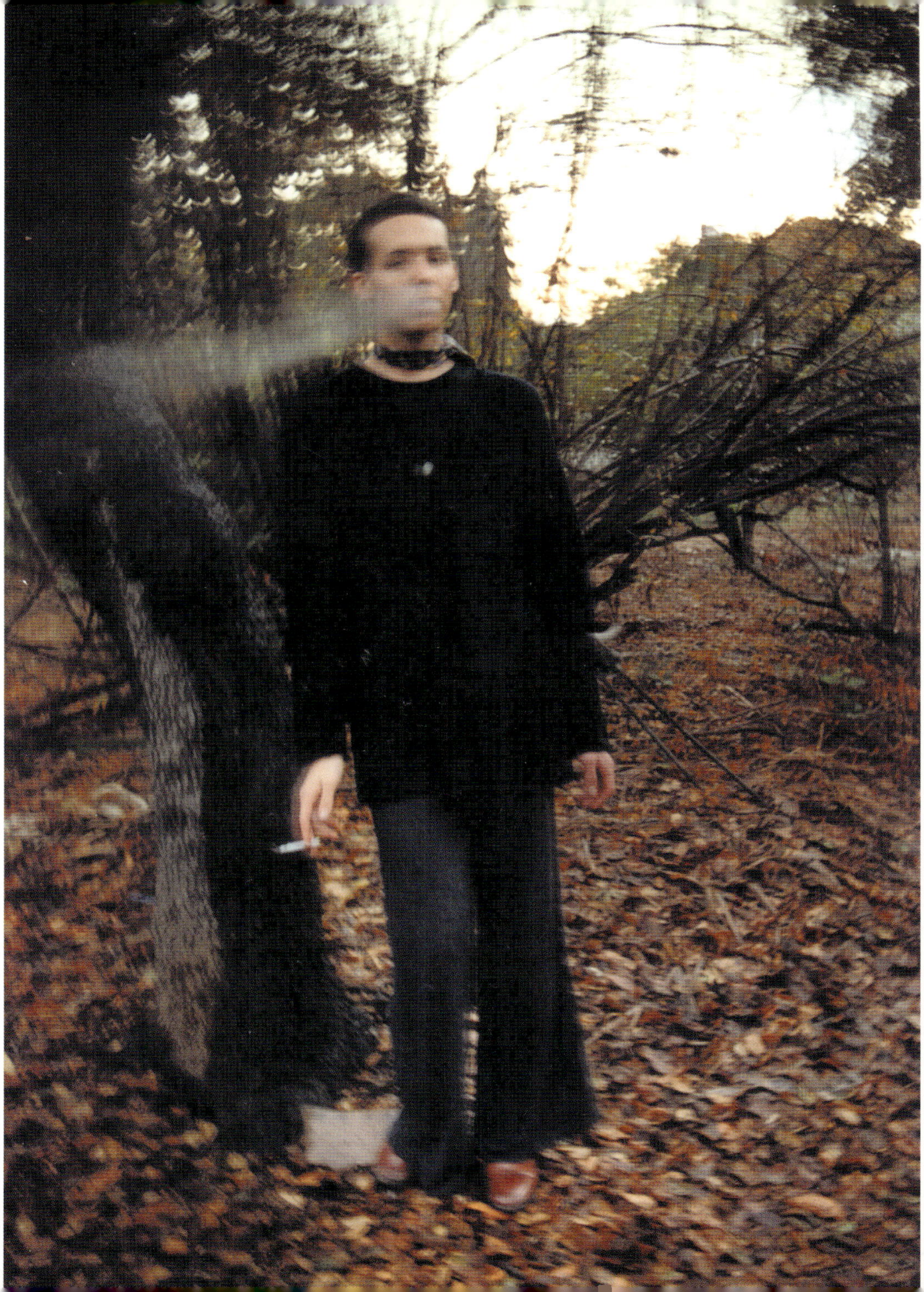

Wolfgang Fetz

Saint Sebastian. Love, Death and Paradise (Excerpt)

G. W. F. Hegel diagnosed the "voluntary self-abnegation, self-sacrifice and self-privation" of the martyr personality as a "rawness of spirit and a barbaric power of abstraction", which offends "against all defined sensitivities of humanity". "The greatest part of this group is made up of … bodily tortures, which are partly applied to the faithful by enemies and persecutors of the faith for reasons of hatred and vengeance and are partly carried out voluntarily in total abstraction, for the purpose of atonement. In both cases the person accepts them in a fanatical form of tolerance, not as an injustice but rather as a blessing. … However, since in such cases the conversion of the inner person can only be shown in the ugliness and mistreatment of the outer person, it is all too easy to offend the aesthetic sense, and the details of this group are consequently a very dangerous subject for art."

The conversion of Sebastian, the Diocletian body-guard officer and faith healer, carried out on the martyr's stake of D'Annunzio is, however, in spite of Hegel's prosaic view, a conversion into beauty (though not into conventional morality). When the *illustrious person* (in contrast to the legend) dies in masochistic submission, the site of the martyrdom is filled with the fragrance of lilies. Traditionally, the lily is the symbol of innocence and purity; in the ancient world the lily plant *Asphodelus ramosus* was seen as the flower of death. At an earlier phase of the martyrdom, the Emperor intended to have Sebastian smothered under a huge bunch of roses. The recurring flower symbolism has a sublime relationship to the saint's injuries. The complicity between victim and perpetrator, the pleasure in suffering and causing suffering transforms the wounds, which are "in themselves ugly, loathsome, disgusting external things" (Hegel), into hallucinogenic blossoms. We are dealing here with a kind of double exposure: the "fanaticism of saintliness" (the appeal to God) and the unforeseen orgiastic alliance between Sebastian and the archers overlay each other to create an excessive image. The ascension of the martyr, the corrida, turns into a triangular story, a saintly trio infernal. For Hegel beauty and "an inwardness that has processed the pain or that is presented in suffering and contains it even in the transfiguration of the moment of pain as the most substantial concern" are separated from each other by an insuperable categorical boundary. In short: the aesthetic (the good and the true) is incommensurable with the cruel or with perverse lust. At about the same time as that when Hegel was delivering his *Lectures on Aesthetics* (from which our quotations have been taken), Thomas de Quincey was writing an essay with the refreshing title: *On Murder Considered as One of the Fine Arts* (1827). There he suggests that we consider murder not from a moral but from an aesthetic point of view, "in relation to good taste". In this way he sets up the moral and the aesthetic in opposition to each other. The fascination of crime as an aesthetic act undermines "the dominance of morality" (Nietzsche) in aesthetics. The (classical) pairing of ethics and aesthetics is replaced by the (romantic) pairing of crime and aesthetics. In other words, aesthetics strip away all its heteronomous rules and begins to make itself autonomous. That this move to autonomy takes place with the vehicle of the evil, the perverse and the illegal may seem paradoxical at first. In fact, however, it is precisely in its liaison with the forbidden, the ostracised, that the magnetic power of the aesthetic is revealed; the aesthetic does not become evil, but evil becomes aesthetic. In the case of Sebastian the scandal, the evil, is in the offensive, schizophrenic entanglement of religious feeling and sado-masochistic ritual under the banner of aestheticism.

The principle of the aesthetic guerrilla, the assurance of its own claims by offensively and strategically passing over the categorical dogmas, penetrates the structure of the *Martyrdom* into its deepest fibres. *Le Martyre de Saint Sébastien* forms a dense network of "forbidden" constellations: the Italian D'Annunzio is writing in French; the French Debussy is composing in the style of Palestrina, using hints of Japanese and Arabian music; the (Jewish) woman is a (Christian) man, the arrow wound in Sebastian's flesh is a cunt, Christ is a heathen dandy etc. Sebastian's body functions as the focal point of (apparently) incompatible codes, he is a cultural hooker: the "dangerous" rhetoric of the work can be understood as a paradigm for eccentric intuition. As Manuel de Falla remarked in relation to Debussy's reception of Spanish music, he "repeats its reality without its authenticity." Transferred to the present case, I would interpret this observation as follows: it is the recipient, the indiscreet witness, who takes over the offensive reality of a "storyline" (or, in the case of an artist, creates it) without getting involved, without covering himself with blood and filth. It is the criminal mind (as an aesthetic event), not the factual criminal act, which is under discussion here. *Le Martyre* and authenticity are in the same relationship to each other as Oscar Wilde ("there is no real incongruity between crime and culture") and the artist-poisoner Thomas Griffiths Wainewright, to whom Wilde devoted a *Study in Green.* It is hard to deny that the martyrdom is touched by "the piquancy of frivolous corruption" (Karl Rosenkranz). For all the explosiveness at its core, it may very well be enjoyed with one's cup of breakfast chocolate.

Excerpt from: PAUL ALBERT LEITNER: *Die Reise zum heiligen Sebastian*, Wien: Sonderzahl 1993, p. 12 f.

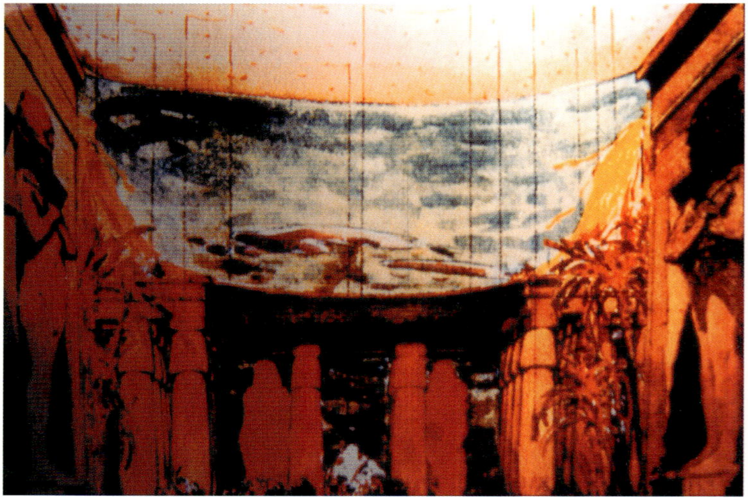

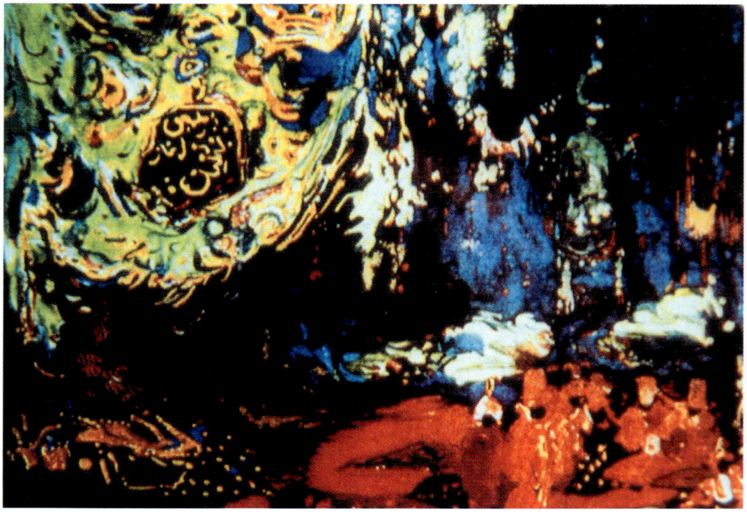

fig. 1: LÉON BAKST, Stage design for the ballett *Cléopâtre* with music by Anton Arensky and other Russian composers, 1909

fig. 2: LÉON BAKST, Stage design for the ballett *Schéhérazade* with music by Nikolaj Rimsky-Korsakov, 1910

Carlo Santoli

Léon Bakst, Stage designer for the première of *The Martyrdom of Saint Sebastian* by Gabriele D'Annunzio[1]

Genesis of the theatrical work.
In his house in Arcachon, Gabriele D'Annunzio worked at *Le Martyre de Saint Sébastien* particularly in summer 1910 and March 1911. For the creation of his tragedy he turned his attention to reading old texts by French writers, which he found both in the libraries and in the bookshops of Paris. These were books of many kinds, of hagiographical or religious character, novels or old epic poems, especially about the birth of Christianity or the decadence of paganism[2], which he read very avidly, absorbing the ancient language and penetrating deeply into the spiritual richness:

Every day I take a bath in mysticism: I have read all of Saint Frances of Sales: I read of old rites. This work absorbs me: his thought stirs me and stops me from sleeping.[3]

Inspired by the Russian Ballet of Sergei Diaghilev, and especially by his productions *Cléopâtre* (fig. 1) und *Schéhérazade* (fig. 2)[4], D'Annunzio not only based his "dramatic expression on dance and on the technique of gesture"[5], but also revealed an exceptional "capacity for fusing the set and choreography with the musical composition into a unique synthesis."[6]

In Ida Rubinstein's dressing room he knelt at her feet, as he recalls in a notebook:

In Paris [...] on the evening of the Russian ballet Cleopatra. *A visit to the diva's dressing room, led by Montesquiou*[7]. *There was Barrès, there was Rostand, there were other French writers, feeling embarrassed, dressed up. With my usual boldness, on seeing the magnificent naked leg close by, I threw myself on the floor, caring nothing for my evening dress and tails, and kissed her feet, rising up the fine shin as far as the knee, and then on and up the thigh as far as the groin, with agile, fleeting lips and the light breath that plays the aulos or double flute. What a scene! What a scandal! I raised my eyes. I saw the face of Cleopatra under the huge blue wig, bent toward me, smiling with a dazzling mouth. I stood up in a dull silence and murmured as if in a day-dream: Saint Sebastien?*[8]

Ida Rubinstein was greatly admired by all, while Jean Cocteau was to say that she is "like an oriental fragrance, too strong and too beautiful".[9] The Russian scene painter, Léon Bakst, spoke of her as follows:

She is a fabulous being [...] I adore her like a beautiful tulip, insolent and dazzling, proud of herself and dispersing pride all around her. I am firmly convinced that the rays of Fortuna will illuminate her to the end.[10]

In spite of her ambition, she was nonetheless aware that she could not take on a role of the highest level in the world of dance in the presence of an artist like Anna Pavlova, Tamara Karsavina or Vaslav Nijinskij. Without a doubt, the Martyre de Saint Sébastien marked a decisive turn in the artistic career of the dancer. The chosen interpreter of the ineffable Saint Ephebe, and the financer of the future play, told the following story, remembering that time:

1910! The Russian Ballet was in triumph. Paris was enchanted. It seemed that the only truth in the universe was poetry. With the point of his ebony cane, Montesquiou made a sketch in the sand of the pavilion of the muses, searching for his own dream. Noone was more suitable than Gabriele D'Annunzio to enter into this enchantment [...]. Montesquiou persuaded D'Annunzio, who had, so to speak, made himself the messenger[11]*, to attend a production of* Cléopâtre.

The author of Fuoco came. Leaving the playhouse, he telegraphed to a friend: 'I have seen Cleopatra. I cannot control my agitation [...]' -

Gabriele D'Annunzio came and found me and told me he wanted to write a mystery play for me, which would have both speech and mime, inspiring me with the play of light from the stained glass windows in Chartres Cathedral ...[12]

The value of the work can indeed be sought in its scenic representation. One can speak of "spatial poetry" or of the creation of a new figurative language, of "total theatre" which harmoniously links the occidental and the oriental. The scene painter Léon Bakst knew the art of enchantment: following the suggestions of D'Annunzio, created particular influences, astonishing the audience, which was no longer made up of simple spectators but virtually entered the scene, becoming an actor or character, reawakening the whirlwind of emotions and passions.

Through his scenery Bakst wanted to freshen up the myth of classical times and of oriental culture. The warm, intense colours are metaphors of a sensualism borrowed from the legends of the orient, to which the artist was powerfully drawn. It was a matter of acclimatising the *Martyre de Saint Sébastien* in a civilisation like that of pagan Rome in the third century AD, interwoven with Orientalist influence from art, culture and religion.

The play succeeded in richly evoking the time, although showing a baroque style, laboured and celebratory. It wanted to be an unrestrained, unlimited drama. The emphasis on scenic apparatus reinforced and complemented the representational aspect, making the distant past come to life again in an aura of aestheticised mysticism.

The figurative motifs and some comparisons with famous paintings

As in Bernini, it was also Bakst's intention that the spiral motif of the pillars would

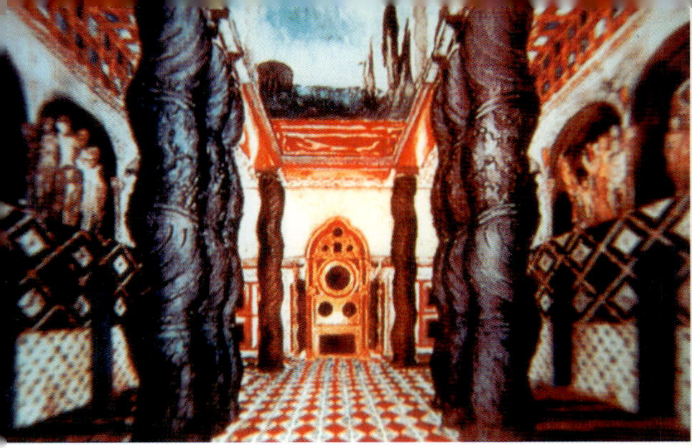

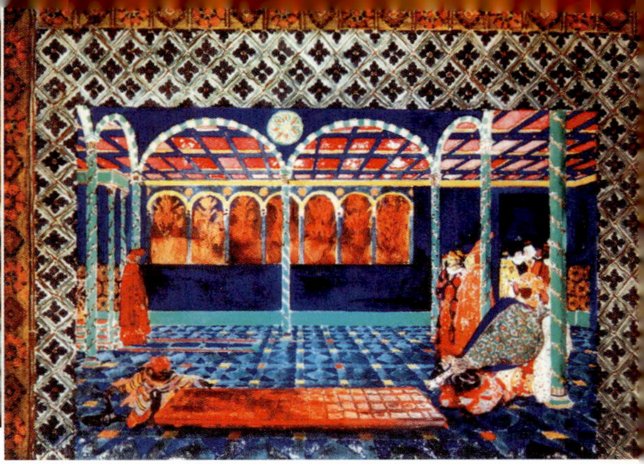

fig. 3: LÉON BAKST, Stage setting for 3rd act (*Le Concile des Faux Dieux)* of *Le Martyre de Saint Sébastien* by Gabriele D'Annunzio with music by Claude Debussy, Théâtre du Châtelet, Paris, 22 May, 1911

fig. 4: LÉON BAKST, Stage setting for 1st act of *Le Martyre (Le Premier Palais, Le Cour des Lys)*, 1911

serve to draw the eyes of the spectator/observer upward where there was no enclosing ceiling like an impediment to vision but an open sky (see the sketch for the third act: *Le Concile des Faux Dieux*, fig. 3). Making appropriate use of the various shades of colour, one could say that Bakst opened up spaces "of a height never again achieved and measured spaces of a vastness and profundity which have remained unequalled."[13]

This repeats the same phenomenon as that found in the tonal pictures of Tiepolo and Veronese. And so the result will be "the identification of infinity in space with infinity in light".[14]

It is significant that he arrives at this point in this sketch, as in that for Act I (*Le Premier Palais, La Cour des Lys*, fig. 4), after beginning with perspective. It depends on the play of withdrawal-and-advance on vertical and parallel planes made only of light, which forms and delineates the almost phosphorescent design of colours in the larger arches, inside which smaller arches are formed, subsiding into the empty and free space behind the fifth of the more withdrawn arches.

An analogous effect of sinking into space is achieved in the set for the fourth act (*Le Laurier Blessé*, fig. 5) across the perspective and the chromatic gradation, curved to communicate the intense and dramatic emotion.

Bakst makes theatre to go beyond theatre, not accepting a picture complete in itself but wanting a visual art which goes beyond simulation. In fact, the visionary colourist reality of this back-drop is a different reality, which supersedes that of nature and history. In short, it is the reality of convulsive movements of the soul, the consuming passions of man, the dramatic interior world of all times.

Some comparisons with famous paintings also bring significant results. For example,

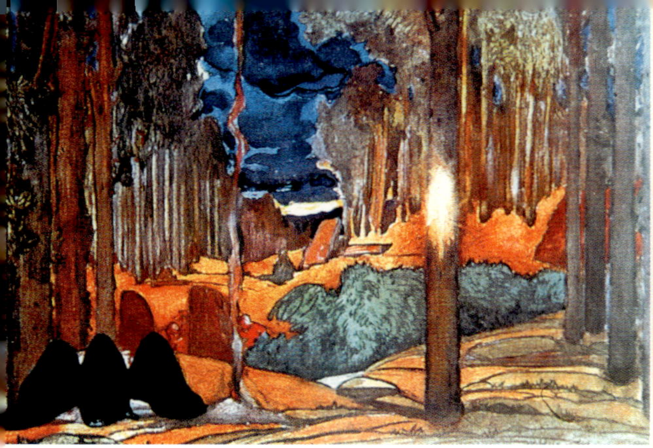

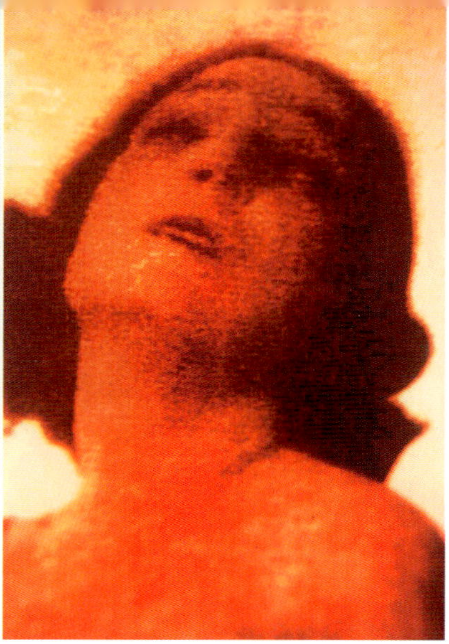

fig. 5: LÉON BAKST, Stage setting for 4th act of *Le Martyre (Le Laurier Blessé)*, 1911

fig. 6: Ida Rubinstein in the role of Saint Sebastian, Teatro alla Scala di Milano, 4 March 1926

the "erotic" beauty of the actress: Ida Rubinstein, like the feminine heroines of Moreau, attracted and quickly seduced the public. This beauty was expressed in chromatic, physical features, in a purity of design of the kind in which Dante Gabriele Rossetti was a master.

Bakst searched for spirituality and found grace in explosive light in which the figures were outlined, determining a theatrical effect on the spectators. To illustrate this assertion, let us consider the faces arranged against the light. The first is that of the interpreter of Saint Sebastian (fig. 6), the second is found in the painting *Beata Beatrix* of Dante Gabriele Rossetti.

In the second act the whole crowd kneels before the saint, appearing like a crowd reproduced in Flemish pictures. In the darkness of the of the mitre crypt there are women in big rust-coloured cloaks hemmed in black, their necks gripped tightly in linen *bandelettes* and bonnets[15] with two horns hiding their hair; there are also men, wounded and leaning on crutches, and witches weighed down with luxuriant robes of orange brocade, as if they were a sudden animation of one of those triptychs of Henri Blès (called the Maître des Moulins).[16]

The third act shows the court where the emperor offers the saint all riches and glory. In this place the women, the priests, the Orientals crowd around the beautiful figure of Sebastian, very slim in his black garment. This is the same interpretation as that of antiquity, the same architectonic vision of the ancient world. The emperor, the priests, the maidservants wearing the purple, the toga or the hood, in stead of the saint, the archers, the people wearing costumes of the fifteenth century.[17]

With the sumptuousness of their clothing the characters (fig. 7) recall other pictorial works: the *Camera degli Sposi* (fig. 8), *L'Incontro* of Andrea Mantegna, with reference also to painting by Pisanello[18] and Cossa[19].

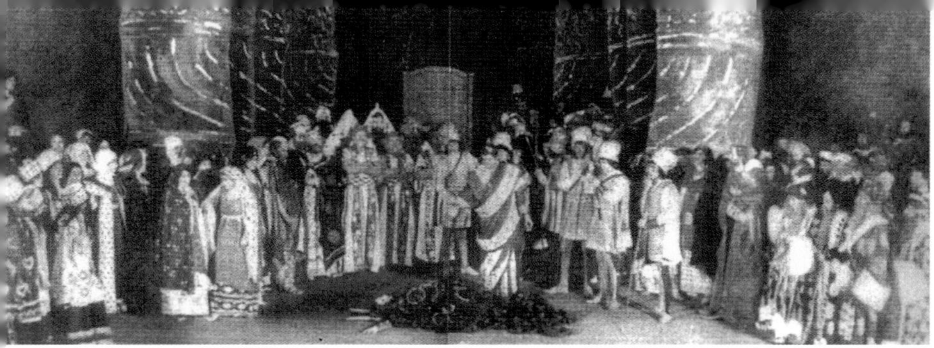

fig. 7: LÉON BAKST, stage photo of 3rd act of *Le Martyre*, 1911

The fourth act – which, according to Diego Angeli, recalls a scene in a picture of Benozzo Gozzoli[20] – opens on a dark forest of green bay trees against which the blue tunics of the archers and the pale, naked body of the saint stand out.[21]

A particular note in the fourth act (fig. 5) is its suggestive chromaticism. The light crossing the colours determines a succession of vertical and parallel axes through them, which grow thicker on the trunks of the trees to right and left – compared with the central space of the large glade – so that one's gaze penetrates into the depth of the field.

A flash of bright light, like a serpentine, moves the scenic space vertically, coming from above, in startling contrast to the deep dark tresses of the trees. Like a thunderbolt that suddenly strikes the earth, this flash produces a psychological effect, which shakes the soul, recalling the lightning that rends the sky in Giorgione's *Tempesta*. The diffuse brightness on the ground at the centre of the picture disperses the darkness of the high leaves on the trees, creating a scenic result of great effectiveness.

It may be considered that the culminating moment of the drama of the sudden martyrdom of Saint Sebastian (see the scenic reconstruction in the original drawing: fig. 9) coincides with that flash, like the flash of a camera shot[22] at the dark trunk of the tree which is aligned with the other trunks at the side with the same regularity of individuation of space as Piero della Francesca in *Battesimo di Cristo* (fig. 10) aligns the vertical elements of the body of Christ and the tree trunks in the foreground.

Be that as it may, in order to differentiate the mysterious light effect that strikes the landscape, originating in the human figure, Bakst introduces in the bottom left corner three obscure, black shapes, three female persons, approaching to form a group in a scenic effect against the light. Seen from the back, these shapes appear to be the figures of spectators who are watching in astonishment the rural scene of pure and magical luminosity of colour. The final result of the enchantment profits from a silence which reigns supreme over the naturalistic scene in the absence of the human figure, now that the three shapes of the three women go almost unobserved, vague like blots obscured by the clear masses of luminous colour.

The primitive fascination of uncontaminated nature seems to be produced by the power of the light. In an ideal dimension one might assume that in representing this

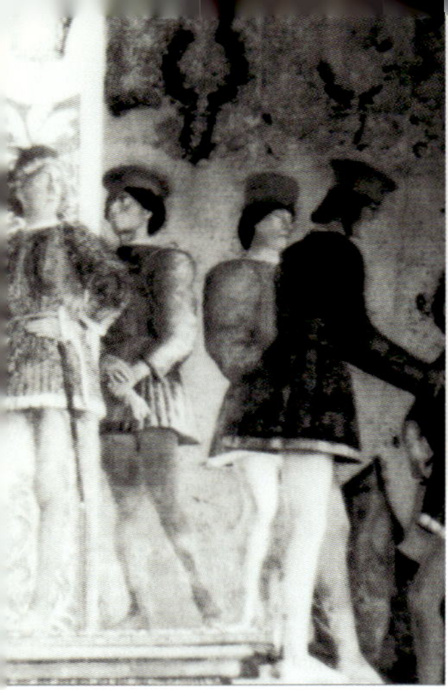

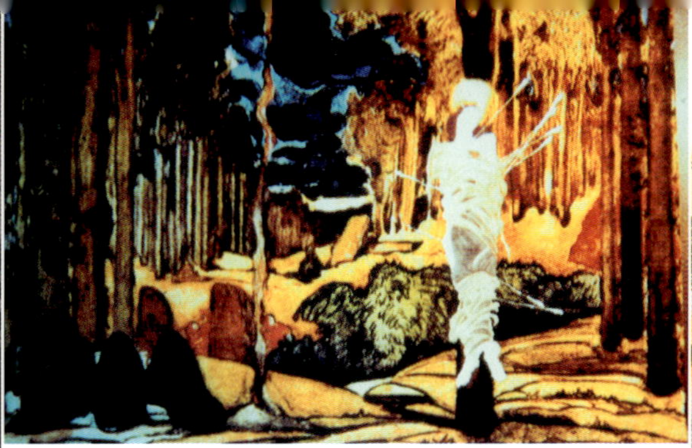

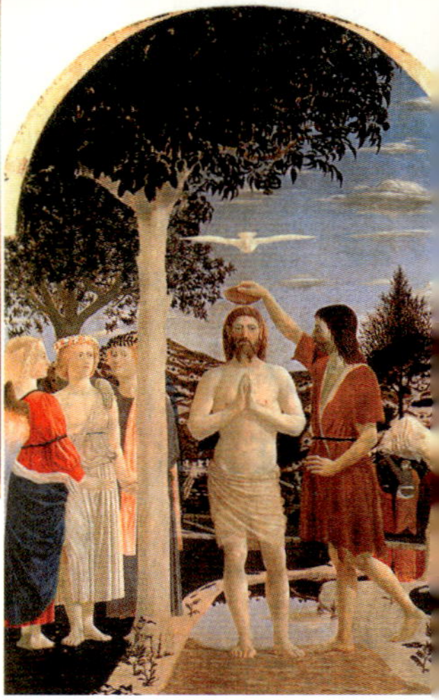

fig. 8: ANDREA MANTEGNA, Detail of the Courtyard *Camera degli Sposi*, Castello di San Giorgio

fig. 9: Stage reconstruction of 4th act of *Le Martyre de Saint Sébastien* after an original design by Léon Bakst

fig. 10: PIERO DELLA FRANCESCA, *Bettesimo di Cristo*

drawing Bakst, either deliberately or else quite unconsciously, wanted to contrast symbolically the value of light (alluding to Life) with the value of darkness (alluding to Death).

And the mystery of faith that renews itself: the three dark figures, as mysterious as the darkness that defines them, express the same intimate concentration of mind in the pain and prayers of the three weeping women at the foot of the cross, on which the man Christ first suffered a martyrdom similar to that which Saint Sebastian now suffers tied to the bay tree.

In terms of iconography, the concentration on the trunk of the tree in the foreground (corresponding to the horizontal piece of the cross), is signalled by the flash of light, and the three pious women and the same silent but eloquent concentration intervening at the cross of Jesus, and the three female figures of the pious women. The enchanted silence of a quasi-supernatural representation of nature, expressed by their unspoken language (not made up of words but of symbolic signs and tonal statements), becomes the transmission of a visual sensation, to which, inevitably, an emotional sensation corresponds.

The colour is actually loaded with pathos and can also correspond with the pursuit of that sensuality peculiar to D'Annunzio, simultaneously erotic and exotic, from the moment when the magic of the warm colours – which pervade the scene in question – recalls the oriental world in a composition of typically occidental vertical planes.

The prevalent tonality of a diffuse red which, in the infinite modulation of light covers over the internal scenic picture (fig. 5) like a photographic film, in truth constitutes the emotional connecting path between the evoked surrounding and the crowd, who, more than just spectators, relive and suffer the same drama of passion as that presented. The red may express – according to Bakst in a letter to D'Annunzio on 10 November 1910[23] – a passion that both draws one in and upsets one. In this way he already anticipated some aspects of Expressionism and confirms those of Symbolism, reuniting them with the same regard for red as a vehicle for conveying passion and scenic drama that Moreau would have had (cf. *Moïse sauvé des eaux*, approx. 1893 – fig. 11). Passion is submerged in the red of the background as in blood.

In an interview granted to Rose Strunsky, Bakst revealed some very interesting elements, speaking sometime afterwards of the production of the Martyre:

[...] It is with line and colour that I give life to my emotions [...] And then in the stage set the aspect of pure mysticism emerges, as in D'Annunzio's Saint Sebastian [...] Since it deals with an essentially Christian subject, I made use of the cross in a thousand variations as the basis of my linear ornamentation, hidden and concealed in the costumes, in the properties and in the ornaments of the beautiful work of D'Annunzio, but also in the lines of the landscape and of the set constructions. In general my method is to adopt a simple motif and to repeat it in infinite variations in such a way as to create a harmony of line and colour [...].[24]

The value of light.

Light assumed a pregnant and polyvalent significance in the first production of the Martyre. Bakst showed that he was concerned with the development taking place in the Middle Ages in the stained glass windows of the most important French cathedrals: Notre-Dame de Paris, Sainte-Chapelle and Chartres. Considering the scenic elaboration of the first act (fig. 4), he used the cathartic and radiant function of light, placing it in verticals and parallels withdrawing or advancing it in space according to precise scientific rules of perspective. It is not by chance that he uses the representation of a casement ceiling in central perspective, with all the lines converging at the vanishing point (in this connection see Leonardo's Last Supper), as is also shown in the introduction of the geometrical "chessboard" decorative motif newly attained by means of perspective (cf. The scene for Act II: *La Chambre Magique*, fig. 12).

Bakst also demonstrated that he had assimilated the value of light in its tonal function: arranging the architectural skeleton of the slender spiral columns – which support the arches in the absolute centre and in full light – son that the lead to the front of the stage (the law of the tonalists is: "the most radiant colour moves towards the spectator in comparison with the darker colours, which retreat"). For a theatrical representation based on effects of light, knowing this law is an indispensable pre-condition. Therefore, the internal order of the architectural-constructional design of the scenes in question results in a characteristic and studied distribution of more radiant colours (in the foreground) and less radiant colours (the background or on intermediate planes). Thus colour becomes the organisational and expressive element of scenic space.

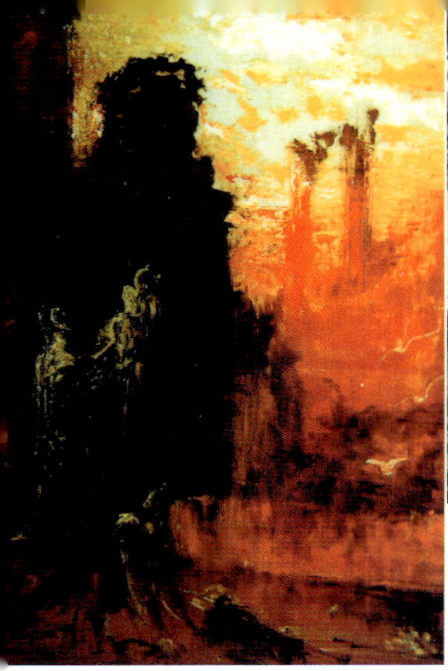

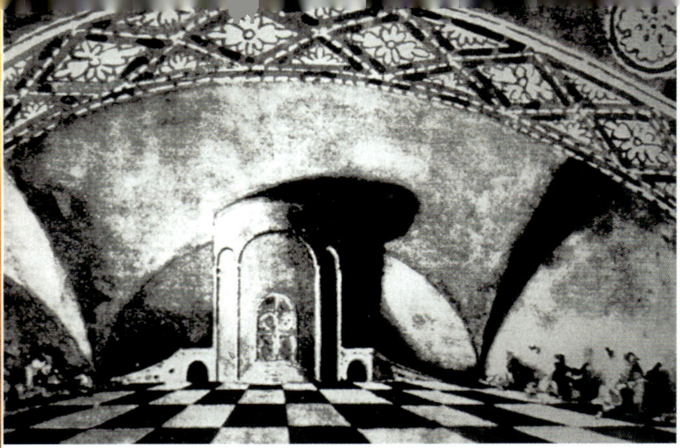

fig. 11: GUSTAVE MOREAU, *Moïse sauvé des eaux*, around 1893

fig. 12: Stage set 2nd act of *Le Martyre (La Chambre Magique)*, 1911

Just as in a Rubens painting, in the stage set for the first act Bakst created brilliant chromatic effects taking on the purpose of ensuring intense emotion through visual perception. If the "theatre is a representation, the profound nature of reality is the staginess of Rubens."[25]

Another feature of the originality of this figurative language is the coexistence of two antithetical worlds: oriental and occidental (fig. 7). If the structural and architectural installation of light-colour accorded with a rational plan of formal balance, which is a part of the character of occidental art, the power of emotional suggestion in the light, evoking dream and fable, is a part of oriental art.

The colours which pervade the shapes of the characters' bodies (fig. 13) in an "inlay" technique recall not only the character of a large picture but also that expressed in the oriental miniature. In a virtual dimension it is perhaps not dangerous to assert that Bakst purposely enclosed all the scenic architecture of the first act in a typically oriental frame, a Persian one in particular. The motif of uninterrupted ornamentation frames the scene as if in an exquisitely oriental taste, where decorative frames enclose the principal scene in the codices of Persian miniatures. The same flowery element in the space where two big arches meet at the centre of the drawing already described may rise as a symbol of the powerful bond uniting oriental and occidental cultures.

Considering then the luminous and warm chromatic texture at ground level it is impossible not to see a clear reference to the function of light when a touch of colour is released in the dark and is able to inflame it as happened in the painting of El Greco. If

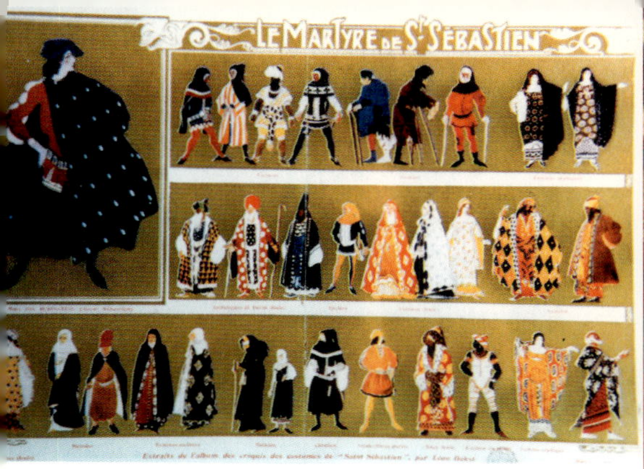

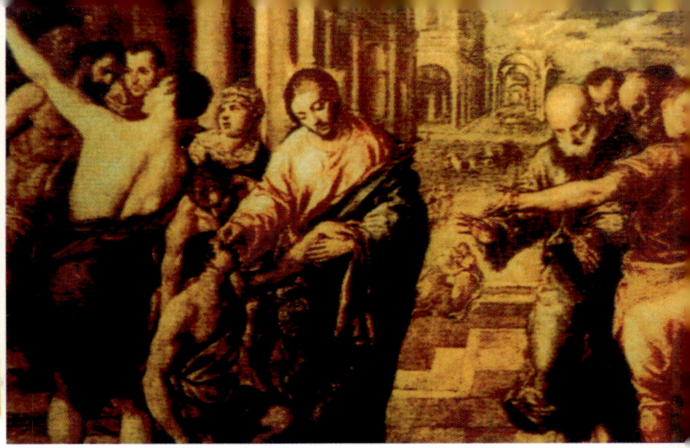

fig. 13: LÉON BAKST, Costume sketches drawn for the prmiere of *Le Martyre*

fig. 14: EL GRECO, *Christ Healing The Blind Man*, around 1750

we compare the *Guarigione del Cieco* (fig. 14) with the drawing for the fourth act (fig. 5), the reddish halo diffused over the entire surface of the picture expresses the same "burning and visionary luminosity"[26]. There are interesting analogies in this composition between the serpentine flash – like a thunderbolt striding the ground – and "the hallucinatory luminous flashes of the extended altar"[27] in the painting of El Greco. The same empty space – as if it had risen again from the whirlpool – inserts itself in depth by an enchanted and mysterious path.

We may therefore conclude that the intuition of Montesquiou is worthy of note, according to whom Bakst succeeded with his stage sets in performing the miracle of transposing the form of light in the stained glass windows of the French cathedrals (with special reference to those of Chartres) onto superimposed planes[28].

"Before our eyes we have moving glass images."[29]

The entire play, however, reveals itself in a dazzling display, even if its reception by critics and the public was not very warm. Mario Corsi writes:

> *The magnificent invocation of the* Martyrdom of Saint Sebastian *was received with a certain coolness and the scene when the archers shoot hid itself perhaps in too much darkness. However Debussy's final scene was greeted with enthusiasm. It was very inspired and D'Annunzio's poem closed with a marvellous symphonic page. And so the audience called the performers to the footlights again and again. Altogether the curtain calls at the ends of the acts amounted to some twenty.*[30]

Apart from Montesquiou and Léon Blum[31], most of the critics expressed themselves as opposed to the play.

Among such observations from Italian critics who were present at the production, we remember the important opinion expressed by Ermanno Amicucci:[32]

The entire poem is interwoven with a miracle of depiction and in particular a splendid language, a sonority of metres and rhymes and of assonance which struck me dumb with amazement. The soul of D'Annunzio, the art of the fine maker of discourse, the mastery of colour of this great imaginative creator were fused in the poem in a sumptuous, mysterious harmony with all the voluptuousness and all the sadness, the fevers and health, the vices and virtues. Under this ostentatious harmony there is the tormenting doubt of terrestrial life and of the future life: there is religious ardour. Gabriele D'Annunzio – I have heard it repeated by more than one person here in Paris – has entered French literature through the Arche de Triomphe. With these words we can judge the literary form of the Martyre de Saint Sébastien.[33]

The play of light and colour and also the sonorous words made up the fascination of the poem. In spite of revealing a negative opinion on the theatrical work, the critic George Le Ferre maintained that Bakst had also succeeded in achieving this enchantment:

I don't like this pastiche play, irritating from every point of view. However the decor and the costumes of Bakst are enchanting. Here, pushed to the greatest extreme of perfection is the triumph of painted decor. The colours of Mr Bakst "sing" at the moment in the first act when the actors seem to be at the heart of a flowering tree.[34]

Conclusion.
In a work "synthesising the arts", *Le Martyre de Saint Sébastien* matches its full title. It is a Jungian theatre: permeated with the collective unconscious and with a communicative language delivered in an original style halfway between Impressionism and Expressionism.

The scene is enlivened with the vivid rhythm of artificial colours with the passage of light through darkness, in which is enclosed the dramatic intensity of the action. One has the sensation of attending a "dance of colours", which ends in transmuting itself into a composition essentially devised on chromatic harmony. It is a "poetics of the miraculous and the sublime", which passes through the enchantment of colours and their sensuous forms exciting the audience to astonishment and admiration.

The figurative language becomes a projection of a *nostos* towards a legendary past, which the spectator can recover, freed from the labyrinth of his times.

With his research work Bakst was able to render magisterially the aesthetic of the miraculous and the tragic, alternating visual emotions and emotional sensations. The scenic art took on a choral valence, becoming communicative, narrative, able, however, not only to tell the fascinating story of an epoch but also to restore to the collective significance and suggestion, emotion and passion.

This is the originality of the *Mystère*, where experience and various outcomes of the classical oriental world and the occidental world flow together and coexist harmoniously, from the Middle Ages to the historical avant garde of the 1900s.

1 *Le Martyre de Saint Sébastien* was performed several times. In addition to the first French production at the Théâtre du Châtelet in Parils (22 May 1911), there were performances at La Scala, Milan, on 4 March 1926, in France at the Chorégie d'Orange in 1949, at La Scala again on 23 May 1951, at the Festival of Lyon-Charbonnières in 1952, at the Théâtre de l'Opéra in Paris on 8 February 1957, at La Scala on 24 June 1986, at the Teatro La Fenice in Venice on 27 April 1995, at the Teatro Lirico di Cagliari in 1997, at the Teatro Massimo in Palermo am 20.. March 1999 and lastly at the Teatro San Carlo di Napoli on 12 December 2001. A photographic documentation (drawings and stage photos) can be found in the catalogue volume *L'Arte del Tragico. L'avventura scenica del ‚Martyre de Saint Sébastien' di Gabriele D'Annunzio dal 1911 ad oggi* by Carlo Santoli (Preface by Annamaria Andreoli), Naples: Edizioni Scientifiche Italiane 2000.

2 With regard to the works that "mainly influenced" the poet, Guy Tosi provides some very interesting information: "They ranged from *Martyrs* by Chateaubriand to the monumental *Histoire des Persécutions* by Paul Allard, from the *Metamorphoses* of Apuleius to the classical work of Franz Cumont on *Die orientalischen Religionen im römischen Heidentum*, from the Bible to the apocrypha Gospels, from *Salambô* and the *Tentation de Saint Antoine* by Flaubert to the *Poèmes antiques* of Leconte de Lisle and his translations of Greek bucolic poetry. Not to forget Swinburne's *Poems and Ballads* in the French translation of Gabriel Murey and *L'art religieux du XIII siècle en France* by Émile Mâle." Cf. Guy Tosi, "D'Annunzio écrivain francais", in: *Quaderni del Vittoriale*, Nr. 5-6, October-December 1977, p. 112. We must also remember Oscar Wilde and Dante Gabriel Rossetti, founders of the Pre-Raphaelite movement, by whom Claude Debussy was inspired and whose poem "The Blessed Damozel" he set to music as "La demoiselle élue".

3 G. Sozzi: *Gabriele D'Annunzio*, Florence 1964, p. 247.

4 The performeances too place in 1909 and 1910 in the Théâtre du Châtelet.

5 Giovanni Isgró: *D'Annunzio e la ‚mise en scène'*, Palermo: Palumbo 1973, p. 171.

6 Ibid.

7 Robert De Montesquiou-Fezensac (Paris 1855 – Menton 1921), French poet.

8 Cf. Francesco Cimmino: "Gabriele D'Annunzio, Appunti inediti sul San Sebastiano", in: *Dialoghi*, August 1953. Reprinted in Eurialo De Michelis, *Tutto D'Annunzio*, Milan: Feltrinelli 1960, p. 366. According to another notebook the idea occurred to him no less than 25 years earlier: "At the age of eighteen years (or perhaps twenty-one), Febea saw me naked on a tree trunk in the hanging garden of the Villa Medici between the terrace and the lookout, and cried: 'Saint Sebastian'" (ibid., p. 366). Febea was Olga Ossani, a Neapolitan journalist and author of *Capitan Fracassa*, for which purpose she used the pseudonym. In memory of this event from his youth D'Annunzio sent her a letter signed "Saint Sebastian". The project of *Le Martyre de Saint Sébastien* goes back to 1908; the Treves publishing house secured the publication rights. This secret is associated with the poet's emotional relationship with the Russian countess Nathalie de Goloubeff, whom D'Annunzio called Donatella. With her he visted churches and museums and admired pictures and sculptures representing Saint Sebastian. In a letter to his mistress, presumably written in November 1908, he expresses himself as follows: "I kiss fervently the wound of Saint Sebastian" (ibid, p. 366).

9 Cf. A. Gold and R. Fizdale: *Misia*, Milan: Mondadori 1981, p. 157.

10 Paolo Alatri: *Gabriele D'Annunzio*, Turin: UTET 1983, p. 309.

11 In the original *annunciatore* – a pun on D'Annunzio [translator's note].

12 Cf. Ida Rubinstein: "Souvenir d'un poète", in: *Scenario*, April 1938, p. 194.

13 Giulio Carlo Argan: *Storia dell' arte italiana*, vol. III, Florence: Sansoni per la scuola 1993, p. 386.

14 ibid.

15 *Bandelette* = ribbon, hennin = Burgundian bonnet.

16 These are the opinions of Diego Angeli, who was a spectator and chronicler of the first performance, taken from "La prima del 'Mistero di San Sebastiano' of Gabriele d'Annunzio a Parigi", in: *L'Illustrazione Italiana* of 28 May 1911. Diego Angeli (Flroence 1869 – Rome 1936) was a journalist for *Marzocco* and chief editor of *Convito romano* of De Bosis.

17 Cf. ibid.

18 Cf. *San Giorgio libera la figlia del re* in Cappella Pellegrini, Chiesa di Sant' Anastasia, in Verona.

19 Cf. *Affresco del Salone dei Mesi* in the Palazzo Schifanio in Ferrara.

20 The reference is to a painting from the cycle *Storie di Sant' Agostino* in the College Church of San Gimigniano (1463-65).

21 Cf. DIEGO ANGELI, op. cit.

22 That was also a hint for the designer of the stage set as to where the Saint was to be positioned.

23 Cf. ANJUTA MAVER LO GATTO: "Otto lettere inedite di Léon Bakst a D'Annunzio", in: *Quaderni del Vittoriale*, No. 7, January-February 1978, p. 54 f.

24 *New York Tribune*, 5. September 1915, p. 1 of the Special Supplement.

25 Cf. GIULIO CARLO ARGAN: *Storia dell'arte italiana*, vol. II, Florence: Sansoni per la scuola 1993, p. 245.

26 ibid.

27 GIULIO CARLO ARGAN: *Storia dell' arte italiana*, vol. III, op. cit., p. 198.

28 In an interview with *Corriere della Sera* on 3 May 1911 D'Annunzio declared that he interpreted the Legend of the Saint "with the imagination of a master glazier, but at the same time followed by instinct the sequence of the popular belief [...] the master glaziers provided the images of these transfigurations in the thousand subdivisions of the glass window for the light of the sky and the soul of the people. In particular, the glass windows of the thirteenth century were no more nor less than visible stories. The were composed in the liveliest of all narrative styles. One might think, for example, of those in the Chartres Cathedral: do they not look like the very coloured and illuminated pages of the blessed Jacopo da Varagine? [...] The master follows the text from episode to episode and develops it from the bottom up."

29 ROBERT DE MONTESQUIOU: "L'archange d'or ou l'archer percé de ses fleches", in: *Le Théâtre*, Nr. 299, 1. June 1911.

30 Cf. MARIO CORSI: *Le prime rappresentazione dannunziane*, Milan: Treves 1928, p. 118.

31 LÉON BLUM (Paris 1872 – Jouy-en-Joses, Paris 1950), theatre critic and man of letters.

32 ERMANNO ARMICUCCI (Tagliacozzo 1890 – Rome 1955), journalist and politician.

33 Cf. MARIO CORSI, op. cit., p. 118 f.

34 From a press cutting found in the Arsenal Library, Paris.

Germaine Greer

The Boy (Excerpt)

The early church might not have been able to turn mortals into gods, but it did have the option of making them immortal and placing them in heaven by the process of canonization. The shortest road to canonization was martyrdom. Much more mysterious in its way than Antinous's translation to godship is transformation of a middle-aged martyr to an ephebe, as happened in the case of Sebastian, by far the most frequently depicted saint in the Catholic Calendar. The *Golden Legend* relates that, at the time of his martyrdom in c. 304 CE, Sebastian had been in the army for nearly twenty years, so he was no stripling. The emperor Diocletian, not knowing him to be a Christian, had appointed him to a captaincy in the elite Praetorian Guard. When the succeeding emperor Maximian set about the suppression of Christianity, he ordered Sebastian's execution. Sebastian was tied to a stake, shot full of arrows and left for dead, but the ministration of Irene, the saintly widow of another Christian martyr, saved his life. Sebastian actually met his martyrdom many years later by being beaten to death.

In the earliest representations Sebastian stands alone in his niche or on his panel, a full-length upright figure, sometimes armoured, sometimes clad in a mixture of Roman and later armour and civilian dress, holding the arrows that were used in his torture. He is often paired with St Roch, who displays (like Adonis) a wound in his groin. Half-lengths and busts based on the full-length figures were later commissioned for the devotions of private clients. These imaginary portraits show Sebastian as a youth of transcendent beauty, as can be seen in the best known examples by Lorenzo Costa, Boltraffio and Raphael. Benozzo Gozzoli, Andrea Mantegna and Carlo Crivelli show Sebastian stripped to his breech clout and so full of arrows "as to appear like a hedgehog". So far the saint's demeanour is one of godly containment; he cannot actually move, being bound hand and foot to his stake or tree or column, but in any case he remains tranquil, simply turning his eyes to heaven. Botticelli's Sebastian and the early examples by Giovanni Bellini are of this kind. Cima da Conegliano dispenses with the stake and with all the arrows but one, presenting us with an apparently uncomplicated image of a beautiful boy with a single arrow piercing his thigh. His colleague Giovanni Bellini adapts the same image for his *Sacred Allegory*, though this time the single arrow is stuck in the saint's breast-bone and his beatified body under its tumbling golden curls is dazzlingly fair.

Then Titian pairs St Sebastian with St Roch for the right-hand side of his altarpiece of St Mark Enthroned for the Church of the Salute in Venice in 1510; he positions Sebastian right on the edge of the picture space looking out and downwards. A single arrow has pierced his ribs while his breech clout has foamed into a sheet, hugely knotted over his genitals and draped behind him like a train. The young man is not only disturbingly human but apparently distracted from the main business of the picture which is the veneration of St Mark, so that he seems to inhabit the same realm as the viewer. Titian must have known that many women would come to kneel and pray before this beguilingly sensual picture of a saint, and so must the painters of the many other altarpiece groups in which a young, nude Sebastian upstages the line-up of celestial worthies.

In later depictions, Sebastian is no longer collected or composed, but a-thrill with emotion, whether weeping like Sodoma's Sebastian, on whom an angel prepares to bestow the martyr's crown, or convulsed and gasping like Garofalo's Sebastian, or breathing forth his soul like the succession of ecstatic Sebastians by Guido Reni. Reni's Sebastian is a lover whose body is racked less with agony form the arrows of his persecutors than with his soul's longing for the beatific vision that will be his at the moment of death. As exactly the same metaphors of breathing forth the soul are used for orgasm, the erotic content of the image is obvious, but Reni challenged himself to purge such crass associations by sheer painterly control. None of the commentators on the pictures of the transfixed Sebastian sees fit to point out that historically Sebastian was not on the point of death when the arrows entered his body and the whole conceit is gratuitous. Until the seventeenth century Sebastian invariably retained his breech clout, which is as much an identifying attribute as his arrows but he had long been excuse for any study of a full-length male nude or nude male torso, especially if the arms were thrown up and the body convulsed in agony or ecstasy.

In another version, rather truer to written history, Sebastian has been taken down from his tree and his wounds are being tended by St Irene. Giordano, Manfredi, Stanzioni, Schedoni, Preti, Cerrini and many other artists of the Baroque period painted versions of this subject. Because the female figure could not be seen in too close contact with the boy's naked body, St Irene is often no more than a head and an arm, gingerly approaching the languishing saint, with none of the two-handed aggression needed actually to extract an embedded arrow from flesh, bone and sinew. Sometimes the problem is solved by presenting Irene as an old woman, with the added benefit that the contrast with her grizzled features makes Sebastian appear yet more beautiful. Another way of solving the problem was to transform Irene into a couple of ministering angels. When these dwindle into cherubs, Sebastian's perforation seems closer to erotic play than ever.

Text excerpt from: Germaine Greer: *The Boy*, London: Thames & Hudson 2003, pp. 204–299

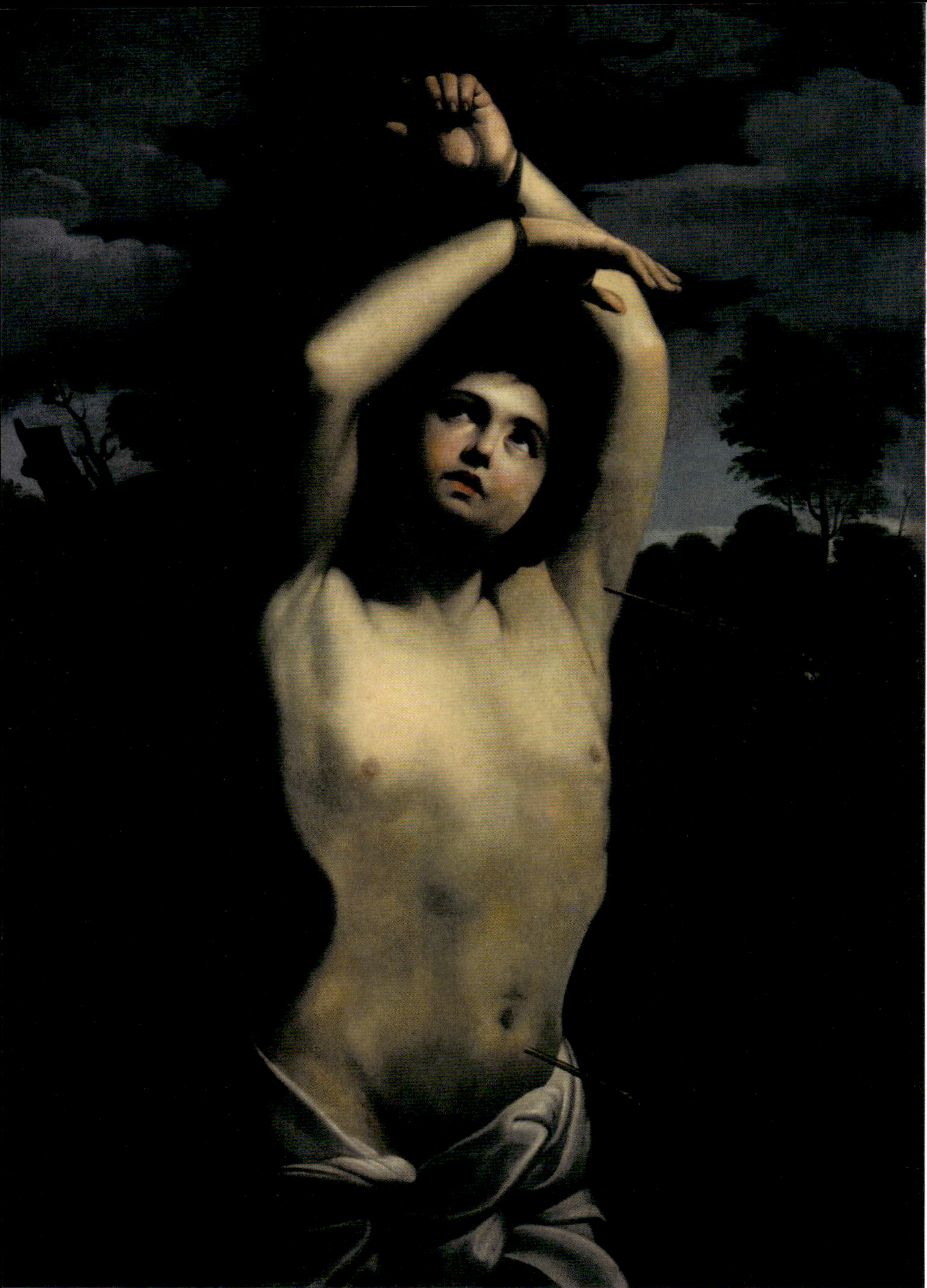

ANONYMOUS, after Guido Reni, *Saint Sebastian*, 18/19th century

Gerald Matt

Saint Sebastian A Journey to the Centre of Pain or "If you love me, then kill me!"[1]

"Pleasure is the only fraud I would like to continue"
Walter Serner, *Die Letzte Lockerung*[2]

The land is mined, the saint already too richly furnished, his path of torment and fervour has been marked by everything from baroque excess to ascetic austerity. Images that whisper cheaply like darkly weeping Swinburnean cascades of feeling, heaving and pompous blood-pink melodramas from Hollywood's ancient myth-smithy; Sebastian, the fleshy-hedonistic masochist, submerged in lusty clair-obsure; Sebastian, the virtuous, pietistic, transfigured being, the anaemic Nazerene stripling, remote in an oily glow, receiving the rain of arrows; Sebastian, martyred, bent over in pain, in photographic realism; Sebastian, the welcome booty of a voyeuristic lovingly veiled style of nude painting. Sebastian, the dying Adonis, Sebastian, the Cupido who charms the hearts of men and women; the James Dean of the history of martyrdom; the stuff people knit their myths from, the mystery play of Gabriele D'Annunzio, an acted, danced and spoken drama with roles for singers and symphonic episodes, composed by Claude Debussy, placed under a spell by Léon Bakst with an oriental stage set and lascivious costumes, an exotic, fascinating work of art, wrapped in liturgical vocabulary, whose sado-erotic symbolism led the Bishop of Paris to threaten the audience with excommunication at the first performance in the Chatelet in 1911. D'Annunzio's *Le Martyre de Saint Sébastien*, which Robert Wilson in 1988 dipped into his cool aseptic light at the Metropolitan Opera, and which was transformed into a blood-soaked ghost-train by the anarchic pack of rowdies La Fura dels Baus in the Teatro di San Carlo in 2001.

Saint Sebastian, a polymorphous projection of human obsessions and vices, drawing a trail of pain through centuries of art history from Guido Reni to Keith Haring. And even today he is still the object of voyeurism and identification for people who need an aesthetically perfect being in order to transcend their disgust with the world. Saint Sebastian is worth a journey.

Pensione Fraschetti, rooms for rent, not including breakfast. Double bed with an extra plank bed, payment in advance, Via Ottaviano within view of the Vatican. Here in the hall Sebastian sings his song of pain as a pin-up picture between a porcelain Madonna Dolorosa and a postcard showing the face of the Pope. Nobody goes past him without raising their eyes and pausing a moment. History and stories nestle in the subconscious: such as a memory of the Japanese super-aesthete Yukio Mishima, who, as he was to narrate in his novel *Confessions of a Mask*, experienced his coming-out in front of Guido Reni's Sebastian, and who committed Seppuku when his fascist dreams had burst, in order to follow his hero to the last. Mishima, who made a "Bella Figura"[3] before his photographers Kishin Shinoyama and Eikoe Hosoe, and to whom Paul Schrader dedicated his melodrama of a failing megalomaniac.

Or another of Salvador Dali, who found "his" Sebastian "in Italy at the end of a black and white marble-lined staircase"[4] and who signed his letters to Lorca as San Sebastian. In his programmatic text "San Sebastian" he declared: "Even so, I can't get past the impression that I have known him all my life."[5] The two friends Dali and Lorca, honoured the saint and drew him. Sebastian the seducer, Sebastian the seduced: that is also the story of Pier Paolo Pasolini's "Teorema", a middle-class drama, where friendship and love lead to confusion, destruction and death.

He stands before us, lightly clad, his beautiful body tanned; the muscles reveal the soldier; his colouring is healthy, his eyes full of submission: Sebastian, the pathfinder for dramatic fates; Sebastian, the appropriate costume for the tragic actor.

Under the title "Sebastian Melmoth", another name for Oscar Wilde, Hugo von Hofmannsthal published one of his actor-biographies, in which he sees the glamour and pain of the poet as a part of an inner being and a fate. Like Sebastian, Wilde walked "towards his catastrophe, with steps like those of Oedipus, the blind seer"[6]. The aesthete was tragic. The dandy was tragic. He stretched his hands up to draw the lightning onto himself. When Mishima in Schrader's film (➸, p. 74 ff.) calls on the soldiers to revolt in the name of the Emperor and the fatherland, he is met only with roars of laughter. What remains for him is death.

Pensione Fraschetti, with its tart atmosphere of devotional trash and healthy hypocrisy can be a base-camp for climbing into the interior of the Sebastian myth – as good as any other place. For the saint cannot be nailed down geographically but strolls metaphorically between the adored reliquaries of Catholic Rome and the dirty contact advertisements on the Internet, between the Kunsthistorisches Museum in Vienna (Andrea Mantegna) and the Palazzo Rossi in Genua (Guido Reni), between the Basque San Sebastian and dreamy gossamer threads of D'Annunzio on Lake Garda. Sebastian lives in us as an hysterical heaving of the soul under the spell of a figure "between secularisation of the saint and sacralisation of the profane"[7], as Heusinger von Waldegg once expressed it. Towards the end of the Second World War, Pier Paolo Pasolini made a sketch for a fresco in an Italian village church that reminds one in its substance of Symbolism in Italian art. In a sketchy drawing he portrays a stripling between darkness and light, between pain and purification, he raises the everyday to the level of the sacred. With the image of a simple boy, for whom Pasolini's cousin Nico Naldini stood model, he points to a motif that returns again and again in his work: "The sanctitude of things"[8].

If we wind our way in a drive through the streets and suburbs of Rome, leaving from Via Ottaviano 16 in the early morning, we look for signs and appearances which make us aware of the real presence of Saint Sebastian in the mirror of his images, and at the same time for the "exemplary sufferer"[9], who he has become, according to Susan Sontag, in the hallucinatory storehouse of images in art.

Passing through the Basilica di San Sebastiano on the Via Appia Antica, we enter the catacombs, where the cruelty of the early Christian centuries seems to be condensed into a dammed up column of air, and we remember that arrows of Sebastian were carried as a form of protection from the plague, the scourge of the Middle Ages, as AIDS is the scourge or our own times. A world of partings and destruction about which Derek Jarman says in his film *Blue*:

The virus rages fierce. I have no friends now who are not dead or dying. Like a blue frost it caught them. At work, at the cinema, on marches and beaches. In churches, on their knees, running, flying, silent or shouting protest.[10]

A world that inspired David Wojnarowicz to his work *Peter Hujar Dreaming/Yukio Mishima: St. Sebastian* (➽ p. 93), where he blends his friend Mishima and Sebastian in a nightmare that anticipates the coming tragedy. A world for which Nan Golding created her pictures. A world where arrows become hypodermic needles and fixers become saints.

The purpose determines the form of the arrow-points. For example, breaking through armour requires short, pyramid-shaped points. Some points have three or four blades; there are fork-shaped, outspread double daggers; there are barbed arrows, whose barbs eat so firmly and deeply into the muscles that they can be removed only by a surgeon; arrows that break off in the martyr's flesh and cause death by suppuration and gangrene; arrows from sharpened sickles that find their dreadful way through the body unresisted. Walter Serner, the Dadaist, who possibly stood model for his painter friend Christian Schad's head of Sebastian, commented on the expressionistically distorted painting in his journal *Sirius* in 1916, saying: "as if the martyr's pain had to be shattered into many little scraps and splinters and only the arrows are sharp and firm"[11].

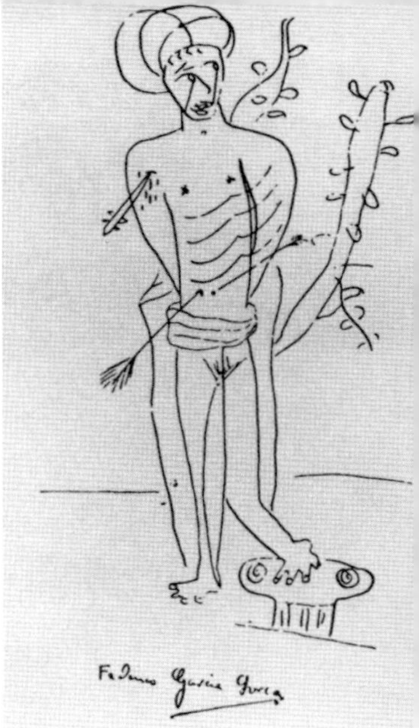

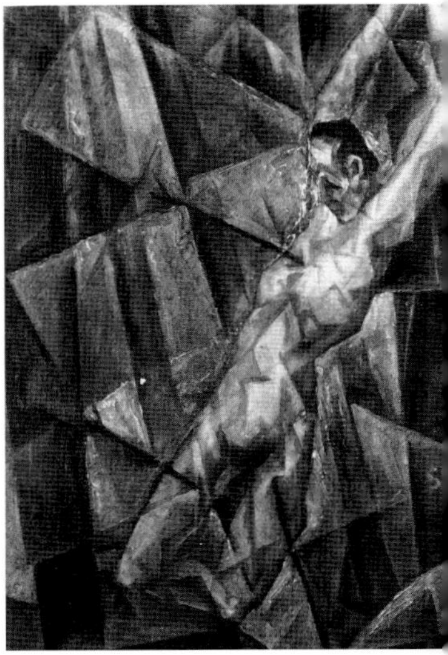

fig. 1: FEDERICO GARCIA LORCA, *Saint Sebastian*, around 1927

fig. 2: CHRISTIAN SCHAD, *Saint Sebastian*, 1916

And there is pain and yet more pain, Bob Flanagan (➻ p. 40 ff.) as Saint Sebastian, Cherry Rose as a soldier and lover. Pain as pleasure. If the shot succeeds, the blades plough broad furrows through the flesh. Arteries are cut through and death follows from internal injury. With a dull, full impact, one arrow after another thuds into the beautiful body.

For the viewer, the arrows grow from the saint's body, like delicate flowers from a well-fertilised bed. Sebastian ardently awaits the arrows. He longs for his martyrdom within the stylistic range of heroic decline and transfigured suffering. In Chris Burden's *Doorway to Heaven* (➻ p. 26) the arrows are transformed into glowing-hot beams of light. His body, illuminated by a painful short circuit to resemble Christ, is a messenger from heavenly hallucinatory spheres. Ron Athey (➻ p. 18 f.) even has the saint nailed to a cross. Sebastian as a substitute for the tabooed erotic aura of the dying son of God.

We walk on to the church of San Sebastiano, and let ourselves come under the spell of the Giorgetti statue, stretched out in semi-darkness, casting demonic shadows like an artefact from the Cabinet of Dr. Caligari.

On the dream-paths of unstilled longing, we see artists of all ages, from Fra Bartolomeo, through Egon Schiele, to Julian Schnabel seeking inspiration in the excess of feeling. Like D'Annunzio in his time, who asked his friend Olga Assani to tie him naked to a tree in the garden of the Villa Medici, thus giving his obsession with Sebastian contours with his own body. Later he carved these words into the mantelpiece above the fireplace of his Villa La Capponcina: "Et quid volo nisi ardeat" (and what do I want other than burning?)[12]

But anyone disturbed by the beautiful death-pangs becomes an art-historical quantité negligeable. And there are very few examples, such as that of Anna Maria Pachecho's *Study for Saint SebastianI/II* (➻, p. 70), where Saint Irene takes Sebastian into her arms to remove the arrows and later to nurse him to health. Even here there are clear parallels to the pieta motif: Sebastian as Jesus, Irene as Maria. But even Saint Irene can only delay the heroic death. Barely conscious, Sebastian goes back to confess his faith (Sebastian, the Notorious), and ultimately to be killed and thrown into the cloaca maxima.

In Mishima's thinking Seppuku – as the most painful way to die – is proof of the unlimited and undefeatable courage of a Samurai. In Seppuku the individual finds the opportunity to prove the power of his will in the total experience of pain and pleasure, which leads to an ecstatic union with the Red Sun, the symbol of Japan. He who overcomes fear and pain remains the victor (Sebastian the Triumphant). Suffering and death are the indispensable ingredients on the path to sainthood. When Walter Pater sees human beings as condemned to death with a period of time that they can spend full of passion or in withering lethargy, Sebastian savours the martyr's death as the last great sensual experience, a moment of highest passion and intensity. Mishima sees in

Seppuku the last masturbation, while the English aesthete and philosopher Walter Pater warns us: "Only be sure, it is passion."[13]

In her video installation, the Indonesian artist Fiona Tan tries to thwart the ubiquitous morbidity of the Sebastian story. In so doing she takes up the Japanese rite of initiation, Toshya, and shows young women, just turned twenty, shooting with their bows at a distant target we cannot see.

The shooting power of a bow under average conditions can be compared roughly with that of a 9 mm pistol. The penetrating power of a shot arrow depends on the strength of the bow, the weight of the arrows and the distance. And so the bow brings death and also awakens love and creates fire. Its string twangs like a harp. The asymmetry of the bow contains an image of time and the symbol of death. The bowstring bonds the universe with the archer who bends it.

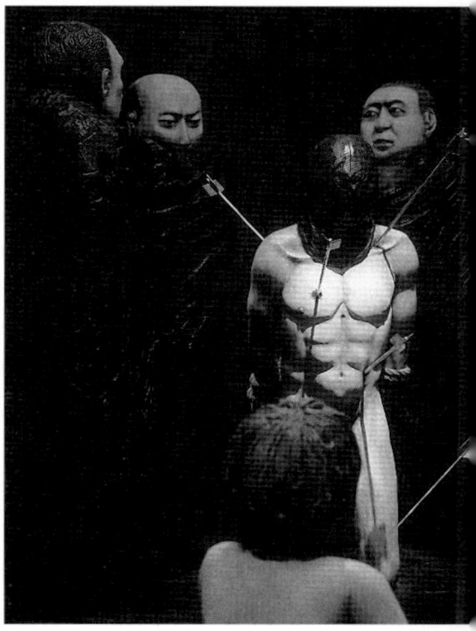

fig. 3: ANA MARIA PACHECO, *The Dark Night of the Soul*, 1999

Now, the Numidian archers hold the arrow behind its feathers. With the right hand they carefully move the arrow past the bow to the string. Then they place the left hand over the grip on the bow and take the string with the forefinger of the right hand. Sinking their shoulders, they breathe out, their knees relaxed, their elbows slightly bent and their backs slightly curved. Only those who are properly relaxed will hit the target. They stand motionless, in perfect stillness, as if in a meditative exercise.

The archer forgets himself, his body, the tension of the bow and his hand, with which he holds the arrow and the string. Only if the archer and the bow are in harmony with each other is perfection reached, and the shot will strike. When all tension has gone, the archer's will dissolved, emptiness surrounds him, he is outside the world.

Then the string jerks back. The arrow shoots towards its target. Unerringly, the strikes prove the concentration and precision of the archers. The archer brings death, but is himself ready to die at any moment. In the *Orologium sapientie*, a medieval text, "learning to die" is the basis of mental health and, indeed, of all other virtues. In Japanese schools of archery, students follow the "path of the bow", the "kyudo", a teaching of the dying process in Japanese mysticism.[14] In the *Hagakua*, the text which was so important to Mishima and which was created from the ethos of the Samurai in the eighteenth century, one can read: "Die in thought every morning and you will no longer fear death." And: "Imagine the moment when you will, perhaps, be penetrated by arrows."[15]

And so the archers submit like martyrs – the leader of the imperial archers is one of them – to the law of death; only together can they perform the ritual act. In his *Journal du Voleur* Jean Genet goes so far as to transfigure the ritual of killing into a quasi-religious mystery.[16] Through murder the victim is transformed into God.[17]

When in the corrida the *terico de la muerte*, the third of death, begins, the matador and the bull are joined in a combined ballet, in the *suerta de la muleta* the "play with the read cloth". The matador places the dagger from the front and top between the shoulderblades directly into the heart. In the ritual everything is pre-ordained and takes its proper, indisputable place.

A pilgrimage to Saint Sebastian is a journey to the centre of pain. A condensation of apperception at the extreme edge of conscious awareness. The sacred and the profane, transcendence and vice must be chemically bound in constantly changing proportions. A remedy for the evil of the times: the dullness of experience between illusions and loss of the world, Sebastian the Smuggler. There is Ron Athey's work *Sebastian Suspended* (➼ p. 19), who is leaving the notorious boredom of everyday life behind him by blowing his genitals up with a salt solution and having arrows driven through his body. There is the Sebastian, who is travestied, in Witkin's work *Queer Saint* (➼, p. 88) as a woman fitted out with the ingredients of sadomasochistic games. And there is the *St. Sebastienne.* of Louise Bourgeois, a self-portrait, Saint Sebastian as a woman (➼, p. 22 ff.).

And we are back in the Châtelet, back with D'Annunzio and Ida Rubinstein. Ida Rubinstein's graceful, long legs, her narrow wasp-like waist and her boy's body make her the ideal of a hermaphroditic beauty. D'Annunzio is excited by her erotic androgynous aura when he sees her dancing in the role of Cleopatra. "She has the legs of Saint Sebastian, which I have been searching for for years"[18], he informs his biographer and amanuensis Antongini. "The desire for a Doppelgänger of the opposite sex is an ancient one"[19], reflects the *Man without Qualities.* "It desires the love of a being that is completely like us but is nonetheless different from what we should be, a magical figure." 20 Francesco Clemente's painting, *Two Lovers*, shows a man on whose shoulders the legs of a woman penetrated by arrows are crossed. Both have the facial features of Clemente, a motif we find again in his work, *Meditation*, where a man is being stabbed by two women. "I believe I am a woman, and I think that women are men and men women, but, of course, that is one of the oldest themes in painting."[21]

Robert Wilson also takes up the open identity of the Sebastian figure by double-casting the role of his protagonist with a male and a female dancer.

In the androgynous beauty of Sebastian Plato's pre-historic tragedy of the separation of the sexes by the gods, who are jealous of their power, is cancelled out. The saint reflects the longing for union in fateful separation, that search for perfection. Sebastian, the fetishist saint of an erotically fluctuating sub-culture; the saint who draws misfortune onto himself to keep it from others; a protective saint for the age of AIDS, Sebastian the Chameleon, as Ron Athey calls him, a man between the frontlines of identity, a figure which also interests Rona Yefman (➵, p. 98 ff.) in her work.

Sebastian, the Vamp, Sebastian, figure of artifice, in whom D'Annunzio's cult of the ego, his idea of ideal beauty, finds its means of identification. Sebastian, the dandy, whose beauty flowers to fullness in the pangs of death; a Narcissus, who prefers death to certain decay, a bird of paradise, who find a congenial artistic response in the sculptures, pictures and graphic images of Luigi Ontani (➵, p. 62 ff.). In his coloured photographs,,. Luigi Ontani is seen as his own actor. With a touch of the Gesamtkunstwerk, he leaves the border between art and life behind him, thereby becoming an artistic reincarnation of the saint. In *Death in Venice* the Sebastian figure represents the "Lust of Decline" which is, as Thomas Mann also says "the most beautiful symbol"[22] While Dorian Gray destroys his portrait, Sebastian seeks death through his archers. Sebastian is their leader, the protective patron of the archer's guilds. His archers are beautiful and strong, soldiers like those set by the Israeli photographer Adi Nes before the murderous backgroun of the conflict in Palestine. His archers love him, and they try in vain in D'Annunzios *Le Martyre de Saint Sébastien* to persuade him to save himself by fleeing. He wants to die, to die for the love of death. And his archers kill him with love for him.

In Derek Jarman's film *Sebastiane* (➵, p. 52 ff.), from 1976, Sebastian is the object of soldier's desire. Here again, Severus, who is called the leader of the archers, falls in love with him. When Sebastian rejects him he gives the order to his followers to execute him. Whether in street-boy romanticism or in bloodred friendship of men and soldiers, Sebastian is also enjoyed as a homoerotic icon, Sebastian, the lovely young man, who "looks on beauty with his eyes"[23], who is "already destined for death"[24], Sebastian the Dying, whose cruel death is rewarded with heaven. In their work *Cherry Blossom* (1974) Gilbert and George seem to rise far above the cruel world, like saints, surrounded by Mikado-style arrows. Sebastian's Ascension.

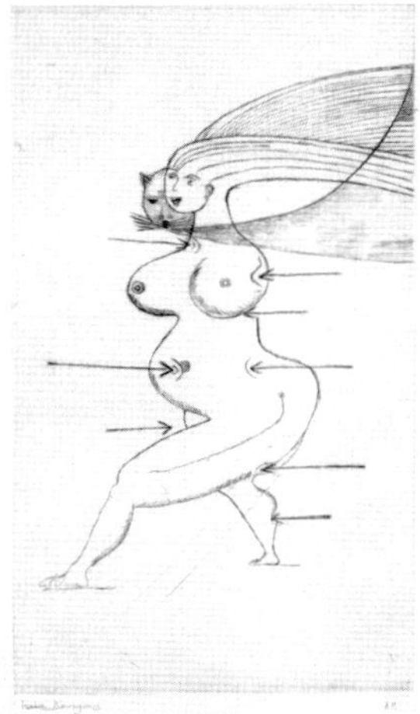

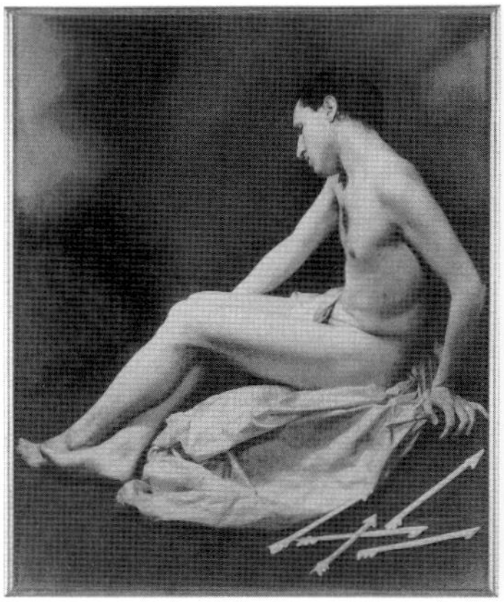

fig. 4: LOUISE BOURGEOIS, *Sainte Sebastienne*, 1990

fig. 5: LUIGI ONTANI, *San Sebastiano d'après J. J. Henner*, Madras/Indien, 1976

Shortly before the end of the First World War, D'Annunzio, who was fascinated by the joy of the Apocalypse, wrote to Olga Levi: "I was a small part of the struggle, I, who want to be the entire struggle … When ordinary life has me again, I suffer and grow angry … Death puts its cloak around me, touches me and hurries away … What shall I do with peace?"[25] For Gabriele D'Annunzio, the "Poeta di vita totale"[26], destruction and death are the only effective formula for renewal. In pure action man finds salvation. In the *Atto puro* the tragedy culminates and in its performance there is purification and triumph at the same time. Unlike D'Annunzio'.,-s fictitious characters Giorgio Aurispa, Andrea Sperelli and Tullio Hermil, Sebastian proves capable of the great act. Sebastian does not wait for life, he takes it into his hands. Not until the hour of his death does life truly come to him. His death is controlled catharsis; his will to sacrifice himself is unconditional; in the excess of evil the ritual of purification is performed, the power of his murderers is theatrical. "Do it beautifully," Hedda Gabler[27] requires of Eilen Loevberg when she kills herself; the arrows sink elegantly into the beautiful body of the saint, erected signs of his power and his triumph. With great beauty the saint wilts away in Bavo Defurne's black and white silent film paraphrase (➼ p. 32 ff.). Full of an emphatic joy in suffering the painter Odilon Redon bursts out: "The artist is distinguished from the dilettante by the pain he feels. Suffering exalts. Strike and go on striking. The wound will be fruitful."[28] In the words of Dr. Gachet, van Gogh's physician, there is also the purest pathos, the idea of giving up life for faith in art: "The phrase 'love of art' is not the right one. It should be faith, faith to a martyr's death."[29] In the end, Stephan Balkenhol in *Martyrs* (➼, p. 20 f.) draws the saint from these metaphysical spheres of the pathetic nineteenth century back into the banality of everyday life. Sebastian, the man from next door, carved out of wood, in working clothes, Sebastian as Everyman.

We have reached the end of our *Grand Tour* through the undomesticated landscapes of our imagination. Back in the house of the luxuriant Anna Fraschetti, who flings out every word like a trumpet call: reality principle versus a weave of dreams. And before we sink into the arms of Morpheus, we take up the volume of Rainer Maria Rilke's poetry which is lying on the little bedside table: "And the arrows come: now and now / and as if they leapt out of his loins."[30]

1 Gabriele D'Annunzio: *Das Martyrium des Heiligen Sebastian. Ein Mysterium in 5 Handlungen*, Berlin 1933.
2 Walter Serner: *Die letzte Lockerung. Ein Handbrevier für Hochstapler und solche die es werden wollen*, Munich 1984, p. 49.
3 Yukio Mishima: *Geständnis einer Maske*, Reinbek bei Hamburg 1984
4 Salvador Dali: "Der Heilige Sebastian. Für Federico Garcia Lorca", in: Axel Mathez and Tilbert Diego Stegman (Eds.): *Salvador Dali. Gesammelte Schriften*, Munich 1974, p. 52-57.
5 ibid.
6 Herbert Steiner (Ed.): *Hugo von Hofmannsthal. Prosa II*, Frankfurt-on-the-Main 1957, p. 135.
7 Joachim Heusinger von Waldegg: *Der Künstler als Märtyrer. Sankt Sebastian in der Kunst des 20. Jahrhunderts*, Worms 1989, p. 15.
8 Cf. "Die Heiligkeit der Dinge. Aussagen zu den Zeichnungen und Bildern von Pier Paolo Pasolini", in: *Mitteilungen des Instituts für moderne Kunst Nürnberg*, No. 28/29, April 1982.
9 Susan Sontag: "Der Künstler als exemplarisch Leidender", in: same: *Kunst und Antikunst. 24 literarische Essays*, Reinbek bei Hamburg 1968, p. 75 – 83.
10 Derek Jarman: "Blue", in: *Chroma*, Berlin 1995, p. 142.
11 Cf. Matthias Eberle (Ed.): *Christian Schad*, Exhibition Catalogue, Staatliche Kunsthalle Berlin, Berlin 1980, p. 34.
12 Gabriele D'Annunzio, see [1]
13 Walter Pater: *The Renaissance: Studies in Art and Poetry. Conclusions*, London 1890, p. 90 see also Wolfgang Iser, Walter Pater: *Die Autonomie des Ästhetischen*, Tübingen 1960.
14 Thomas Marcotty: *Bögen und Pfeile*, Munich 1958, p. 88.
15 Yukio Mishima: see [3]
16 Cf. Joel Black: *The Aesthetics of Murder*, Baltimore 1991, p. 199-209.
17 Jean Genet: *Journal du voleur*, Paris, Gallimard 1949, p. 225.
18 Gabriele D' Annunzio, see [1]
19 Robert Musil: *Der Mann ohne Eigenschaften*, Hamburg 1952.
20 Francesco Clemente, as quoted in: Ursula Prinz: *Androgyn. Sehnsucht nach Vollkommenheit*, Exhibition Catalogue, Neuer Berliner Kunstverein, Berlin 1986, p. 213
21 Thomas Mann: *Tod in Venedig*, Frankfurt am Main 1998.
22 August Graf von Platen, from "Tristan und Isolde" as quoted: Ralph-Rainer Wuthenow: *Maske, Muse und Meduse, Europäischer Ästhetizismus*, Frankfurt 1978, p. 287
23 Gabriele D'Annuncio, see [1]
24 ibid.
25 Michael Meyer (Ed.): *Ibsen, Plays 2*, London 1980, p. 316.
26 Joachim Heusinger von Waldegg, see [7], p. 11.
27 ibid. p. 97.
28 Rainer Maria Rilke: "St. Sebastian" in: same: *Neue Gedichte*, Leipzig 1907/8.

RON ATHEY

1961 born in Groton, Connecticut
Has been living and working in Los Angeles since 1963

Exhibitions/Performances/ Videos/Films (Selection)
2002 *Joyce*
2000 with Catherine Opie, Thread Waxing Space, New York; *St. Sebastian*, T.G. Body Probe, London
1997 *Martyrs & Saints*, with director Simeon Hutner; The Body: Expression/Impression, Philadelphia Museum of Art
1996 *Incorruptible Flesh*, ACME Gallery, Santa Monica
1994 *Four Scenes from a Harsh Life*

STEPHAN BALKENHOL

1957 Born in Fritzlar/Hessen
Lives and works in Frankfurt and Meisenthal, France

Exhibitions (Selection)
2001 *Zeichnungen und Skulpturen*, Kunstforum Bâloise
2000 *HERAUSFORDERUNG TIER. Von Beuys bis Kabakov*, Städtische Galerie, Karlsruhe; Stedelijk Museum, Amsterdam together with Rüdiger Schöttle; *HausSchau. Das Haus in der Kunst*, Deichtorhallen Hamburg
1996 Saatchi Gallery, London; *Szenenwechsel X*, Museum für Moderne Kunst, Frankfurt; *Views from Abroad*, Whitney Museum of American Art, New York

Publications (Selection)
Stephan Balkenhol. Sculptures and Drawings, Hirshhorn Museum and Sculpture Garden Smithsonian Institution, Washington D. C., The Montreal Museum of Fine Arts (Eds.), Stuttgart 1996

LOUISE BOURGEOIS

1911 Born in Paris, France
Has been living and working in New York City since 1938

Exhibitions (Selection)
2001/02 *Louise Bourgeois at the Hermitage*, The State Hermitage Museum, St. Petersburg, , Russia (10/9/01-1/13/02) and travelling schedule
1993 American Pavilion, Venice Biennale, Venice, Italy (6/9/93-10/10/93); with an expanded travelling exhibition *Louise Bourgeois: The Locus of Memory*
1989/90 *Louise Bourgeois: A Retrospective Exhibition*, Frankfurter Kunstverein, Frankfurt, Germany (12/2/89-1/28/90) and traveling schedule
1982/83 *Louise Bourgeois: Retrospective*, Museum of Modern Art, New York, NY (11/3/82-2/8/83) and travelling schedule

Publications (Selection)
The Prints of Louise Bourgeois, New York (The Museum of Modern Art), Deborah Wye, Carol Smith (Eds.), 1994
Louise Bourgeois, Destruction of the Father, Reconstruction of the Father. Writings and Interviews, London 1998

CHRIS BURDEN

1946 born in Boston, Massachusetts
Lives and works in Topanga, California

Exhibitions (Selection)
2001 Arts Club of Chicago
2000, 1996, 1994, 1993 Gagosian Gallery, New York, Beverly Hills, London
1999 Tate Gallery, London; Magasin 3 Stockholm Konsthall, Stockholm; 48th Biennale von Venedig
1998 *Out of Actions: Between Performance and Objects, 1949–1979*, Museum of Contemporary Art, Los Angeles
1991 *Dislocations*, Museum of Modern Art, New York
1977 documenta VI, Kassel

Publications (Selection)
Chris Burden, Beyond The Limits (Jenseits der Grenzen), Peter Noever (Ed.), Ostfildern 1996

BAVO DEFURNE

1971 born in Oostende, Belgium
Lives and works in Brussels

Films (Selection)
1999 *Kampvuur*
1998 *Matroos*
1996 *Saint* (short film)
1995 *Particularly now, in Spring* (film)
1993 *Trailer*; *Ludodrome*
1992 *Rohypnol*; *Particularly now, in Spring* (video)
1990 *Atlantis*

KIRBY DICK

Films (Selection)
2003 *The End*
2002 *Derrida*
2001 *Chain Camera*
1997 *Sick: The Life and Death of Bob Flanagan, Supermasochist*
1996 *Guy*
1988 *Private Practices: The Story of a Sex Surrogate*

CERITH WYN EVANS

1958 born in Wales
Lives and works in London

Exhibitions (Selection)

2003 *mini MATRIX*, Berkeley Art Museum, San Fransisco
2002 documenta XI, Kassel
2001 *The Art Newspaper project*, Venice Biennale
2000 *Cleave 00. Art Now*, Tate Britain, London
1998 *From the Corner of the Eye*, Stedelijk Museum, Amsterdam
1997 *Sensation*, Royal Academy of Arts, London, Hamburger Bahnhof, Berlin

BOB FLANAGAN

1952 born in New York
1996 died in Los Angeles

Exhibitions/Performances (Selection)

1993 *Sickness to Health Through S&M*, Feature Gallery, New York
1992 *Visiting Hours*, Santa Monica Museum of Art
1991 *100 Reasons* (mit Sheree Rose und Mike Kelley), Rosamund Felsen Gallery, Santa Monica; *Night Gallery* (man being slapped in a video segment of an installation by Daniel Martinez), Center on Contemporary Art, Seattle
1990 *Under Grand Music*, Reading of a text on Ludwig van Beethoven, The Museum of Contemporary Art, Los Angeles
1982 *A Matter of Choice* , video collaboration with Sheree Rose, Otis Art Institute, Los Angeles

Publications (Selection)

A Taste of Honey with David Trinidad, Cold Calm Press 1990
Slave Sonnets, Cold Calm Press 1986, cover art by Mike Kelley

EIKOH HOSOE

1933 born in Yonezawa-shi, Yamagata, Japan
Lives and works in Japan

Exhibitions (Selection)

2000 *Eikoh Hosoe. Photographs 1950–2000*, Yamagata Museum of Art; *Innovation in Japanese Photography in the 1960s*, Tokyo Metropolitan Museum of Photography
1990 *Photography. The World of Eikoh Hosoe*, Museum of Modern Art, Osaka, Kunsthalle Tokio, travelled as *Eikoh Hosoe: Meta* in the U.S. and Europe
1988 *Photography. The World of Eikoh Hosoe*, Ikeda Museum of 20th Century Art, Ito
1985 *Black Sun. The Eyes of Four*, Museum of Modern Art, Oxford

Publications (Selection)

Mark Holborn: *Eikoh Hosoe: Masters of Photography*, New York 1998
Eikoh Hosoe: *BA RA KEI: Ordeal by Roses*, New York 1985

DEREK JARMAN

1942 born at Northwood, Middlesex
1994 died February 19th

Films (Selection)
1993 *Blue*; *Glitterbug*
1992 *Wittgenstein*
1991 *Edward II*
1990 *The Garden*
1989 *War Requiem*
1986 *Caravaggio*
1975 *Corfe Film*; *Sebastian Wrap*; *Gerald's Film*; *Picnic at Rae's*

Publications (Selection)
Derek Jarman: A Portrait. Artist, Filmmaker, Designer, Barbican Art Gallery, Hatton Gallery at Newcastle University, London 1996
Derek Jarman: *Chroma*, London 1994

SIGALIT LANDAU

1969 born in Israel

Exhibitions (Selection)
2002 *Paradise, Video-Zone*, Herzliya Museum of Art
2001 Thread Waxing Space, New York; *Spunky*, Exit Art, New York
1999 *The Natives are Restless*, Chisenhale Gallery, London
1997 *Resident Alien – 2*, documenta X, Kassel
1996 *Voorwerk 3*, Witte de With Center for Contemporary Art, Rotterdam

ADI NES

1966 born in Israel
Lives and works in Tel Aviv

Exhibitions (Selection)
2003 *Adi Nes. Recent Photographs*, Jack Shainman Gallery, New York; *Attack! Kunst und Krieg in den Zeiten der Medien*, Kunsthalle Wien
2002 FIAC Art Fair, Paris; *Adi Nes. Photographs*, Museum of Contemporary Photography, Columbia College, Chicago; *Adi Nes: Photographs*, Museum of Contemporary Art, San Diego
2001 *Adi Nes. Recent Photographs*, Tel Aviv Museum of Art
2000 *Adi Nes. Photographs*, Dvir Gallery, Tel Aviv

Publications (Selection)
Adi Nes. The Soldiers Series, 1994–2000, Dvir Gallery, Tel Aviv 2002
Adi Nes. Recent Photographs, Tel Aviv Museum of Art, Tel Aviv 2001

LUIGI ONTANI

1943 born in Vergato, Italy
Lives and works in Rom and in Grizzana Morandi

Exhibitions (Selection)
2003 *Luigi Ontani. Genthara*, Stedelijk Museum voor Actuele Kunst, Gent
2001 *Luigi Ontani. San SeBestiAno*, Florenz; *Luigi Ontani. 1965–2001. GaneshamUSA*, P.S.1 Contemporary Art Center, New York
1996 *Luigi Ontani*, Frankfurter Kunstverein; *Luigi Ontani: Installationen in den historischen Räumen*, Museum Villa Stuck, München
1982 *Luigi Ontani. San Petronio il Demonio*, Galleria Comunale d'Arte Moderna, Bologna; *Italian Art Now: An American Perspective*, The Solomon R. Guggenheim Museum, New York

Publications (Selection)
Luigi Ontani. 1965–2001 GaneshamUSA, Carolyn Christove-Bakargiev (Ed.), 2001
Luigi Ontani, Peter Weiermair (Ed.), Frankfurter Kunstverein; Frankfurt am Main; Museum Villa Stuck, München; Kilchberg-Zürich 1996

ANA MARIA PACHECO

1943 born in Goiás, Brazil
Lives and works in London

Exhibitions (Selection)
2002 Salander-O'Reilly Galleries, New York
2001 *Absences*, Galleri F 15, Moss (Norwegen)
1999 *Ana Maria Pacheco in the National Gallery*, National Gallery, London; Ashmolean Museum, Oxford
1994 Birmingham Museum & Art Gallery (The Gas Hall)
1991 *Some Exercise of Power*, Camden Arts Centre, London, The Museum of Modern Art, Oxford

PIER PAOLO PASOLINI

1922 born in Bologna
1975 died in Ostia

Films (Selection)
1970 *Medea*
1968 *Teorema*
1964 *Il Vangelo secondo Matteo*
1963 *La rabbia*; *La ricotta*
1962 *Mamma Roma*; *Il sogno di una cosa*
1961 *Accatone*

Publications (Selection)
Pier Paolo Pasoloini: *Teorema oder die nackten Füße*, 1968, Munich 1983
Pier Paolo Pasolini: *Ragazzi di vita*, 1955, Berlin 1990

PAUL SCHRADER

1946 born in Grand Rapids, Michigan, USA
Lives and works in New York

Films (Selection)
2004 *Exorcist IV. The Beginning*
2002 *Auto Focus*
1995 *Witch Hunt*
1985 *Mishima. A Life in Four Chapters*
1978 *Blue Collar*

KISHIN SHINOYAMA

1961–63 studied photography at Nihon University, Tokyo
1961–68 photographer at Light Publicity Company, Tokyo
since 1968 freelance in Tokyo
1968 Tanjo (Birth), Ginza Nikon Salon

Publications (Selection)
KISHIN SHINOYAMA: *Santa Fe, featuring Miyazawa Rie*, Tokyo 1991
KISHIN SHINOYAMA: *water fruit featuring Higuchi Kanako*, Tokyo 1991

WOLFGANG TILLMANS

1968 born in Remscheid
Lives and works in London since 1996

Exhibitions (Selection)
2003 *If One Thing Matters, Everything Matters*, Tate Britain, London
2001 *Aufsicht*, Deichtorhallen Hamburg, Museo d'Arte Contemporanea, Castello di Rivoli, Turin, Palais de Tokyo, Paris, Louisiana Museum of Modern Art, Humlebæk
1999 *Space between Two Buildings/Soldiers – The Nineties*, Maureen Paley/Interim Art, London
1998 Andrea Rosen Gallery, New York
1996 *Faltenwürfe*, Galerie Daniel Buchholz, Köln

Publications (Selection)
Wolfgang Tillmans, J. VERWOERT, P. HALLEY, M. MATSUI (Eds.), London, New York 2002
if one thing matters, everything matters, London 2003

ROBERT WILSON

Born in Waco, Texas
Lives and works in New York

Exhibitions/Installations/Operas (Selection)
2003 Neue Nationalgalerie, Berlin
1993 Museum Boijmans Van Beuningen, Rotterdam
1992 Instituto Valenciano de Arte Moderno
1991 Museum of Fine Arts, Boston; Centre Georges Pompidou, Paris; Contemporary Arts Museum, Houston
1984 *the CIVIL warS. a tree is best measured when it is down*, Olympic Arts Festival, Los Angeles
1971 *Deafman Glance*

Publications (Selection)
Robert Wilson, Franco Quadri/Franco Bertoni/Robert Stearns (Eds.), New York 1997
Collaboration Robert Wilson, Parkett 16, Zürich 1988

For further information, see www.robertwilson.com.

JOEL-PETER WITKIN

1939 born in Brooklyn, New York
Lives and works in Albuquerque, New Mexico

Exhibitions (Selection)
2003 Galeria Juana de Aizpuru, Madrid; Circulo de Bellas Artes (Photo España), Madrid
2002 *Joel-Peter Witkin. Compassionate Beauty*, Stadtmuseum Jena; Ricco Maresca Gallery, New York; Galerie Baudoin Lebon, Paris
1999 Santa Fe Art Museum
1995 Museo d'Arte Contemporaneo, Catello di Rivoli, Turin; Salomon R. Guggenheim Museum, New York
1983 Stedelijk Museum, Amsterdam

Publications (Selection)
Germano Celant, *Joel-Peter Witkin*, Zürich 1995
Joel-Peter Witkin, *The Bone House*, Santa Fe 1998

DAVID WOJNAROWICZ

1954 born in New Jersey, USA
1992 died

Exhibitions (Selection)
1999 *Fever. The Art of David Wojnarowicz*, New Museum, New York
1996 The American Center, Paris
1991/85 Whitney-Biennale, Whitney Museum of American Art, New York
1990 *David Wojnarowicz. Tongues of Flame*, Illinois State University Galleries, Normal, Santa Monica Museum of Art, Exit Art, New York
1984 *Indigestion*, PPOW, New York
1980 *Hunger* Leo Castelli's Staircase, with Julie Hair, New York

Publications (Selection)
Fever: the Art of David Wojnarowicz, The New Museum of Contemporary Art, New York 1999
David Wojnarowicz, Close to the Knives: A Memoir of Disintegration, New York 1991

RONA YEFMAN

1972 born in Israel
Lives and works in Tel Aviv

Exhibitions (Selection)

2002 *Rubb-it*, Chambers, Herzliya Museum of Art

2001 *Florasent, No. 2*, Tel Aviv; *Looking In Looking At, Self Portrait*, The M.A. Program Gallery, Tel Aviv; Bezalel Academy of Arts and Design, Jerusalem; *Top Secret! Leaps of Consciousness*, Haifa Museum of Art; ARCO Art Fair; *Inwards*, Gordon Gallery, Tel Aviv

2000 *Babe. A Family Album*, The Blansh & Romi Shapiro Gallery, Bezalel Academy of Arts and Design, Jerusalem

1999 *Bunny on the Roof*, Borchov Gallery, Tel Aviv; Städtisches Museum Flensburg; Museum of Photography, Tel-chay

E-Mail: shemesh1@hotmail.co.il

GERMAINE GREER was born 1939 in Melbourne, Australia.
Publications (Selection)
The Female Eunuch (1970), *The Madwoman's Underclothes: Essays and Occasional Writings*, 1968–85 (1990), *Kissing the Rod: An Anthology of Seventeenth-Century Women's Verse* (1989), *Women, Sex, & Desire: Understanding Your Sexuality at Every Stage of Life* (1996), *The Whole Woman* (1999)

WOLFGANG FETZ was born 1958. He studied art history and philosophy. He is the chief executive of the cultural department of Bregenz, state Vorarlberg, and has been a member of the administrative board of the "Magazin 4" Art Association in Bregenz since 1992. He is curator and editor of numerous exhibitions and publications on contemporary art.

RICHARD A. KAYE is an Associate Professor at the Department of English at Hunter College in New York City. He is the author of *The Flirt's Tragedy: Desire Without End in Victorian and Edwardian Fiction* (University of Virginia Press, 2002) and the forthcoming *Voluptuous Immobility: St. Sebastian and the Decadent Imagination* (Columbia University Press, 2004).

GERALD MATT
Born in 1958, Matt studied Law, Business Administration and Art History. He was the City of Vienna's adviser in cultural-political matters and is the chief executive of the Kunsthalle Wien since 1996. Since 1992 he has been a member of the administrative board of the "Magazin 4" Art Association in Bregenz, state Vorarlberg. He has curated numerous exhibitions in Austria and elsewhere and produced publications relating to exhibitions, art and economics. Since the year 2001 he has been teaching Cultural Management at theUniversity of Music and Performing Arts in Vienna.

CARLO SANTOLI was born 1968 in Avellino and obtained his doctorate from the Sorbonne (Paris) with an honourable mention in November 2002. His doctoral research thesis was entitled *Gabriele D'Annunzio's French theatrework and the decorative art of Léon Bakst*. He is author of *L'Arte del Tragico. L'avventura scenica del Martyre de Saint Sébastien di Gabriele D'Annunzio dal 1911 ad oggi* (2000), *Gabriele D'Annunzio e Arturo Toscanini* (1999) and *Gabriele D'Annunzio, la musica e i musicisti* (1997). He is founder and scentific director of Sinestesie: www.rivistasinestesie.it

List of Works

Anonymous, after Guido Reni
Heiliger Sebastian, 18./19. Jh.
Oil on canvas, 173,7 x 135,5 cms
Courtesy LETTER Stiftung, Cologne

ALEXANDRE ARSÈNE

L'Art décoratif de Léon Bakst, Paris, 1913
Book
Courtesy Österreichische Nationalbibliothek, Benützungsabteilung

RON ATHEY

Sebastian Suspended, 1992
Polaroid, 334,5 x 113 cms
Courtesy of the artist

Saint Sebastian, 1997
Photograph, 152,4 x 104 cms
Courtesy of the artist

STEPHAN BALKENHOL

Märtyrer, 2003
Wawa wood, coloured frame,
170 x 45 x 45 cms
Courtesy Collection John and Amy Phelan, New York;
Courtesy Mai 36 Galerie, Zurich

LOUISE BOURGEOIS

St. Sebastienne, 1947
Watercolour and pencil on paper,
48 x 39 cms
Courtesy Collection Wendy Williams, New York

Ste Sebastienne, first version, state V, variant, 1990–93
Drypoint, printed in black, with ink additions
Sheet dimensions: 63 x 46 cms
Publisher: Peter Blum Editions, New York
Printer: Gravure Inc, New York (Christian Guérin)
Edition: not editioned
The Museum of Modern Art, New York, Gift of the artist 1993

Ste Sebastienne, first version, state VI, variant, 1990–93
Drypoint, printed in black, with ink additions
Sheet dimensions: 65 x 50 cms
Publisher: Peter Blum Editions, New York
Printer: Gravure Inc, New York (Christian Guérin)
Edition: not editioned
The Museum of Modern Art, New York, gift of the artist 1993

Ste Sebastienne, first version, state XII, 1990–93
Drypoint, printed in black, with ink additions
Sheet dimensions: 56 x 38,2 cms
Publisher: Peter Blum Edition
Printer: Harlan & Weaver Intaglio, New York (Christian Guérin)
The Museum of Modern Art, New York, gift of the artist 1993

Ste Sebastienne (The Arrows of Stress), 1992
Drypoint, 120,7 x 94 cms
Courtesy Peter Blum Edition, New York

Stamp of Memories I, 1993
Drypoint etching with engraving and relief
Artist proof, 65 x 43,8 cms
Courtesy Peter Blum Edition, New York

Stamp of Memories II, 1994
Drypoint etching with engraving and relief
Artist proof, 65 x 43,7 cms
Courtesy Peter Blum Edition, New York

St. Sebastienne, 2002
Fabric and stainless steel,
43,1 x 30,4 x 30,4 cms
Courtesy Cheim & Read, New York und Galerie Karsten Greve, Cologne

CHRIS BURDEN

Chris Burden Deluxe Photo Book, 1974
82 pages, 44 b/w photographs,
9 colour photographs,
30,5 x 25,5 x 5,5 cms
Courtesy Chris Burden and Gagosian Gallery, New York

GABRIELE D'ANNUNZIO

Das Martyrium des Heiligen Sebastians. Ein Mysterium in fünf Handlungen, Berlin, 1913
Book
Courtesy Private Collection

BAVO DEFURNE

Saint, 1996
16mm/ DVD, b/w, 11 mins.
Courtesy Laika Films, Brussels

KIRBY DICK

Sick: The Life And Death Of Bob Flanagan, Supermasochist, 1997
DVD, 86 mins.
Courtesy Kirby Dick

CERITH WYN EVANS

As its object I chose my own ampits..., 2003
Courtesy Jay Jopling/White Cube, London

KEITH HARING

St. Sebastian, Poster, 27 x 26,7 cms
Courtesy Collection of Richard Kaye

EIKOH HOSOE

Ordeal by Roses (BA RA KEI) # 1, 1961
Gelatin silver print, 60 x 50 cms
Courtesy Howard Greenberg Gallery, New York

Ordeal by Roses (BA RA KEI) # 15, 1961
Gelatin silver print, 50 x 60 cms
Courtesy Howard Greenberg Gallery, New York

Ordeal by Roses (BA RA KEI) # 25, 1962
Gelatin silver print, 60 x 50 cms
Courtesy Howard Greenberg Gallery, New York

Ordeal by Roses (BA RA KEI) # 32, 1961
Gelatin silver print, 60 x 50 cms
Courtesy Howard Greenberg Gallery, New York

Ordeal by Roses (BA RA KEI) # 34, 1962
Gelatin silver print, 60 x 50 cms
Courtesy Howard Greenberg Gallery, New York

DEREK JARMAN

Sebastian Wrap, 1975
DVD, 6 mins. 17 secs.
Courtesy James Mackay, London

Sebastiane, 1976
DVD, 82 mins.
Courtesy In-motion Pictures, London

Blue, 1993
DVD, 75 mins.
Courtesy Salzgeber & Co. Medien GmbH, Berlin

SIGALIT LANDAU

Passion Victim, the Peacock, 2003
Iron and newspaper, 270 x 210 x 80 cms
Courtesy Galerie Frank, Paris

ANDRÉ LEVINSON

The Story of Léon Bakst's Life, London, 1923
Book
Courtesy Österreichische Nationalbibliothek, Benützungsabteilung

ADI NES

n. t., 1995
Photograph, 90 x 90 cms
Courtesy Dvir Gallery, Tel Aviv

n. t., 1999
Photograph, 90 x 90 cms
Courtesy Dvir Gallery, Tel Aviv

n. t., 1999
Photograph, 60 x 90 cms
Courtesy Dvir Gallery, Tel Aviv

n. t., 1999
Photograph, 60 x 90 cms
Courtesy Dvir Gallery, Tel Aviv

n. t., 1999
Photograph, 60 x 90 cms
Courtesy Dvir Gallery, Tel Aviv

LUIGI ONTANI

San Sebastiano d'après J. J. Henner, Madras/India, 1976
Watercolour on photograph, 60 x 50 cms
Courtesy of the artist

San Sebastiano nel bosco di Calvenzano, 1970
Photograph, 70 x 104 cms
Courtesy Sammlung Fabio Sargentini, Rome

S. Sebastianello al Paradiso Attico, 1982
Watercolour on photograph, 76 x 108 cms
Courtesy Sammlung Fabio Sargentini, Rome

ErmEstetica di San Sebastian Sagittario, 1994
Ceramic sculpture, 177 x 52 x 52 cms
Courtesy Sammlung Ghirlandi Lega Baldini

San Sebastian Ontano del Pavone Indiano, Delhi/India,
Watercolour on photograph, 38 x 31 cms
Courtesy of the artist

San Sebastiano of BroOKlyn, New York/USA, 1985
Watercolour on photograph, 52 x 42 cms
Courtesy of the artist

ANA MARIA PACHECO

Study for Saint Sebastian I, 1998
Drypoint, 98,5 x 77 cms
Courtesy Pratt Contemporary Art, UK

Study for Saint Sebastian II, 1998
Drypoint, 98,5 x 77 cms
Courtesy Pratt Contemporary Art, UK

PIER PAOLO PASOLINI

Teorema, 1968
Film, 92 mins.
Courtesy Laura Betti

LUCIANO ROMANO

Le Martyre de Saint Sébastian
at Teatro di San Carlo in Naples by La
Fura del Baus, 2001
6 photographs
Courtesy Teatro di San Carlo, Naples

PAUL SCHRADER

Mishima, 1985
35mm Film/ DVD, 121 mins.
Courtesy Warner Bros. Film GmbH,
Hamburg

KISHIN SHINOYAMA

Mishima Yukio, 1968
Photograph, 45 x 55 cms
Courtesy of the artist

Mishima Yukio, 1969
Photograph, 45 x 55 cms
Courtesy of the artist

Mishima Yukio, 1969
Photograph, 45 x 55 cms
Courtesy of the artist

Mishima Yukio, 1969
Photograph, 45 x 55 cms
Courtesy of the artist

Mishima Yukio + Tate No Kai, 1970
Photograph, 45 x 55 cms
Courtesy of the artist

Mishima Yukio, 1970
Photograph, 45 x 55 cms
Courtesy of the artist

WOLFGANG TILLMANS

Swiss Police, 1994
Ink jet print- 137 x 200 cms
Courtesy Galerie Daniel Buchholz,
Cologne

ROBERT WILSON

Saint Sebastien, Act I, 1988
Charcoal and graphite on paper, 30,5 x
43,2 cms
Courtesy Paula Cooper Gallery, New York

Saint Sebastien, Act I, 1988
Graphite on paper, 56,5 x 76,2 cms
Courtesy Paula Cooper Gallery, New York

Saint Sebastien, Act III, 1988
Charcoal on paper, 30,5 x 43,2 cms
Courtesy Paula Cooper Gallery, New York

Le Martyre de Saint Sébastien, 1988
Sketch
Courtesy Sammlung Stephan Götz,
Stuttgart

Saint Sebastien, Act I, 1988
Washed Indian ink drawing, 21 x 30 cms
Courtesy Sammlung Stephan Götz,
Stuttgart

Saint Sebastien, Act II, 1988
Washed Indian ink drawing, 21 x 30 cms
Courtesy Sammlung Stephan Götz,
Stuttgart

Saint Sebastien, Act III, 1988
Washed Indian ink drawing
Courtesy Sammlung Stephan Götz,
Stuttgart

Saint Sebastien, Act IV, 1988
Washed Indian ink drawing, 21 x 30 cms
Courtesy Sammlung Stephan Götz,
Stuttgart

Saint Sebastien, Act V, 1988
Washed Indian ink drawing, 21 x 30 cms
Courtesy Sammlung Stephan Götz,
Stuttgart

Marc Enguerand, *Le Martyre de Saint Sébastien*, staged by Robert Wilson at
Opéra National de Paris 1988
6 Photographs
Courtesy of the artist

Programm book *Le Martyre de Saint Sébastien* von Gabriele D'Annunzio und
Claude Debussy, staged by Robert Wilson
at Opéra National de Paris, Paris 1988
Courtesy RW Work Ltd., New York

JOEL-PETER WITKIN

Sander's Wife, 1981
Silver print, 51 x 41 cms
Courtesy Baudoin Lebon, Paris

Penitente, New Mexico, 1982
Silver print, 71 x 71 cms
Courtesy Baudoin Lebon, Paris

Blackman Rome, 1996
Silver print, 47,6 x 40,5 cms
Courtesy Baudoin Lebon, Paris

Queer Saint, Paris, 1999
Silver print, 101,6 x 76,2 cms
Courtesy Baudoin Lebon, Paris

DAVID WOJNAROWICZ

Arthur Rimbaud in New York (Shooting Up, Pier), 1978–79
Silver print, 40 x 34 cms
Courtesy of the Estate of David Wojnarowicz and PPOW, New York

Peter Hujar Dreaming/Yukio Mishima: St. Sebastian, 1982
Acrylic and spray paint on masonite, 101,5 x 101,5 cms
Courtesy Evan Lurie, New York

Bad Moon Rising, 1989
Acrylic, photograph, collage on masonite, 94 x 95,5 cms
Courtesy Collection of Walter Sudol and Steven Johnson

I Feel a Vague Nausea, 1990
B/w photographs, acrylic, string and text on board, 152,5 x 121 cms
Courtesy of the Estate of David Wojnarowicz and PPOW, New York

RONA YEFMAN

Gal with arrows, 2003
Photograph, 110 x 80 cms
Courtesy Sommer Contemporary Art, Tel Aviv

Rocks, 2003
B/w photograph, 110 x 70 cms
Courtesy Sommer Contemporary Art, Tel Aviv

Smoke, 2003
Photograph, 110 x 70 cms
Courtesy Sommer Contemporary Art, Tel Aviv

Young, 2003
Photograph, 110 x 80 cms
Courtesy Sommer Contemporary Art, Tel Aviv

Folter der hundert Teile,
4 Photographs
Courtesy Gerd Bergfleth, Matthes & Seitz Verlag, Munich

La Revue Musicale, No. 234, Paris, 1957
Magazine
Courtesy Musiksammlung der Österreichischen Nationalbibliothek, Wien

Slide-show compiled by Carlo Santoli, providing a purview of the iconography of *Le Martyre de Sainte Sebastién* in the 20th century, taking as its starting point the première of the opera of the same name by Gabriele D' Ánnunzio and Claude Debussy at the Théâtre du Châtelet in Paris in 1911.

PICTURE CREDITS

All images by Stephan Balkenhol, Louise Bourgeois, Alfred Courmes, Federico Garcia Lorca, Pier Paolo Pasolini, Christian Schad © VBK WIEN, 2003

Courtesy Ron Athey: 18, 19
Courtesy Sammlung Ghirlandi Lega Baldini: 64
© Banco de México: 15
Bibliothèque nationale de France: 107, 108, 109, 112, 113
Collection of Barry Blinderman: 95
Courtesy Sammlung Louise Bourgeois : 23, 24, 127
Courtesy Galerie Daniel Buchholz, Cologne: 82, 83
Courtesy Chris Burden, Topanga: 26, 29
Foto: Christopher Burke: 22, 23, 24, 25, 127
Courtesy Carnegie Museum of Art, Pittsburgh; Gift of Mervin Jules in Memory of Hudson Walker: 14
Foto: Marco Fedele di Catrano: 67
Centre Pompidou-MNAM-CCI, Paris © Photo CNAC/MNAM Dist. RMN: 13
Foto: Geoffrey Clements: 84
Courtesy Courtesy Cheim & Read, New York: 25
Courtesy Paula Cooper Gallery, New York: 84
© Bavo Defurne: 32, 33, 34, 35
Courtesy Kirby Dick: 40, 41, 42, 43
Courtesy Palazzo Ducale, Mantova, su concessione del Ministero per i Beni e le Attività Culturali: 110
Courtesy Dvir Gallery, Tel Aviv: 58, 59, 60, 61
Foto: Frank Elbaz: 56, 57
Foto: Marc Enguerand: 87
© Cerith Wyn Evans: 36, 37, 38, 39
Courtesy Galerie Frank, Paris: 56, 57
Courtesy Frith Street Gallery, London: 125
Courtesy Gagosian Gallery: 27, 28, 30, 31
Courtesy Sammlung Stephan Götz, Stuttgart: 86
Courtesy Howard Greenberg Gallery: 44, 45, 46, 47, 48, 49, 50, 51
Courtesy Galerie Karsten Greve, Cologne: 25
© Eikoh Hosoe: 44, 45, 46, 47, 48, 49, 50, 51
Foto: Jean-Luc Ikelle-Matiba: 120
Courtesy In-motion Pictures: 50, 51, 52, 53
Courtesy Jay Jopling/White Cube, London: 36, 37, 38, 39
Courtesy Sammlung Walter Sudol und Steven Johnson: 92
Courtesy Laika Films: 32, 33, 34, 35
Courtesy Sigalit Landau: 56, 57
Courtesy Baudoin Lebon, Paris: 88, 89, 90, 91
© LETTER Stiftung, Cologne: 120
Courtesy Evan Lurie, New York: 93
Courtesy Mai 36 Galerie, Zurich: 20, 21
Courtesy Musée Gustave Moreau, Paris; Foto: C. Jean: 112
© National Gallery, London: 110
Courtesy Galleria Nazionale, su concessione del Ministero per i Beni e le Attività Culturali: 113
Courtesy Sammlung Luigi Ontani: 61, 63, 66, 67, 127
Courtesy Sammlung John and Amy Phelan, New York: 20, 21
Courtesy Pratt Contemporary Art: 68, 69, 70, 72, 125
Courtesy Carlo Santoli: 110
© Edition Manfred Salzgeber: 51
Courtesy Sammlung Fabio Sargentini, Rome: 62, 65
Courtesy Kishin Shinoyama: 78, 79, 80, 81
Courtesy Sommer Contemporary Art, Tel Aviv: 98, 99, 100, 101
© Museen der Stadt Wien: 13
Courtesy Fiona Tan: 125
Courtesy Teatro alla Scala, Milano: 108
Thyssen-Bornemisza Collections: 107
Union Centrale des Arts Décoratifs, Paris: 104
Foto: Uwe Walter: 20, 21
Courtesy Warner Bros. Film GmbH, Hamburg: 74, 75, 76, 77
Whitney Museum of American Art, New York; Purchase, with funds from the Photography Committee 95.88: 94
Courtesy Sammlung Wendy Williams, New York: 22
Courtesy Estate of David Wojnarowicz und PPOW, New York: 96, 97

In case that the Kunsthalle Wien has not been able to contact all copyright holders despite strenous efforts to do so, claims will be happily sttled upon request.

TEXTREFERENCES

The texts are reprinted by kind permission of the following:

Text extracts (pages 12-14) from Wolfgang Fetz: Sankt Sebastian. Liebe, Tod und Paradies, in: Paul Albert Leitner: Die Reise zum Heiligen Sebastian © Wolfgang Fetz
Text extracts (pages 204 - 209) from Germaine Greer: The Boy, published by Thames & Hudson, 2003 © 2003 Germaine Greer. Text reproduced by kind permission of Thames & Hudson Ltd., London
Text extracts from Derek Jarman: Blue © James Mackay, London
Text extracts from Yukio Mishima: Confessions of a Masc © Rylie, London
Text extracts (pages 81 - 82) from Pier Paolo Pasolini: Theorem, translated by Stuart Hood, translation © Quartet Books

IMPRINT

This catalogue was published on the occasion of the exhibition "Saint Sebastian. A Splendid Readiness for Death", Kunsthalle Wien, 2003/2004

Curators: Gerald Matt and Wolfgang Fetz
Curatorial Assistance: Angela Stief
Production: Simone Sentall

Director: Gerald Matt
Managing Director: Bettina Leidl
Head of Exhibitions: Sabine Folie

Producers: Kunsthalle Wien, Gerald Matt and Wolfgang Fetz
Editors: Wolfgang Fetz, Gerald Matt, Angela Stief
Translations: Tom Appleton, Roger Buergel, Susanne Noack, Birgit Strauß, Nelson Wattie
Copy Editing: Tom Appleton, Birgit Trinker
Graphic Design: Dieter Auracher

The exhibition and catalogue were made possible with the generous support of
Instituto Italiano di Cultura and The British Council

Production, Printing, Distribution:
Kerber Verlag
Windelsbleicher Straße 166, D-33659 Bielefeld
Tel. +49 (0)521 95008-10 Fax +49 (0)521 95008-88
info@kerber-verlag.de
http://www.kerber-verlag.de

US Distribution:
D.A.P., Distributed Art Publishers Inc.
155 Sixth Avenue 2nd Floor
New York, N. Y. 10013
Tel. 001 212 6 27 19 99
Fax 001 212 6 27 94 84

ISBN 3-936646-45-7

Printed in Germany